*f*P

ALSO BY RUSSELL JACOBY

The Repression of Psychoanalysis

Dogmatic Wisdom

Social Amnesia

The End of Utopia

The Last Intellectuals

Dialectic of Defeat

Picture Imperfect

BLOODLUST

*On the Roots of Violence from
Cain and Abel to the Present*

RUSSELL JACOBY

Free Press
New York   London   Toronto   Sydney

Free Press
A Division of Simon & Schuster, Inc.
1230 Avenue of the Americas
New York, NY 10020

First Free Press hardcover edition April 2011

FREE PRESS and colophon are trademarks of Simon & Schuster, Inc.

For information about special discounts for bulk purchases,
please contact Simon & Schuster Special Sales at
1-866-506-1949 or business@simonandschuster.com.

The Simon & Schuster Speakers Bureau can bring authors
to your live event. For more information or to book an event,
contact the Simon & Schuster Speakers Bureau at
1-866-248-3049 or visit our website at www.simonspeakers.com.

Designed by Carla Jayne Jones

Manufactured in the United States of America

1   3   5   7   9   10   8   6   4   2

Library of Congress Cataloging-in-Publication Data
Jacoby, Russell.
Bloodlust : on the roots of violence from Cain and Abel
to the present / Russell Jacoby.
p.   cm.
Includes bibliographical references and index.
1. Violence—History.   2. Violence—Psychological aspects.   I. Title.
HM1116.J33   2011
303.609—dc22   1020028150

ISBN 978-1-4391-0024-0
ISBN 978-1-4391-1756-9 (ebook)

For Cristina and "Dice"

CONTENTS

PREFACE

"And Cain talked with Abel his brother: and it came to pass, when they were in the field, that Cain rose up against Abel his brother, and slew him." Such are the details of the first murder in the Judeo-Christian world. Motive? Unclear. Means? Unclear. Penalty? Unclear. The killing of Abel by Cain has been called "the first genocide."[1] Half of mankind slays the other half.

Several millennia later, not much has changed. Despite an ocean of words about violence—its origins, course, and prevention—something has gone virtually unrecognized: its primal form is fratricide. This observation contradicts both common sense and the collective wisdom of teachers and preachers, who declaim that we fear—and sometimes should fear—the "other," the dangerous stranger. Citizens and scholars alike believe that enemies lurk in the street and beyond the street, where we confront a "clash of civilizations" with foreigners who challenge our way of life.

The truth is more unsettling. It is not so much the unknown that threatens us but the known. We disdain and attack our brothers—our kin, our acquaintances, our neighbors—whom we know well, perhaps too well. We know their faults, their beliefs, their desires, and we distrust them *because* of that. The most common form of violence is violence between acquaintances or neighbors or kindred communities within nations—civil wars writ large and small. From assault to genocide, from assassination to massacre, violence usually emerges from inside the fold rather than outside it. A Hindu nationalist assassinated Mohandas Gandhi, "the father" of India (as Nehru called him) and a pioneer of nonviolent politics. An Egyptian Muslim assassinated Anwar Sadat, the president of Egypt and a recipient of the Nobel Peace Prize. An Israeli Jew assassinated Yitzhak Rabin, the Israeli prime minister and also a recipient of the Nobel Peace Prize. Each of these assassins was a good son of his country and religion.

Civil wars are generally more savage and bear more lasting consequences than state-versus-state wars, and they increasingly characterize contemporary strife. Many more died in the American Civil War—at a time when the U.S. population was a tenth of what it is today—than in any other American conflict; its long-term effects probably surpass those of the others as well. Major bloodletting of the twentieth century—hundreds of thousands to millions of deaths—occurred in civil wars such as the Russian Civil War, the Chinese Civil War of 1927–37 and 1945–49, and the Spanish Civil War. In Iraq today—leaving aside causes and blame—the number of people killed in sectarian warfare between Sunnis and Shiites far exceeds the number slain by foreign troops. "By any definition, Iraq is already in a state of civil war," stated two political scientists in 2007.[2] The ongoing civil wars in the Democratic Republic of the Congo have already caused millions of deaths, with the world taking little notice.

World War II, a signal example of twentieth-century international conflict, also presents a paradigmatic case of fratricide: the extermination of the Jews. Anti-Semitism as it developed in Germany (and Austria) did not target a bizarre or foreign population. On the contrary. The German Jews were extraordinarily well assimilated and successful. They were the very opposite of outsiders. In the professions of law, medicine, journalism, science, music, and banking, they belonged to the establishment. German anti-Semitism targeted neighbors, not strangers.

The situation in Eastern Europe, where most Jews lived and most of the slaughter took place, did not always differ from that of Western Europe. Many Eastern European Jews were integral to society. A film by the Polish documentary filmmaker Agnieszka Arnold, *Where Is My Older Brother, Cain?*, revisited the killing of the Jews in Jedwabne, a small town in northeastern Poland. Excellent relations had prevailed between Jews and Poles in that region. "Everybody was on a first-name basis," recalled a resident interviewed by Arnold.[3] But one summer day in 1941 half of the population killed the other half, the entire Jewish population of approximately 1,600 people; the Jews were mainly herded into a barn, which was set afire. The Princeton historian Jan T. Gross, who investigated the mass murder, titled his account *Neighbors*.[4]

The extermination of European Jews prefigures more recent mass killings—in Cambodia, in Bosnia, in Rwanda—perpetrated not by foreigners but by neighbors. Serbs and Muslims lived together for centuries in Bosnia and had intermarried and worked together. Even to one another, Hutus and Tutsis in Rwanda were not clearly distinguishable. As the French Africanist Gérard Prunier put it, the Rwandan genocide possessed a "neighborly quality" and proceeded "home-by-home." He suggests that in order to fathom it, "one should imagine a world in which many of the German SS would have had Jewish relatives"—a perspective that subverts the conventional idea that genocide arises from hatred of the "other."[5] This notion is almost exactly wrong. The German Christians and the German Jews, the Serbs and the Muslims, the Iraqi Sunni and the Shiites, the Hutus and the Tutsi knew each other well. Fratricide does not arise from a lack of understanding. Its origins may be just the opposite.

On the fifth anniversary of September 11, 2001, a news article reported that during the previous year homicides in the

United States had increased to about seventeen thousand.[6] We obsess about strangers piloting airplanes into our buildings, but in the United States in 2005 six times the number killed in the World Trade Center were murdered on the streets or inside our own homes and offices. The news of the uptick in homicides—a 4.8 percent increase—received virtually no attention, perhaps for obvious reasons. Its news value was hardly comparable to that of suicidal bombers and their victims. The murders stretched out over a year and across the country; in kind and degree they also recur more or less each year.

These regular losses serve to remind us that the majority of criminal violence takes place between people who know each other. Domestic violence speaks for itself. Cautious citizens may push for better street lighting, but they are much more likely to be assaulted, even killed, in the light of the kitchen by someone familiar than in a parking garage by a complete stranger. A study of homicides in New York City from 2003 to 2005 found that three-quarters of the perpetrators knew their victims.[7] National crime reports confirm that the majority of homicides happen between friends or associates. For rape and assault, the numbers tilt even more toward the familiar. You have more to fear from a spouse, an ex-spouse, or a coworker than you do from someone you don't know.[8] City gangs overwhelmingly target other city gangs, a few blocks away.[9] Like, not unlike, prompts violence.

Where I live in Los Angeles, the public schools look forbidding. High chain-link fences almost entirely surround them. During the day a police car lingers in front of the entrance to the high school. The fear, of course, is of an eruption of violence, but school violence does not usually emanate from intruders. Who is kept out by the fences? The police in the idling car hope to deter the students inside the school.

The proposition that violence derives from kith and kin overturns a core belief that we assault and are assaulted by those who are strangers to us. If this were so, the solution would be at hand. Get to know the stranger. Talk with the stranger. Reach out. The

cure for violence is better communication, perhaps better education. Study foreign cultures and peoples. Unfortunately, however,
our brother, our neighbor, enrages us precisely because we understand him. Cain knew his brother—he "talked with Abel his
brother"—and slew him afterward.

If threat emerges not from the strange but from the familiar, is
it nonetheless possible that the strange and familiar may be connected? Sigmund Freud argued this some time ago. He contended
that the link between the German words for "uncanny" (*unheimlich*) and "familiar" (*heimlich*) suggests an inner connection between the two. What frightens us as strange might be something
eerily familiar. The work of Freud may help to chart the underground sources of fratricidal violence. We hate the neighbor we are
enjoined to love. Why? Perhaps small disparities between people
provoke greater hatred than do the large ones. Freud introduced
the phrase "the narcissism of minor differences" to describe this
phenomenon. He noted that "it is precisely the little dissimilarities
in persons who are otherwise alike that arouse feelings of strangeness and enmity between them."[10]

Freud first broached the narcissism of minor differences in "The
Taboo of Virginity," an essay in which he also took up the "dread
of woman." Is it possible that these two notions are linked? That
the narcissism of minor differences, the instigator of enmity, arises
from differences between the sexes? The literary and philosophical critic René Girard may also help illuminate the menace posed
by the familiar. His work has long centered on what he has called
"mimetic desire" and its relationship to violence. Girard challenges
the usual inclination to prize likeness in society. "In human relationships words like *sameness* and *similarity* evoke an image of
harmony," he writes.[11] But for Girard similarity leads to aggression
and rivalry. Not differences but their absence is the danger.

These ideas of similarity and its discontents run against the
common understanding of global conflict. We like to believe that
world hostilities are driven by antagonistic principles about how
society should be constituted. To hold that differences of scale—

relative economic deprivation, for instance—not substance divide
the world seems to trivialize the stakes. Rather, we prefer the
scenario of clashing civilizations, such as the hostility between
Western and Islamic cultures. Presumably fundamentalist Muslims advance tenets that conflict with those of the West. Perhaps
extremist Muslim anger, however, stems not from differences between the two cultures but from their diminution. What infuriates
these fundamentalists is not the West's distance from them but its
encroachment; they seethe at copying Western society. Osama bin
Laden rails at Muslims for "imitating" Westerners. "The Jews and
Christians have tempted us with the comforts of life and its cheap
pleasures and invaded us with their materialistic values."[12]

The subject of violence has generated a library of books and
studies. Scholars usually distinguish interpersonal violence such as
homicide and rape from collective violence such as wars and riots.
Historians like to look at particulars—this murder, that war—and
wind up with slender conclusions. Sociologists and political scientists like to look at multiple events and wind up with many conclusions, usually self-evident and jargonized. "My aim is a general
theory of violence as situational process," writes one sociologist,
who considered thirty varieties from muggings to sports hooli-
ganism. "All kinds of violent confrontations have the same basic
tension . . . called non-solidarity entrainment."[13]

Of late the sociobiological approach to violence, never completely out of fashion, has returned with a vengeance. Almost fifty
years ago Konrad Lorenz's *On Aggression* and Robert Ardrey's *The
Territorial Imperative* proposed biology-driven theories of violence. Advances in genetics and evolutionary biology have given
new force to this perspective. Psychology as well has embraced
biology and chemistry. Psychoanalysis, which overthrew the biological, has in its turn been overthrown by the biological. Psychological ailments, it is now believed, mainly derive from chemical
imbalances in the brain. Psychiatrists rarely analyze their patients;
they write prescriptions for them.[14]

Darwinian thought, with its emphasis on the struggle for sur-

vival, is on the ascent in political and social studies. The sociobiological theories emphasize a heritable propensity for violence at
both the individual and the social level. A book on foreign policy
subtitled *On the Evolutionary Origins of War and Ethnic Conflict*
harnesses Darwin to global strife. "The time is right," states political scientist Bradley A. Thayer, "to bring Darwin into the study
of international relations."[15] In an encyclopedic study of war, the
Israeli scholar Azar Gat defends an evolutionary perspective.
"There is nothing special about deadly human violence and war,"
he writes. For Gat, "throughout nature" violent competition is "the
rule."[16] Meanwhile, studies of criminal violence invoke genetics.
A well-regarded book on homicide in the United States by historian Randolph Roth closes with the primatologist Frans de Waal
declaring that humans have by nature an unparalleled capacity for
violence.[17]

There is nothing in this book about Darwin or DNA. The biological may indeed play a role in violence—it plays a role in everything—but it is not my focus. I am wedded to history, but I want
to do more than string together events or facts. I will not pretend
that I am reinventing the wheel. But perhaps I am nudging the
vehicle in a new direction. I am putting together histories and reflections in order to expose the fratricidal roots of violence. I offer
some ideas about these as they pertain to such twentieth-century
configurations as German anti-Semitism and Islamic terrorism.
In the following chapters I say nothing more about criminal and
domestic violence, whose fratricidal dimension seems obvious.

Bloodlust is an essay, not a tome. I want to suggest, not fore-
close; provoke, not pronounce. I look with awe, even envy, on the
seven volumes and three thousand pages of William T. Vollmann's
Rising Up and Rising Down, which explore violence and its justification.[18] If it fell off a high shelf—not impossible in Vollmann's
earthquake-prone California—his compendium could easily kill
someone, a contretemps he probably discusses somewhere. In volume one he writes about ornamental daggers; in volume three,
boiling lobsters; in volume six, Apache suicides. My pages could

vanish without a trace inside his. I salute his omnivorous intellect, but my working principle differs from his: prune away rather than pile on.

This book dips in and out of history, but it remains an essay—an effort to shed light on the origins of violence. In no way do I propose a universal theory of violence, nor do I present solutions. What I offer is occasional illumination and understanding, perhaps a mixed blessing. In dictionaries as in life, *apprehension* is linked to *apprehensive*. And yet, to quote T. W. Adorno, "thought is happiness, even where it defines unhappiness."[19] In thinking about the bad, we reach for the good.

Los Angeles
May 2010

BLOODLUST

1

"KINSMEN, NEIGHBORS, AND COMPATRIOTS"

Shortly before sunrise on Saturday, March 27, 1546, Alfonso Díaz, a Spaniard and minor officiant at the Vatican, arrived in Neuburg on the Danube, a village outside Augsburg, Germany. His brother, Juan, was in Neuburg to supervise the printing of a book by a leading architect of the Protestant Reformation. Like virtually all Spaniards, Juan had begun life as a Catholic, but during his studies in Paris he drew close to the Protestants and eventually moved to Strasbourg, a Calvinist stronghold, to join them. Alfonso had remained in the Church.

Alfonso and a companion approached the inn where Juan was staying. They carried a letter for him.[1] As his companion rapped on the door, Alfonso stood out of sight. The servant who answered the door was instructed to awaken Juan, because of an urgent message from his brother. A first-person account by one Claudio Senarcleo describes the scene. "Juan was asleep in a room with me, when the young domestic came in and awakened him. He jumped out of bed, clad only in a light nightgown, and went into the front room to receive the 'messenger' with Alfonso's letter." Alfonso stayed hidden from view as Juan received the letter. "Dawn was beginning to break, and Juan went over to the window to read it."

Alfonso stated in the letter that Juan was not safe in Neuburg; he was the object of a plot, and he should leave immediately. Senarcleo's account continues:

> While his attention was thus engaged, the assassin took out the hatchet he carried hidden inside his jacket and plunged it up to the handle into the right side of Juan's head, near the temple. In an instant all the sensory organs in the brain were destroyed, so that Juan could not utter a sound. So as not to disturb any of us with the sound of a falling body, the assassin caught Juan's body and eased it quietly to the floor, where it lay with the hatchet protruding from the head. All this was done so quickly and silently that none of us knew anything about it.[2]

Events three months earlier had set the fratricide in motion. As part of the Protestant contingent, Juan Díaz had attended a colloquy to hammer out religious unity in German states riven by the Reformation. (Like other such conferences, it ended in failure.)[3] At this gathering Juan had encountered an old Spanish acquaintance, Pedro de Malvenda, a member of the Catholic delegation, who was shocked to discover Juan among the Protestants. "What! Juan Díaz in Germany, and in the company of Protestants! . . . No, I am deceived; it is a phantom before me, resembling Díaz, indeed, in stature and in feature, but it is a mere empty image!"[4]

For Malvenda, Spain was the national embodiment of Catholicism. "To conquer one Spaniard," he reportedly declared, "was more momentous . . . than to win ten thousand Germans or numberless proselytes from other nations." Díaz must not "destroy the purity of the word 'Spanish.'" At the conference he sought in vain to bring Díaz back into the Church. He begged him to confess his sins and ask for repentance from Charles V, Holy Roman Emperor and (as Carlos I) King of Spain. Malvenda also alerted

Alfonso Díaz in Rome; he had known little of his brother's religious peregrinations and at once hurried to Juan's side. Senarcleo reports that Juan

> was touched by this sign of fraternal love . . . and he received Alfonso with great respect and affection. Alfonso told Juan how he had made the long and arduous journey from Rome to persuade Juan to give up his heresy and return with Alfonso to Rome and the true faith. He spoke of the dangers of persisting in his heresy, and of the dishonor Juan was bringing to the family name.[5]

Juan could not be convinced. Alfonso then sought to persuade him at least to return to Spain, where he might practice his new faith among his countrymen. Juan "was sorely tempted to follow the advice of his brother whom he loved." However, he conferred with colleagues who counseled against it. They feared he would be persecuted and even arrested. They could have been right. By the 1540s the Inquisition in Spain had turned its attention from the so-called *conversos*—Jews who converted to Christianity—to Christians who had fallen under the influence of Luther, Erasmus, and other reformers. Juan would be a tempting target.[6]

Faced with this refusal, Alfonso made the decision to kill his brother, an act he may well have contemplated as soon as he heard of Juan's apostasy. He withdrew with his associate to a village a few miles away. They dined with a priest and visited a local carpenter, with whom they evaluated an array of hatchets. "The carpenter produced several," Senarcleo reports, "which they carefully hefted for efficiency, finally choosing one which they thought would be satisfactory, i.e., small enough to hide under a coat."

The murder of Juan Díaz by his brother provoked Protestant outrage and Catholic applause. The Spanish humanist Juan Ginés de Sepúlveda wrote that news of the murder was "disagreeable to none of our countrymen."[7] Of course, the Protestants did not see it that way. As a leading Protestant reformer, Martin Bucer, declared in his preface to Senarcleo's chronicle, the "generation of Cain" tracked down Juan Díaz, who was "killed with exquisite perfidy by his twin and only brother."[8] Bucer was not alone in his reference to Cain and Abel. Senarcleo's title translates as "The True Story of the Death of the Spaniard, Saint Juan Díaz, whom His Blood Brother Nefariously Murdered, Having Followed the Example of the First Parricide Cain as He Did to His Own Brother Abel."[9] Accounts of the murder often allude to Cain. John Foxe's popular sixteenth-century *Book of Martyrs* called this "terrible murder" something that "was never heard of since the first example of Cain who, for religion, slew his own brother Abel."[10]

After the murder, Alfonso and his hired assassin fled, but they were captured. Judicial machinations by the emperor and the pope obtained their release.[11] The murder then vanished from history, remembered, if at all, in passing, in histories of sixteenth-century Spain and the Inquisition, old compilations of Protestant martyrdom, and oddball story collections for young Christians.[12]

Twenty-six years after Díaz killed Díaz, Paris was in a festive mood. French Protestants—or Huguenots—and French Catholics had been warring for decades, bloodying the country. But a celebration scheduled for August 18, 1572, promised reconciliation. Catherine de Medici, the mother of the Catholic king of France, Charles IX, had arranged for her daughter Margaret of Valois to marry the Protestant Henri, King of Navarre, a union that might heal France by ending the bloodletting between Christians. All the leading Huguenots arrived to join in the festivities. In her memoirs, Margaret recalled the wedding as a glorious occasion.

> I was set out in a most royal manner; I wore a crown on my head with the 'coet', or regal close gown of ermine, and I blazed in diamonds. My blue-coloured robe had a train to it of four ells in length, which was supported by three princesses. A platform had been raised, some height from the ground, which led from the Bishop's palace to the Church of Notre-Dame. It was hung with

cloth of gold; and below it stood the people in throngs to view the procession. . . . We were received at the church door by the Cardinal de Bourbon, who officiated for that day, and pronounced the nuptial benediction.[13]

Among the prominent Huguenot guests was their military leader, Admiral Gaspard de Coligny. He wrote to his wife, "Today the marriage of Madame the King's sister and the King of Navarre was celebrated. The next few days will be passed in feasting and in presenting masques and combats."[14] But "the next few days" proved something less than celebratory. On August 22, a would-be assassin shot and gravely wounded Coligny. The shooter escaped. Who sent him? We still do not know, but it seems he was linked to the Catholic House of Guise.[15] With the attempted assassination of the Huguenot leader, Paris turned tense. Charles's brother advised Coligny to assemble his friends and supporters in case of further trouble.

At this point, historians and participants differ as to who orchestrated what.[16] Perhaps the king's council feared a Huguenot reprisal and to prevent it decided to slaughter its leaders in the capital the next day. Perhaps—and this is what contemporary Protestants believed—a plan to kill them had already been drawn up. After all, hadn't they been lured to the city for the nuptials and then locked inside as the city gates closed? One sixteenth-century chronicler believed that the "things that followed" proved the strategy had been hatched long ago. "For those whiche might haue by flight escaped out of the suburbs were nowe holden fast inough, being enclosed not only within the walles of the towne, but also within the compasse of one narrow strete."[17]

In any event, "Sometime in the afternoon or evening of 23 August it was agreed that the Huguenot leaders must die," reports the historian Barbara Diefendorf. They had just been wined and dined in the Louvre but now were targeted to be killed. As the nineteenth-century French historian Jules Michelet put it, "The dinner companions and associates of last night, the officers and captains of the guard, were to be their executioners in the morning."[18] Did Catherine de Medici, who engineered the marriage of her daughter to a Protestant king to bring peace to France, support this plan? Who played the key role? "The truth will never be known," Diefendorf concludes. "Everyone who was party to these events had reason later to lie."[19] There are no independent sources. Many key documents were destroyed. The nineteenth-century historian Lord Acton, who examined the role of Austria, Italy, and the pope in the massacre, noted the missing evidence. "No letters written from Paris at the time have been found in the Austrian archives," he wrote in an essay, "The Massacre of St. Bartholomew." "In the correspondence of thirteen agents of the House of Este at the Court of Rome, every paper relating to the event has disappeared. All the documents of 1572, both from Rome and Paris, are wanting in the archives of Venice. In the Registers of many French towns the leaves which contained the records of August and September in that year have been torn out."[20]

Before dawn on August 24, the feast of St. Bartholomew— with more wedding celebrations planned for that day and those following—the bells of Saint-Germain l'Auxerrois, the parish church of the French monarchy, began to peal. That was the signal. The city gates had already been shut. The young duke of Guise, twenty-two years old, head of the hard-line French Catholics, led an armed militia to Coligny's quarters, where they broke into his second-story bedroom. As the duke waited below, his men slew Coligny, who reportedly said that he wished it were "a man rather than this dirty adolescent who causes my death." The duke demanded proof that the deed was done and his followers—a motley collection of French and foreign soldiers—hurled the body from the window into the street. With Coligny's identity confirmed, the duke sent his men off to dispatch the other Huguenots.[21]

The day began, but did not end, with the murder of several dozen Huguenot leaders in their beds. The killing of the Protestant elite triggered a general massacre. Over the next few days rabid Catholics tracked down Protestants throughout Paris. With great ferocity mobs ferreted out Huguenots and hacked them to death. To what extent this bloodbath was expected and organized or spontaneous and unanticipated remains vigorously contested by both contemporary and later commentators. One Mathurin Lussault was killed the moment he opened his door on the evening of the twenty-fourth. When his son came downstairs after him, he too was stabbed, and died in the street. Lussault's wife tried to escape by jumping out of a second-story window and broke both her legs. She was discovered in a neighbor's yard and the mob "dragged her by the hair a long way through the streets, and spying the gold bracelets on her arms, without having the patience to unfasten them, cut off her wrists." Impaled on a spit, her corpse was paraded through Paris before being thrown into the Seine.[22] In three days several thousand Protestants were slain in Paris. After that the bloodletting spread to the provinces, where tens of thousands died. "I am sure that the wild beasts are kinder than those in human form," concluded one Protestant observer of the rampage. He noted that "Huguenot-hunting" had become a popular pastime.[23]

The St. Bartholomew's Day Massacre stands even today as a symbol of religious vengeance, as well as fratricidal violence. Two centuries later Voltaire, a sworn critic of religious sectarianism, claimed he took ill every year on its anniversary. Some points, however, are still worth making about these events. The conflict was especially brutal, because—not in spite of—the fact that the participants were neighbors. This lesson is difficult to acknowledge. Kinship produced enmity, not affection. In Paris in 1572 neighbors savaged neighbors. These people knew one another—or at least were accustomed to passing one another in the street. They were not strangers or foreigners. As with the Díaz brothers—indeed, as is frequently the case in history—proximity engendered not warmth but rage.

The slaughter cannot be discounted as solely an irrational effusion of popular anger, since it found approval among the learned and the powerful.[24] King Charles and his mother both commended the mayhem. The Church was delighted by it. The papal nuncio in Paris, Anton Maria Salviati, wrote that he "desired to fling himself at the pope's feet for joy." He was pleased that God had promoted the true faith "so honorably" and that the French monarchy had been able to "extirpate the poisonous roots with such prudence."[25]

A Swiss monk at a Jesuit college in Paris reported to his abbot: "I do not think that I shall weary you in telling you at length of an occurrence as unexpected as it is helpful to our cause, one that not only captures the world's admiration but also raises it to the highest pitch of joy." He assured the abbot that he could "rejoice" with confidence because the information derived from "unimpeachable sources." He described "an immense slaughter" that filled the Seine with "naked and horribly maltreated bodies." All the Protestant booksellers "who could be found" had been killed and "thrown naked into the waters." Petrus Ramos, a Huguenot philosopher, who "leapt from an upper story bedroom," floated unclothed in the river, his body "pierced" by many daggers. "In a word, there is no one (not excepting the women) who is not killed or wounded." The monk was filled with gratitude. "Everyone agrees in praising the prudence and magnanimity of the king, who, having as it were fattened the heretics like cattle with his kindness and indulgence, has suddenly had their throats slit by his soldiers."[26]

The news of the massacre pleased Pope Gregory XIII no end. The guns of Castel Sant'Angelo were fired, and Rome was illuminated for three days. A thanksgiving mass was celebrated and the pope thanked God for having "granted the Catholic people a glorious triumph over a perfidious race."[27] A papal medal was struck to commemorate the occasion; it showed Gregory on one side and on the other an exterminating angel with a sword attacking a fleeing foe.[28] It was inscribed "*Ugonottorum Strages.* 1572," or "Huguenots Slaughtered 1572."[29] Nor was that all. Adjoining the Sistine Chapel in the Vatican Palace, the Sala Regia had just been built. The room was intended to serve as the pope's principal audience chamber, where he would meet ambassadors and other diplomats.

No commission, however, had been awarded for decoration of the wall behind the throne.

This task was now assigned to the painter and architect Giorgio Vasari, with instructions to honor the glorious killing of the heretical Huguenots.[30] Vasari painted three frescoes titled *Massacre of the Huguenots*. The first shows the attempted assassination of Coligny; the second, titled *The Slaughter of Coligny and His Men*, shows the admiral thrown from a balcony while his followers are hacked to death; and the third, *Charles IX before Parliament*, shows the king approving the murder.

The art historian Philipp Fehl has noted that these frescoes have been oddly neglected by commentators. Even "guide books to the Vatican pass them over or, at best, barely mention their subject."[31] Evidence of this point can be found in the classic *Catholic Encyclopedia*, where the paintings receive a brief and sanitized mention. The *Encyclopedia* notes that Gregory XIII engaged Vasari to paint scenes "commemorative" of "the triumph of the Most Christian King over the Huguenots." In its description of the room, it states that the "very powerful frescoes" represent "momentous turning-points in the life of the Church" but offers no more information.[32] Acton, himself a Catholic, remarked that "the shameful scene may still be traced upon the wall, where, for three centuries, it has insulted every pontiff that entered the Sistine Chapel."[33] Another historian has observed that the Sala Regia, with its gloating frescoes, has become something of "an embarrassment" to the Vatican nowadays, and is rarely opened to the public.[34]

The slaughter pitted Christian against Christian, Frenchman against Frenchman. As Michelet wrote, the conflict consisted of "neighbor against neighbor, people who knew each other."[35] The rise of the Huguenots had in fact split families, alienating parents from their children and brothers from brothers. "Families like the Budés and Hotmans were set against one another," the historian Donald Kelley observes of two leading French families. "While François Hotman and his son Jean were serving Protestant interests abroad, for example, his brothers and cousins in Paris were actively supporting the Catholic League."[36] François Hotman himself remarked that "learned men" had read "many histories" but none contained comparable tales of internecine violence. In the past, "cruelties" had been visited upon "foreigners and strangers," but now French citizens attacked one another.[37]

Fratricidal struggles often tap deep reservoirs of fury. This too, though difficult to accept, marks civil strife across the ages. "No one can imagine the rage and frenzy of those who slaughtered," reported the Venetian ambassador in Paris.[38] Coligny's head was cut off, the body butchered, and the remains dragged through the streets and then strung up for all to view. "Away with him, cut off his head and handes," runs a couplet from Christopher Marlowe's *The Massacre at Paris*, "And send them for a present to the Pope."[39] To this day learned scholars discuss the actual disposition of the head, which seems to have disappeared.[40] (The rumor that the head was delivered to the pope, which Marlowe might have believed, has no basis.) The Parisian crowd specialized in castrating corpses and slicing open pregnant women. "They spared neither the women nor the children," reported an admirer.[41] The Venetian ambassador found it "strange and barbarous to see people in every street composedly, deliberately committing acts of cruelty upon inoffensive fellow-countrymen, often acquaintances, even relations."[42]

The Venetian ambassador had it right: the massacre of the Huguenots was barbarous. In these years a series of words— *barbarian, savages, massacre,* and *cannibal*—were coined or redefined and brought to bear on the European religious civil wars. *Barbarian,* from the Greek, originally referred to anyone who wasn't Greek. By extension it designated foreigners or persons who were culturally and linguistically strange. The term came home, however, in the sixteenth century. *Barbarian* moved from describing the foreign inhabitants of the New World to those subduing them and finally to Protestants and Catholics of the Old World who were murdering one another.

The discovery of the New World had prompted a controversy about the nature of its natives that would last for centuries. With frequent references to Aristotle, sixteenth-century theologians argued as to whether the indigenous people were barbarians, natural slaves, or innocent souls.[43] Some of the earliest observers of the Spanish colonizers, however, came to a separate conclusion. The great Dominican priest Bartolomé de las Casas had been a typical colonist in Hispaniola (now Haiti and the Dominican Republic) but underwent a conversion to emerge as a defender of the native Indians, a role that became his career. In 1550 he debated the Spanish humanist Juan Ginés de Sepúlveda, who had welcomed the murder of Juan Díaz and now defended the conquest and enslavement of the Indians.[44] Las Casas did not believe in concessions or compromise. "I will show that the Reverend Doctor Sepúlveda . . . is wrong in law in everything," Las Casas stated, and also wrong "in fact" about everything.

Las Casas followed the style of the day inasmuch as he demarcated, in the spirit of Aristotle, the types of barbarians. For Sepúlveda the barbarian status of the natives justified Spanish domination. The title of one of his essays on the subject captures this sentiment. He supported the papal decree "Which Gives the Catholic Kings . . . Authority to Conquer the Indies and Subject Those Barbarians, and by This Means Convert Them to the Christian Religion and Submit Them to Their Empire and Jurisdiction."[45]

Las Casas, however, turned the term *barbarian* against the civilizers. "Barbarian in the loose and broad sense of the word," he wrote, "means any cruel, inhuman and merciless man acting against human reason . . . so that . . . he becomes . . . unbearably cruel, and plunges into crimes that only the wildest beast of the forest would commit." Las Casas found this definition inapplicable to the Indians but fit for the Spaniards, who unleashed "massacres" against the harmless indigenes. "In the absolutely inhuman things they have done to those [Indian] nations," he wrote, "they have surpassed all other barbarians." He did not mince words. "The

Spaniards who have maltreated the Indians . . . with so many massacres, and evils . . . are barbarians and worse than barbarians."[46]

Nor did Las Casas shrink from giving details to his readers. His *Devastation of the Indies* (1542) described gratuitous dismemberments and torture of the Indians. A Spaniard "summons" a hundred Indians and they come "like sheep." "He commands his soldiers to decapitate thirty or forty of the Indians" and warns the others that the same fate awaits them "if you do not serve me well" or if they try to escape. "Could anything," asks Las Casas, "be uglier, more horrible, more inhuman than this?" He cites sworn first-person testimonies of priests: "I affirm that with my own eyes I saw Spaniards cut off the nose, hands and ears of Indians, male and female, without provocation, merely because it pleased them. . . . I have seen Spaniards urge their dogs to tear Indians to pieces, this I have seen many times."[47]

Who were the barbarians? For Las Casas, Christians can be barbarians if they "manifest fierceness, wildness, savagery, and cruelty." Others too would come to this conclusion. The lawyer and humanist Alonso de Zorita, who wrote one of the earliest descriptions of Aztec life, also turned the intellectual tables. There was no "reason for calling" the Indians "barbarians," he wrote a few years after Las Casas, since they were both innocent and able to learn. "Let those who call them barbarians consider that by the same token they could call 'barbarians' the Spaniards."[48]

In the wake of the religious wars, the word seemed apt for all of Europe. The St. Bartholomew's Day Massacre and wider French civil wars from 1562 to 1598 were marked by a violence previously unseen or unremembered. Huguenots as well as Catholics participated in dismemberments, infanticide, even cannibalism. Richard Vestegan, a Catholic Dutch-English writer, published *Theatre of the Cruelties on the Heretics of Our Time* (1587), an account of horrific Protestant violence. It included detailed engravings of Protestants disemboweling Catholics, mutilating priests, and knifing pregnant women. One image depicts the Huguenots feeding an eviscerated Catholic to farm animals.[49]

Contemporary witnesses concluded that barbarism had arrived in France. For years, observed a French Protestant of the civil strife, "not strangers" but Frenchmen were killing Frenchmen. "The father kills his son, the son his father, the brother his brother, and the parent his parent."[50] A modern French historian summarizes eyewitness accounts and concludes, "Barbarism was no longer something far away or distant; it was among the French themselves." The concept underwent a "radical upheaval" and no longer pertained to a phenomenon distant in time or place.[51] A sixteenth-century Protestant pamphleteer accused the king of violating "the bonds of nature and humanity, which the very barbarians will never do."[52]

The words *massacre* and *cannibal* also entered common parlance during these years and reflected the European internecine wars. *Massacre,* a French word, had originally referred only to a butcher's chopping block, but the religious wars bestowed on it a new meaning, which the English adopted from the French.[53] A Protestant account of a 1572 slaughter in Lyon—in the wake of the St. Bartholomew's Day Massacre—claimed that when soldiers and the official executioner refused to slay imprisoned Huguenots, the governor enlisted seamen and butchers to do the job. "Those fellows went to it with chopping knives and butchers' axes" and "for sport" cut off fingers and hands.[54] The Oxford English Dictionary reports that *massacre* in its present sense was first used in 1578 in connection with the Parisian violence. This association endured. Marlowe probably picked up the word from Huguenots who fled France for England; he incorporated it in several of his plays, most notably *The Massacre of Paris.*[55]

Cannibal too bears the traces of civil strife, and it remains a contested term among anthropologists.[56] The word derives from the Spanish *Canibales,* a form of the name *Caribes,* and dates from the voyage of Columbus, who characterized (and perhaps mischaracterized) the Caribs, inhabitants of the islands in the Caribbean, as man-eaters. An influential report of New World cannibalism originated from a visit to the New World by a Frenchman. Jean de Léry's *History of a Voyage to the Land of Brazil,* an account of a French Protestant expedition to that country in the mid-1550s, has been prized through the centuries. (The twentieth-century French anthropologist Claude Lévi-Strauss packed the book when he first traveled to Brazil.) Léry offered a sober account of the customs, religion, and language of the Tupinamba Indians of Brazil. He revised his account several times and only published it in 1578, some twenty years after his visit. The dates are pertinent since Léry was a Huguenot. Between his Brazilian journey and his published account, the St. Bartholomew's Day Massacre of 1572 intervened.

As a very young man Léry had joined the Brazil expedition as much "out of curiosity to see this New World" as to serve God's "glory."[57] Léry and his companions planned to establish a Protestant outpost in Brazil, but the colony failed to take root. On his return from Brazil, Léry pursued his studies and became a Huguenot minister. At the time of the massacre, he was working as a pastor in a small village on the Loire. The Parisian violence spread through the countryside to Léry's town, where twenty-two Huguenots were killed. With other frightened coreligionists Léry fled to nearby Sancerre, a fortified hill town and Huguenot stronghold. After Catholic forces failed to overwhelm Sancerre, they laid siege to it. The blockade endured for eight months before the starved inhabitants finally surrendered. In his *L'Histoire mémorable de la ville de Sancerre* (1573), Léry tracks the slow descent of the residents. First they ate the horses, cats, and rats and then moved on to leather, paper, and—in at least one case—their own dead. In his description of this he alludes to his experience in Brazil, where he witnessed "savages" who ate human flesh. Until now, he writes, he had never seen such a pitiable event in "our France."[58]

Five years later Léry, still in the grip of the St. Bartholomew's Day Massacre, published his account of his Brazilian journey.[59] He continued to revise and augment the book, which went through numerous editions, in light of the French civil wars. Léry's experience of French savagery in the St. Bartholomew Massacre and the siege of Sancerre infused his interpretation of the cannibalism practiced by Brazil's Tupinamba Indians; he viewed New World barbarism through the lens of Old World barbarism. He concluded his chapter on "How the Americans Treat Their Prisoners of War and the Ceremonies They Observe Both in Killing and in Eating Them" by shifting the subject to European cruelty. Léry describes in detail how Indians eviscerated bodies, roasted body parts, and did other things "to make your hair stand on end." He observes that first the prisoners were killed with a single blow to the back of the skull, aimed "so accurately" that blood was not shed.

Yet Léry does not leave it at that; he is not simply describing exotic behavior. He wants his readers to "think more carefully about the things that go on every day over here, among us." He observes that "one need not go beyond one's own country, nor as far as America, to see such monstrous and prodigious things." He alludes to atrocities of the French civil strife in which Catholics supposedly grilled the livers of Huguenots. "If it comes to the brutal action of really (as one says) chewing and devouring human flesh, have we not found people in these regions over here, even among those who bear the name of Christian . . . who, not content with having cruelly put to death their enemies, have been unable to slake their bloodthirst except by eating their livers and hearts?"

Nor is it just Christians. It is French Christians. "And, without going further, what of France? (I am French, and it grieves me to say it.) During the bloody tragedy that began in Paris on the twenty-fourth of August 1572, other acts horrible to recount" took place, including the butchering of people "in ways more barbarous than those of the savages." He provides examples. "There are thousands alive today who beheld these things never before heard of among people anywhere." He closes the chapter:

> So let us henceforth no longer abhor so very greatly the cruelty of the anthropophagous—that is, man-eating—savages. For since there are some here in our midst even worse and more detest-

able than those who, as we have seen, attack only enemy nations, while the ones here have plunged into the blood of their kinsmen, neighbors, and compatriots.[60]

Two years after the *Histoire*'s 1578 publication, Michel de Montaigne published his essays. He had retired on his birthday at the ripe age of thirty-eight. He explained that "weary of the servitude of the court and public employment," he sought repose among the learned giants of the past, where he hoped to spend "what little remains" of his life. (He died at fifty-nine.) Montaigne wrote amid the French religious wars. In more than a hundred pieces that ponder everything from war to sleep, he never directly mentions the St. Bartholomew's Day Massacre, although he often alludes to the violence of religious strife.[61] In one essay he observes that the violence of civil wars outstrips that of foreign war and that "many today" wish that the "heat of civil commotions among us" could be diverted into a foreign war. "Indeed a foreign war is a distemper much less harsh than a civil war." But Montaigne considered a war to resolve an internal conflict "a wicked" enterprise.[62]

Several of his essays examine the unparalleled violence of "our" civil wars. "If I had not seen it," he writes, "I could hardly have made myself believe" in the violence of people who for pleasure "hack at another man's limbs and lop them off, and would cudgel their brains to invent unusual tortures and new forms of murder."[63] His famed essay "On the Cannibals" draws out most emphatically the implications of the French violence. For this essay Montaigne employs reports from Brazilian colonies (including Léry's) in order to meditate on the differences between foreign and local violence. Like Léry, he turned the intellectual tables.[64] Like Léry, he decried the characterization of the New World natives as barbarous or savage—at least in comparison to the Europeans.

Montaigne describes the ways the Indians eat, dance, and hunt. He also gives an account of their conduct in war, which includes cannibalism, and he contrasts the eating of the dead in the New World with the torture of the living in the Old. It does not trouble him to note the "horrible barbarity" of New World cannibalism. It does trouble him that while we damn their practices, we are "blind" to our own.

> I think there is more barbarity in eating a man alive than in eating him dead; more barbarity in lacerating by rack and torture a body still fully able to feel things, in roasting him little by little and having him bruised and bitten by pigs and dogs (as we have not only read about but seen in recent memory, not among our enemies in antiquity but among our fellow-citizens and neighbours—and what is worse, in the name of duty and religion) than in roasting him and eating him after his death.

In this passage Montaigne alludes to contemporary fratricidal violence in France. "We have seen in recent memory," he reminds his readers, atrocities among "our fellow-citizens and neighbours." In Brazil cannibals devoured enemies in war after they were dead. In France, citizens tortured neighbors until they were dead. He concludes, "So we can indeed call those folk [the Brazilian cannibals] barbarians by the rules of reason, but not in comparison with ourselves, who surpass them in every kind of barbarism."[65]

About the time that Alfonso Díaz was stalking his brother, Juan, another Spaniard, who also studied in France, left the Catholic fold and fell afoul not only of the Inquisition but of the reformers—in this case, the Calvinists—thus making himself, in the words of one historian, a "complete heretic."[66] Inasmuch as Michael Servetus challenged infant baptism and the traditional interpretation of the Trinity, he alarmed both the Catholics and the Calvinists. The Calvinists supplied information to the Inquisition in the hope that Servetus would be convicted of heresy, but he eluded its grasp. When the Inquisition became aware that Servetus was in Germany, it hoped the Protestants would complete what the Catholics had failed to do. "These heretics of Germany, Lutheran or

Zwinglian," wrote an Italian cardinal, "wherever the Spaniard may be, ought to punish him if they are so very Christian and evangelical and defenders of the faith. . . . He is as much opposed to their profession as to the Catholic."[67]

Like Juan Díaz, Servetus had a brother who was a good son of the Church—a priest, in fact—and the Supreme Council of the Inquisition instructed Juan Servetus to bring Michael back to Spain. The council deemed it of "great import for our Christian religion" to "try every possible means to lure" him home. It counseled Juan to keep the entire affair secret and to entice his brother back with promises of favors or employment. If those failed, he should then "exert pressure."[68] Juan apparently did not interpret this last command as permission to assassinate his brother. Almost six years later the Supreme Council still fretted over Juan's failure to retrieve his sibling and wondered where the heretic might be. It need not have worried; Michael Servetus's fate was no better than that of Juan Díaz.

On the run from the Inquisition, Servetus made the lethal mistake of holing up in John Calvin's stronghold of Geneva, where his doctrinal unorthodoxy proved as unacceptable as it had to the Inquisition. The Geneva Council imposed a death sentence. The authorities rejected decapitation as too gentle and condemned him "to be bound" and "attached to a stake and burned with your book to ashes."[69] In October 1553—six years after the killing of Juan Díaz—an executioner secured Michael Servetus to a stake with an iron chain, tied his book to his arm, and lit the firewood.

Unlike Díaz, Servetus left a mark on history; he was a medical doctor, a theologian, and a writer.[70] Because he rejected belief in the Trinity, today the Unitarians honor him as a founder.[71] His death also inspired one of the earliest and most forceful defenses of religious freedom and tolerance, Sebastian Castellio's *Concerning Heretics* (1554). Castellio, a French theologian of great learning and industry, was drawn to Protestantism and became a preacher in Geneva, but he clashed with Calvin, who had turned the city into his theological fiefdom. Castellio departed Geneva and for some years scrounged for a living. He was probably spared the fate of the Spaniard by his untimely death at forty-eight. Montaigne regretted that this "outstanding" scholar died impoverished.[72]

The execution of Servetus horrified Castellio; to him, it exemplified a murderous age in which Christian turned upon Christian. He deemed *Concerning Heretics* necessary "in these unsettled times."[73] This understated the situation. Religious wars were sweeping Europe. Germany had already witnessed a religious-political upheaval of great violence in the 1520s. "I dare not say (for the atrocity is almost incredible)," wrote Castellio, "that more than thirty thousand in about thirty years have been killed for religion" in Germany. "Men have been drowned, not one by one nor two by two, but a hundred and a thousand at a time and even whole shiploads." He noted that "if a prince had lost, I will not say so many horses, but even so many pigs, he would think that he had sustained great damage."[74]

In *Advice to a Desolate France* (1562), Castellio turned to France and noted that the present war differed from those of the past. This one was fratricidal. He addressed his fellow Frenchmen:

> For they are not strangers, those who are fighting you, as was the case in the past when, being attacked from the outside, you at least found some solace at home in the love and unity of your children. But this time your own children are ravaging and afflicting you . . . by murdering and strangling each other within your bosom, without any mercy whatsoever, with enormous swords, fully drawn, with pistols and with halberds.[75]

To the modern citizen, the enmity among the "children" might seem to have been provoked by arcane doctrinal disputes—perhaps as difficult for an outsider to follow as the doctrinal differences between, for example, Sunni and Shiite Muslims. The execution of Michael Servetus turned on what to some might appear to be a fine point about the interpretation of the Trinity—to what extent Jesus as the son of God was "consubstantial and co-eternal" with God.

The transposing of a single adjective might have prevented his death. The Calvinist preacher who led Servetus to his immolation, William Farel, stated that his life could have been spared if the condemned had shifted the position of one word. As the flames leaped up, Servetus cried out, "O Jesus, Son of the Eternal God, have pity on me!" He declined to say, "O Jesus, Eternal Son of God." For Farel (and others) this fact confirmed the justice of the execution. Servetus had blasphemed the Holy Trinity. "We could not get him openly to admit his errors and confess that Christ is the eternal Son of God." On the very path to his death Servetus refused to repent and transpose the adjective *eternal*.[76]

It is easy to forget that the religious violence of the sixteenth century, and that of the Inquisition that preceded and succeeded it, pitted Christian against Christian. "From the beginning," writes a historian of religion, "Christianity was distinctive among religions in its tendency to demonize its enemies, especially one type: the enemy within the fold."[77] Indeed, this was an irony that Sebastian Castellio regularly raised against Calvin—and one that characterizes fratricidal struggles. Small distinctions are what engender the hatred. Castellio noted that Calvin detested Christians to whom he was close, not those theologically distant from him. Those near were a greater threat than those who were remote. Calvin "wishes to hold as heretics all who disagree with him," Castellio declared. But who are those? "His program would call for the extermination of all the Papists, Lutherans, Zwinglians, Anabaptists, and the rest. There would survive only Calvinists, Jews and Turks, whom he excepts."[78]

On a rare occasion the propensity to attack those close could work in favor of tolerance of those less close. Hugo Grotius, the Dutch philosopher and jurist, rendered this hostility of the neighbor into a defense of the Jew a half century later. The Jews, expelled from Spain and Portugal, had been settling in the Dutch Republic, and the city of Rotterdam commissioned Grotius to address their place within the polity. Grotius never offered a robust defense of the Jews and accepted many anti-Semitic myths. Nevertheless, he believed that Jews should be granted freedom of religion under certain restrictions.[79] He did not consider it advisable for domestic tranquility "to admit any persons into the country who differ so greatly from us in their religious convictions." Jews hate Christians and pose threats to them, he believed, but he evaluated the "opposite arguments" and found them persuasive. With good laws and close supervision Jews might be admitted to the Dutch Republic: at least they composed a smaller risk than the Catholics. Grotius considered Catholics "incomparably more dangerous" than the Jews, "who have neither a head nor a Prince of their religion." Amid the fractious religious wars, this Dutch philosopher, who would spend much of his life buffeted about Europe by Christian sectarian wars, offered a comment that illuminates fratricidal enmities. He declared that the more distant religions, such as Judaism, were less of a threat than the closer. "The religion most differing from ours constitutes the least danger to true belief," stated Grotius. He added a pithy, if rephrased, sentence from Tacitus: *acerrima fratrum odia:* "Most bitter are the hatreds of brothers."[80]

That phrase addresses the situation of Christians throughout Europe of the sixteenth century. Fratricidal hatred turned on similarity, not difference. French Catholics reviled French Huguenots, not Turkish Muslims. Defenders of Christ often attacked Christians more violently than they did Turks (the prevailing shorthand for Muslims). The cognate religion—almost the same but slightly different—offended more than did the foreign religion. In Thomas More's *Utopia* almost any religion could be practiced. "Some worship as a god the sun, others the moon, still others one of the planets."[81] But More wrote *Utopia* in 1516—before the threat of Protestant heresies. Within a few years he had entered government service to become lord chancellor of England. The softhearted utopian became the hard-nosed defender of the faith. He wanted Lutherans suppressed.

In his shift More exemplifies the mechanism by which religious affinity, not dissimilarity, engenders animus. To worship the moon might be acceptable; to submit to the Christian Bible but not recognize the pope was a killing offense. In *Dialogue Concerning Heresies* (1528), More answered the common objection that it was "hard and uncharitable" to put heretics "sometimes to shame, sometimes to death." He appealed to the Christian tradition that executed heretics. "Many sore punishments have been devised for them, and especially by fire, not only in Italy and Germany, but also in Spain, and in effect in every part of Christendom." With obvious satisfaction More added that in England, "as a good Catholic realm," heresy had long been "punished by death in the fire."[82] Following his words with deeds, More as lord chancellor consigned several Protestants to death.[83] Within seven years of publishing his *Dialogue,* More would find it his turn as the good Christian realm of England beheaded him.

In his defense of burning heretics, More often invoked the specter of the Turks. Just as Christians protected their countries against invaders such as the Turks, so must we "defend each other from far the more peril," the loss not only of body but of soul. More drew a distinction between the heretic, who claimed to be a Christian, and the heathen, who was not a Christian: the former was the greater risk. The heathen is distant, geographically and theologically. The heretic is nearby and threatens the soul. The heretics "rising among ourselves and springing of ourselves" should be repressed with "force and fear." He calls them "worse than the Turks."[84]

This sentiment turns on its head the usual dichotomy of the neighbor and the "other." The compatriot—not the stranger—represents the danger. For Christian Europe the "Turk" stood as a shorthand insult for the "other"—the barbarous and the violent. But the internecine wars of Christian against Christian undermined that easy categorization. Again and again in the sixteenth century, the phrase that Christian heretics were "worse than the Turks" surfaced. Christian polemics suggested that the violence of the Catholics (or of the Protestants) surpassed that of the Turks and that the Christian heretic posed greater danger than the Muslim.[85] "Rome is today worse than the Turks," opined Luther. The

Vatican concurred that the danger of the Christian heretic surpassed that of the Muslim. "We are occupied," wrote a papal nuncio in 1523, in preparing for "the general war against the Turk," as well as for "war against the nefarious Martin Luther, who is a greater evil to Christendom than the Turk."[86]

Bartolomé de las Casas, who defended the native people in the Americas, charged that the behavior of the Christians in New Spain was "worse" than the behavior of the Turks. The Spaniards killed millions, "young and old, men, women, and children . . . much worse than the deeds committed by the Turks in their efforts to destroy the Christian Church."[87] The year before the St. Bartholomew's Day Massacre, the Papal Holy League defeated the Turkish forces at the naval battle of Lepanto. The Muslim outsiders threatened the pope's domain, but less so than the insiders, the heretical Christians. The pope told the French ambassador at the Vatican that he found the annihilation of the Huguenots "more pleasing than fifty victories" over the Turks.[88]

Jean de Léry captured the shift as well. In a later edition of *History of a Voyage* he added a lengthy new chapter titled "Of Cruelties Carried Out by the Turks, and other Peoples, and notably the Spanish, Much More Barbarous than even the Savages." He offered a catalog of the world's atrocities drawn across the globe from the Spanish colonies to the Turkish empire. He recounted horrible stories of Turkish violence—for instance, that of Mehmed II, the sultan who conquered Constantinople and sliced in half many of the Greek opponents he captured. But for Léry, the violence of the sultans took second place to that of a Christian, Vlad III, the fifteenth-century Romanian prince known as the "Impaler" in his day and as the inspiration of the Dracula story in ours. (Vlad III was the "son of the dragon" or "Dracula" inasmuch as his father, Vlad Dracul, belonged to the Order of the Dragon.) Vlad savaged equally Christians and Turks. A contemporary woodcut shows him calmly dining at a full table as impalements and vivisections take place before him. The caption of the woodcut reads in part that here it can be seen how Vlad "skewered people and roasted them, and boiled their heads in a pot." As Léry put it, Vlad "did not delight in having the victims killed by some simple and easy death, but by impaling them alive, not sparing a single member of their family." For Léry "the horrible cruelties" of Vlad—and of the Turks he fought—surpassed those of the Brazilian natives.[89]

Under the rubric of "French Cruelties Compared to Those of Savages and Turks," Léry returned to France and recounted episodes of atrocities among Christians that included a Calvinist slaughter of Catholics. To underline the exceptional horror of French violence, Léry presents a three-way verbal "tableau" that contrasts three situations. In the first, he describes the Brazilian cannibals subduing, slicing up, and preparing to consume their opponents. In the second, he offers a panorama of Turks impaling their enemies—children along with soldiers—alive. In the third, he describes the French butchering one another in the religious civil wars. Léry details at length the hacking off of limbs and ears and the burying of opponents alive. He declares that he is not exaggerating the French atrocities, and he asks the reader to judge the three pictures, Brazilian, Turkish, and French. "In contemplating these three tableaus, in your opinion, which will be the most dreadful and hideous to look at? Won't it be the last? Certainly yes." He closes with a verse:

> *Laugh, Pharaoh*
> *Ahab and Nero,*
> *Herod too;*
> *Your barbarity*
> *By this deed*
> *Is buried from view.*[90]

"Of all the great religions past and present, Christianity has been by far the most intolerant," declared the late American historian Perez Zagorin in the opening sentence of his history of tolerance.[91] In this judgment he followed Voltaire, who wrote more than two centuries earlier, in his entry on Toleration in his *Philosophical Dictionary*, "Of all religions, the Christian would of course inspire the most toleration, but till now the Christians have been the most intolerant of all men."[92] Neither author included a critical subclause. The intolerance of Christianity has been mainly directed at other Christians—at local heretics, not foreigners and outsiders. Fratricidal violence marks the history of Christianity.

The Crusades—a series of conflicts with foreign Muslims over a distant city, Jerusalem—stand as a major counterpoint. Exceptions do not prove rules, but exceptions can show how rules operate; they can illuminate the limit and power of rules. The Crusades regularly spilled over into attacks on local heretics and local Jews. The crusaders acted in the name of Christianity to recapture Jerusalem, but as they assembled, a question often arose: why travel to distant lands to fight the enemies of Christianity, when they, especially the Jews, exist here in our midst?

Guibert of Nogent, a French twelfth-century Benedictine historian who wrote a history of the First Crusade (1095–99), recounted in his memoirs how the notion to attack Jews surfaced, and indicated its consequences. The crusaders of Rouen complained as they were about to embark on their journey. "Here we are," Guibert reports their saying, "going off to attack God's enemies in the East, having to travel tremendous distances when there are Jews right here before our very eyes, of all races God's greatest enemy." The warriors added the revealing comment, "This is doing our work in reverse." With that, they picked up their weapons, "rounded up" Jews into a church, and "put them to the sword regardless of age or sex."[93]

A few Jewish reports have survived and confirm this sentiment and its murderous impact. As Germans gathered in the Rhineland for the First Crusade, they savaged at least three Jewish communities in Worms, Mainz, and Cologne.[94] Like the crusaders of Rouen, those of Germany questioned why they should travel so far when heretics existed among them. In the words of a Hebrew narrative, the crusaders said, "Look, now, we are going a long way" to avenge ourselves, but "here, in our very midst" are the Jews who murdered Christ. "Let us first avenge ourselves on them and exterminate them from among the nations." This they tried, and the chroniclers offer horrifying details of Jews "slaughtered, stabbed, strangled, burned, drowned, stoned, and buried alive." At Worms the "crusaders and common folk" assembled under the leadership of one Count Emich. The count "had no mercy on the elderly, on young men and young women, on infants and sucklings, nor on the ill." He put the young Jewish men "to the sword" and "their pregnant women he ripped open."[95]

Some fifty years later, on the eve of the Second Crusade, both the learned and the less learned espoused the same argument. "Why travel abroad when Jews live right here?" popular preachers in Germany asked. "Avenge the crucified one upon his enemies who stand before you; then go to war against the Muslims."[96] Peter the Venerable, a French abbot of reach and influence, approved the idea. Peter, who took a genuine interest in Islam and had commissioned a series of translations of Muslim texts, wrote to King Louis VII of France and asked the same question: "Why should we pursue the enemies of the Christian faith in far and distant lands while vile blasphemers far worse than any Muslims, namely the Jews, who are not far away from us but who live in our midst, blaspheme, abuse, and trample on Christ and the Christian sacraments so freely and insolently and with impunity?" At least the Muslims believed in the Virgin birth. The Jews "disbelieve everything and mock at everything!" To be sure, God did not want us to kill them, "but like Cain . . . they must be made to suffer fearful torments, and be preserved . . . for an existence more bitter than death."[97] The mobs that attacked the Jews did not always remain loyal to the textual subtleties that distinguished fearful torments from death.[98]

The mass killing of enemies "who live in our midst" and who are deemed far worse than the Turks did not spring from papal directives—or not yet. Some fifty years later the papacy endorsed this view. The internal threat loomed larger than the external. The peril arose not from neighbors of a related but different religion, Jews, but from those who professed the same religion. With the so-called Albigensian Crusade, the Vatican sought to stamp out deviant Christians—the Cathars—in southern France. A historian of the Albigensian Crusade noted that the pope proclaimed a holy war to cleanse southern France of "men, women and children whom he readily acknowledged looked and acted like Christians—that was the trouble."[99]

While much about the Cathars remains in dispute—even their name[100]—what is not in dispute is the danger they posed to the papacy. The Cathars rejected Church authority and wanted to return to the simplicity and abstinence of the early Church. As a nineteenth-century Church historian put it, to find a crisis as grave to the Church, one must look to the eighth century, when Islam threatened all of Europe, but that threat was "less serious" than that posed by the Cathars. He quotes Pope Innocent III: "The Cathars are worse than the Turks."[101]

In his call for a crusade, Innocent III denounced the Cathars as "pestiferous men." The Church had tried, he wrote to Philippe II, King of France, to correct the heretics, but they did not mend their ways. "And so," concluded the pope, "wounds that do not respond to the healing of poultices must be lanced with a blade." Those who resist correction must be "suppressed." The pope offered a direct comparison to the more distant Muslims or Saracens. He sought a new crusade toward recapturing not Jerusalem but the towns of Languedoc. "You must try to wipe out the treachery of heresy and its followers" with a strong hand, the pope instructed believers. "Attack the followers of heresy more fearlessly even than the Saracens—since they are more evil."[102]

The pope summoned his troops in 1208: "So rouse yourselves, knights of Christ! Rouse yourselves, strong recruits of Christian knighthood! . . . Vindicate such a terrible injury to your God!"[103] To Catholics committed to extirpate Christian heretics, the pope made an offer: "Catholics who take the cross and gird themselves for the expulsion of the heretics shall enjoy the same indulgence and be strengthened by the same holy privilege, as is granted to those who go to the aid of the Holy Land."[104]

The Albigensian Crusade organized to eliminate the Cathar heresy lasted some twenty years. For a contemporary monk, Peter of les Vaux-de-Cernay, who wrote a chronicle of it, its length was a blessing. "The Lord in His compassion did not wish this most holy war to be ended quickly," but wished that his enemies be "subdued gradually." The "prolongation of the war" allowed more sinners to take up arms and the righteous to attain "a higher state of grace."[105] The war was also conducted with unusual ferocity. As the *Catholic Encyclopedia* puts it, the crusade against the Cathars led to "regrettable excess." It does not take much imagination to understand what this expression signifies. The Cathars disappeared from history—burnt, persecuted, and imprisoned.[106]

The crusaders first laid siege in 1209 to Béziers, a commune in the South of France, six miles from the Mediterranean. A few accounts describing the butchery survive. A sea of tents surrounded Béziers, recounts a poet in "The Song of the Cathar Wars." The inhabitants quaked. The "lords from France and Paris, laymen and clergy, princes and marquises all agreed" that the citizenry of the towns that did not surrender would be "slaughtered wholesale." The crusaders had a list of 222 Cathars living in Béziers, whom they wanted delivered to them. The list probably named only the priests, since the village sheltered many more Cathars. The town also contained numerous loyal Catholics.

Béziers refused to hand over its Cathars, which set the stage for an attack. So-called ruffians or camp followers of the crusaders managed to breach the town walls. The crusaders followed. The Cathars sought refuge in a church—to no avail. The church was set afire. "They killed everyone who fled into the church; no cross or altar or crucifix could save them. . . . They killed the clergy too, and the women and children." The poet adds, "I doubt if one person came out alive."[107] Another contemporary account confirms that almost all the inhabitants "from the youngest to the oldest" were killed. Afterward the invaders torched the town.

Peter of les Vaux-de-Cernay comments that it was "right" that these "shameless dogs" were captured and destroyed; moreover, he points out, the city was taken on the feast day of the Blessed Mary Magdalene and thousands were immolated in the very church in which they insulted her. Their fiery deaths delighted him. "What a splendid example of divine Justice and Providence!"[108] The massacre also gratified the papal envoy Arnaud Amalric, who led the crusaders. "Our men spared no one, irrespective of rank, sex, or age," he boasted in a letter to Pope Innocent, "and put to sword almost 20,000 people." Nor did this suffice. "After this great slaughter," he exulted, "the whole city was despoiled and burnt, as divine vengeance raged marvellously."[109] A series of attacks on other French towns followed, although Béziers remained the most bloody.

Amid a fratricidal struggle of French Catholics and French Cathars, how does one tell enemy from friend? This issue bedevils civil conflicts; combatants frequently look the same. Brothers share features. What distinguishes Cain from Abel? Indeed this question echoes down the corridors of history. As Béziers fell to the crusaders, confusion gave rise to an infamous solution as to how to distinguish fraternal friend from fraternal enemy. If the papal envoy Amalric is remembered for anything today, it is for his response to this problem. When the walls were breached, the invaders realized that the Cathars might mingle with Catholics and thereby escape. They asked Amalric, "Sir, what shall we do, for we cannot distinguish between the faithful and the heretics?" Amalric replied, "Kill them all. The Lord knows his own."[110]

Did he actually say that? We don't know. Writing a dozen years later, a German monk, Caesarius of Heisterbach, who may have had a contact at Béziers, attributes the retort to him; the *Catholic Encyclopedia* describes Caesarius as "a gifted and diligent scholar." It also notes that he told fabulous stories about demons and saints but that he "scrupulously avoids whatever may endanger the principles of true piety and sane morality."[111] To put it differently, Caesarius of Heisterbach did not tell this story to criticize Amalric.

If he contrived the words, it was to praise him. This in itself is revealing. A pious scholar of the era invents these sentences to inspire the faithful. Academic opinion concludes that the command captures the spirit of Amalric, if not his actual words.[112] It also captures the spirit of Catholics thrilled by the massacre. Many scholarly canonists offered justification of the violence at Béziers. A contemporary bishop, Johannes Teutonicus, opined that if a city housed heretics, the whole city could be torched.[113]

Amalric probably exaggerated the numbers killed, but this too is revealing.[114] In his letter to the pope he claimed twenty thousand died. Even with additional Cathars from elsewhere, who may have sought refuge in Béziers as the crusaders approached, this seems unlikely inasmuch as the town's population was only about ten thousand. The exaggeration, however, bespeaks the satisfaction in the fratricidal slaughter. Amalric did not minimize the numbers, as he might have, as evidence of his mercy and judiciousness. He inflated the numbers as evidence of his righteousness, to wit, the more dead the better.

More than three centuries later, Sebastian Castellio reflected on the French religious wars and on neighbors attacking neighbors. He translated the Bible into French, and in his preface addressed the issue of how to distinguish enemy from friend. In religious disputes he proposed the model of the battlefield, where combat ceases at night "lest by chance friends be killed instead of enemies." For Castellio, a "moral" can be drawn from this. We live amid the "night of ignorance" with "diverse and even contrary judgments about the same color." Principally these "disturbances" raise religious questions. But good and evil are "confused" and in the conflict the good gets thrown out with the evil. "Hitherto the world has always made this mistake." The blood of thousands has been shed "under the color of religion." The lesson? "It were better, therefore, in view of so much doubt and confusion, to wait before shooting until the dawn."[115]

Few listened to Castellio's advice, however. With his death "silence" enfolded him. "No one breathed the name of Castellio. His friends died or vanished. His writings that had been published became unobtainable." It might be supposed that "his fight had been fought, his life lived, in vain."[116] These are the words of Stefan Zweig, the once popular Austrian Jewish author, still best known in English for his 1942 autobiography, *The World of Yesterday*.

On the run from the Nazis in the 1930s, Zweig believed he had found a kindred soul in Castellio, about whom he had known nothing. A Swiss acquaintance, who still feared to have his name mentioned in connection with Castellio, suggested that Zweig save the reformer from undeserved neglect.[117] Almost four centuries after Castellio's death, Zweig delved into his writings and his fate. He was struck by the parallels between Castellio and persecuted Jewish refugees like himself. Zweig saw in Castellio a fearless champion of freedom of conscience who had stood up to the dictators of the sixteenth century. He lamented that only a single book on Castellio, written by Étienne Giran, a French theologian, was available.[118] Zweig began to work on a book that would highlight Castellio's relevance for the 1930s.

Yet to draw a straight line from Castellio as a sixteenth-century defender of freedom of conscience to Zweig and others beset by twentieth-century Nazis oversimplifies history. The Jews were driven out of Central Europe in the 1930s not because of their heretical ideas about anything or because they defended freedom of conscience. They were expelled because they were Jews. They shared the ideas of their compatriots. They were neighbors, who breathed and exhaled the same culture as non-Jews. Zweig knew this, of course.

As Vienna fell to the Nazis, Zweig observed that the city—more than any other in Europe—had been "formed and molded" by Jews.[119] As he stated later, Germany was "our homeland." Others can say a "strange spirit" or "strange ideology" has taken over Germany, but "we" cannot. This is our language and culture. "The [Nazi] decrees are composed in the German language, the same language in which we write and think. These brutalities take place in the name of German culture, which we have tried in our works to serve."[120] This is the point. The Jews were citizens who did not differ in their ideas from their fellow Germans.

What links the era of Zweig with that of Castellio is less a return to an imperiled freedom of conscience than a return to fratricidal bloodshed. Castellio wrote amid the religious civil wars of the sixteenth century, Zweig amid what might be called a civil slaughter of the twentieth. Castellio protested the execution of Michael Servetus for heresy in particular, but also the internecine killings of Christians in general. The country did not suffer from an invasion by strangers from the outside, Castellio had declared of sixteenth-century France. The French themselves were "murdering and strangling each other." By the mid-twentieth century, German Jews were as foreign to German Christians as four centuries earlier French Huguenots were to French Catholics. Indeed German Jews had assimilated to the point where they had reworked their religion into "a kind of Protestantism," commented Zweig's friend, the writer Joseph Roth.[121] That might have been the problem. The Jews became more suspect the less distant they became. Someone who speaks the same language, dresses the same, partakes of the same culture but departs slightly in religious rituals offends more than someone who speaks a foreign language, dresses differently, and worships a strange god.

The violence of these centuries suggests that minor differences between neighbors, not grand ideas about freedom of thought, spark civil strife. Rancor over these differences feeds the recrudescence of fratricidal violence across the centuries. This truth remains difficult to swallow. We prefer to stigmatize the strangers and the outsiders. But most violence emerges from within the community. Díaz killing Díaz exemplifies the violence of the twentieth as of the sixteenth century. Zweig may have overplayed the parallel between the plight of Castellio and that of refugees in the 1930s, but he glimpsed the common feature, the relapse into fratricidal barbarism. He wondered when, or if, it would end.

His book on Castellio appeared in 1936, titled in English *The Right to Heresy: Castellio against Calvin*. He used as an epigraph a sentence from Castellio: "Future generations will not understand, why, after living in the light, we are forced back into such deep darkness." In Germany in the name of "the people and the state," the Nazi Reich blocked sales of the book.[122] For Zweig things went from bad to worse. When Germany annexed Austria in 1938, his pessimism deepened. An Austrian citizen who found himself in England, he became a stateless refugee. He doubted that the darkness would lift. He wrote to a friend "for us the dawn will never arrive, the night will last forever."[123] Like many refugees, he was preoccupied with applications for permits and visas for himself and family members; he called himself "formerly a writer, now expert in visas."[124] He had difficulty obtaining a resident visa for the United States. To his distress, his American papers bore the stamp "enemy alien."

Six years after publishing his book on Castellio, a weary Zweig, separated from his beloved books and homeland, tried to reestablish himself in Brazil. He rediscovered Montaigne and planned to write about him. But he saw a future only of "wandering and wandering." He saluted his friends: "May it be granted them yet to see the dawn after the long night!" With that, in 1942 he and his wife committed suicide in Petrópolis, a mountain town fifty miles outside Rio de Janeiro.[125] Zweig could not know that two years later Étienne Giran, the French liberal Protestant who had once authored the single available book on Castellio, would die in Buchenwald.[126]

2

UNCIVIL WARS

"Most wars are now civil wars," runs the first sentence of a World Bank publication.[1] Yet the situation may not differ from the past. Of course, much turns on definitions. What is a traditional or noncivil war? Is it a war between states or distinct peoples? Between strangers? World War I offers an obvious example. An assassination of a high state official provokes a clash of sovereign nations. After issuing an ultimatum, Austria-Hungary attacks Serbia. Hostilities spread across Europe, engaging Russia, Germany, Great Britain, and France, and eventually the United States. World War I might be thought of as a classic war, a murderous conflict among autonomous nations and separate peoples.

Yet this description misses something. World War I was a battle of sovereign nations, but did it consist of separate peoples fighting one another? What constitutes a people with its own culture? A typical definition—a UNESCO statement—characterizes a culture as "distinctive spiritual, material, intellectual and emotional features of society or a social group." A culture encompasses not only art and literature but "lifestyles, ways of living together, value systems, traditions and beliefs."[2] By these criteria did the denizens of Britain, France, Germany, and Russia partake of different cultures? Probably not.

What anthropologist would study the French and the Germans, or the Germans and the British, as unique cultures? A Yale University anthropological database that "facilitates" worldwide "comparative studies of human behavior, society, and culture" contains no listings for the English or the French or the Germans.[3] The ten-volume *Encyclopedia of World Cultures* describes more than 1,500 cultures. One volume is devoted to Europe but lavishes attention on minor ethnic groups. In three hundred large-format pages, 60 million Frenchmen merit a single paragraph, while the fifty thousand Vlachs of the Balkans and the fifty thousand Faroe Islanders of Denmark receive careful dissection over many pages.[4] And why not? How many significant differences could an anthropologist find between the people of the major European powers?

The principal belligerents of World War I shared much in the way of history, culture, and religion, as evidenced by the fact that their leaders—the monarchs of Britain, Germany, and Russia— were not simply related but were close cousins. King George V of Great Britain and Kaiser Wilhelm II of Germany were grandchildren of Queen Victoria, who was also grandmother of Alexandra, the wife of Tsar Nicholas II. (The tsarina passed along to her son, Alexei, the gene for hemophilia that had been carried by Victoria.) The tsar himself was George V's first cousin (both were grandchildren of Christian IX of Denmark), and in photographs the two look like twins. Moreover, a dense network of intermarriages connected the European kings and queens of smaller countries from Sweden, Norway, and Denmark to Spain, Belgium, Romania, and Bulgaria.

As children, the royalty of Germany, Russia, and Great Britain romped together on vacations in England and often attended one another's family celebrations. For years the Russian monarch and the kaiser, first cousin to the tsar's wife, exchanged newsy letters full of family events. The kaiser typically signed his "Your most affectionate friend and cousin." He wrote to "Dearest Nicky" in 1913 to announce the marriage of his daughter and begged Nicky to join in the festivities. "I fervently hope that you will be able to leave Russia for a few days to meet many of your relatives; as we have asked your dear Mama, Aunt Alix [Princess Alice of England], Georgie and May [George V and his wife, Victoria Mary] . . . to enable all the 'Geschwister'"—that is, brothers and sisters—"to meet each other."[5] The tsar did manage to steal away—as did King George—to attend the wedding. The *New York Times* story was subheaded "Three Mightiest Rulers Flanked the Couple as They Took Their Marriage Vows."[6]

Two of the "mightiest rulers" wrote a series of telegrams to each other on the eve of the Great War, in an effort to avoid the coming bloodbath. Just months earlier the kaiser had thanked the tsar for "the lovely china pot" he sent for Wilhelm's birthday.[7] Now, in the so-called Willy-Nicky communiqués, the kaiser and the tsar corresponded in their shared language, English, and sought in vain to clear up the misunderstandings and halt the mobilization. They signed their messages "Your devoted cousin Willy" and "Your loving Nicky." Willy avowed that "my friendship for you and your empire, transmitted to me by my grandfather on his deathbed, has always been sacred to me." Nicky appealed to their old bonds.[8] While the term "the cousins' war" has been employed to refer to Anglo-American conflicts, World War I might also be dubbed a war of cousins. Among the rulers at the top and among the soldiers at the bottom, related peoples with shared cultures fought each other.

In the quintessential war novel *All Quiet on the Western Front*, a French soldier lost in a fog-enshrouded no-man's-land stumbles into a shell hole in which Paul, the German soldier protagonist, has sought refuge. Paul instinctively stabs him. The shooting above continues, which forces the living and the dead soldier to spend hours together. Paul reflects on their fate and bitterly regrets his action. He looks through the papers and photos carried by the dead man, a modest printer with a wife and child. "If you jumped in here again, I would not do it," Paul decides. "Forgive me comrade: how could you be my enemy? If we threw away these rifles and this uniform you could be my brother."[9]

World War I followed on the heels of the Balkan wars of 1912 and 1913, which prefigured not only the subsequent atrocities of the twentieth century but its fraternal violence. In the First Balkan War, the so-called Balkan League—Bulgaria, Greece, Serbia, and Montenegro—defeated the outsider, the Ottoman Empire, but in the second the victorious nations fought one another. The defeat of the Turks in the first war had prepared the way, in the words of a Balkan historian, for a "fratricidal war."[10]

The two Balkan wars might be considered a short course in the dialectic of violence. The attack on the outsider makes way for the attack on the insider. To use psychoanalytic logic, first the father is overthrown, and then the brothers turn on one another. The Macedonian historian Christ Anastasoff notes that the united Balkan League fought against the Turks, the hated foreigners, in order to liberate "their brothers in Macedonia," who saw the League as liberators. "The detested and tyrannical Turks were to be driven out." But in the Second Balkan War, he continues, "the war of 'liberation' soon turned into a war of extermination." Balkan brother attacked Balkan brother with unrestrained violence over hapless Macedonia. In Doxato, now part of Greece, witnesses reported that the Bulgarians burned the Greek part of the town and massacred all its residents. "I saw the heaps of charred remains . . . in the gardens and courtyards," declared an English officer, who arrived soon after the killings. He counted six hundred bodies, mostly women and children.[11] "Not even the detested Turks ever indulged in such barbarities," Anastasoff concludes.[12]

The newly founded Carnegie Endowment for International Peace issued a comprehensive report on the Balkan wars. "Nations which had been in alliance and had invoked the aid of Heaven in a war of deliverance," the study declared, "suddenly awoke to fierce hatred of each other. . . . Those who fought side by side . . . were

now ready to kill, mutilate, and to torture each other." In the introduction to the Carnegie study, Paul Henri d'Estournelles de Constant, a diplomat and peace activist, called this second war among
the Balkan peoples "a war of religion, of reprisals, of race . . . of
man against man and brother against brother." The Second Balkan
War, he thought, might be "only the beginning of other wars."[13]

So it would be. The Carnegie report bears the date February 22,
1914. Four months later, in June, the assassination of an archduke
in the Balkans led to World War I, which has also been called "the
Third Balkan War."[14] By an exponential factor the third surpassed
the first two in violence. The loving cousins directed their subjects to kill one another, which they did with gusto. The scale of
the slaughter remains unfathomable. One example: In seven days
on the Western Front, at Passchendaele, the losses matched those
of American soldiers in twelve years of the Vietnam War—some
fifty-five thousand, or almost eight thousand deaths a day. The
cultural links between the belligerents evidently did not prevent
bloodshed. Perhaps the reverse. World War I might be considered
a civil war inasmuch as it was a conflict between kindred, not foreign, peoples. To the degree that World War II emerged out of
its wreckage, some historians view World War I as a chapter in a
twentieth-century European civil war.[15]

However, to stick to conventional criteria of civil wars, which
exclude wars between sovereign nations, intrastate conflicts increasingly characterize the present and the recent past. Not only
are there more civil wars, but they last longer.[16] The conflicts in
Southern Sudan have been going on for decades. Large-scale attacks of one state on another have become rare, the recent wars
waged by the United States in Iraq and Afghanistan being notable
exceptions. States seldom attack states nowadays, and when they
do, the fighting is short-lived (witness Israel's monthlong incur-
sion into Lebanon in 2006).

We live in an era of ethnic, national, and religious fratricide.
A new two-volume reference work on "the most severe civil wars
since World War II" has forty-one entries running from Afghani-

stan and Algeria to Yemen and Zimbabwe.[17] Over the last fifty
years the number of casualties in intrastate conflicts is roughly
five times more than that of interstate wars. The number of refugees from these conflicts similarly dwarfs those from traditional
state-versus-state wars. "Cases such as Afghanistan, Somalia, and
Lebanon testify to the economic devastation that civil wars can
produce," note two political scientists. By the indexes of deaths,
numbers of refugees, and extent of destruction, they conclude,
"civil war has been a far greater scourge than interstate war" in
recent decades.[18]

In the past as well, the toll from civil wars has probably eclipsed
that of conventional wars, although that is easy to forget—and
sometimes deliberately forgotten. More Russian lives were lost in
the Russian Civil War that followed World War I than in the
Great War itself, for instance.[19] But who cares about the Russian
Civil War? A thousand courses and ten thousand books dwell
on World War I but few on the Russian Civil War that emerged
from it. That war, with its fluid battle lines, uncertain alliances,
and clouded beginning, seems too murky. It was a "three-cornered
struggle" with Russian revolutionaries against counterrevolutionaries and national minorities resisting both.[20] (And this shorthand leaves out a fourth corner, that of the Black Army led by
the Ukrainian anarchist Nestor Makhno.[21]) This stew of hostilities is typical of civil wars. With some notable exceptions, modern
civil wars resist the clear categories of interstate wars. The sides are
blurred. Revenge often trumps ideology and politics.

"Not surprisingly there is no treatise on civil war on the order
of Clausewitz's *On War*," writes the historian Arno Mayer, "civil
wars being essentially wild and savage."[22] Carl von Clausewitz, the
Prussian military thinker, wrote in the wake of the wars against
Napoleon. His iconic book evokes the spirit of Immanuel Kant,
whose writings he studied. Its subheadings, such as "The Knowledge Required in War Is Very Simple, but at the Same Time It Is
Not Easy to Apply," suggest its philosophical structure. Clausewitz
subordinated war to policy, which entailed a rational evaluation of

goals and methods. He compared the state to a person. "Policy" is "the product of its brain," and war is an option. "No one starts a war—or rather, no one in his senses ought to—without first being clear in his mind what he intends to achieve by war and how he intends to conduct it." If civilized nations at war, he writes, "do not put their prisoners to death" or "devastate cities," it is because "intelligence plays a larger role in their methods of warfare . . . than the crude expressions of instinct."[23]

In civil wars, by contrast, prisoners are put to death and cities destroyed as a matter of course. The ancient Greeks had already characterized civil strife as more violent than traditional war. Plato distinguishes war against outsiders from what he calls factionalized struggles, that is, civil wars.[24] He posits that Greeks practice war against foreigners ("barbarians"), a conflict marked by "enmity and hatred," but not against one another. When Greeks fight Greeks, he believes, they should temper their violence in anticipation of reconciliation. "They will not, being Greeks, ravage Greek territory nor burn habitations" nor "lay waste the soil" nor treat all "men, women and children" as their enemy. Such, at least, was his hope in the *Republic,* but the real world contradicted it, as he knew. His proposition that Greeks should not ravage Greeks challenged the reality in which Greeks did exactly that. "Our citizens ought to deal with their Greek opponents" in a temperate way, Plato states in conclusion to this discussion, "while treating barbarians as Greeks now treat Greeks."[25] The sentence encapsulates the problem; an ethical "ought" stands like a reed against a brutal reality of how Greeks "now" treat one another. Indeed the notion that "enmity and hatred" can be confined to wars against foreigners evaporated in the rancor unleashed in the Greek civil wars.

Plato did not have to look further than Thucydides' account of the Peloponnesian War to find confirmation of the brutality of Greek-on-Greek strife. In a passage often commented upon, Thucydides wrote of the seesaw battle in Corcyra (Corfu) in 433 BCE, which prefigured the larger war. When the Athenians approached the island in force, the faction it supported seized the occasion to settle accounts with its adversaries. In Thucydides' telling, this was a "savage" civil war of Corcyraean against Corcyraean. For the seven days the Athenians stayed in the harbor, Corcyraeans "continued to massacre those of their own citizens" whom they considered their enemies. "There was death in every shape and form," writes Thucydides. "People went to every extreme and beyond it. There were fathers who killed their sons; men were dragged from the temples and butchered on the very altars." Families turned on families. "Blood ties became more foreign than factional ones." Loyalty to the faction overrode loyalty to family members, who became the enemy.[26]

For Thucydides the "passions of civil war" leave no room for compromise. The impulse of revenge undermines reconciliation. "Personal ambition" and "violent fanaticism" drive the conflict. "The victims [members of the anti-Athenian faction] were accused of conspiring to overthrow democracy, but in fact men were often killed on grounds of personal hatred or else by their debtors because of the money they owed."[27] The Venetian ambassador's report on the St. Bartholomew's Day Massacre two thousand years later used almost the same words. The crowd had no mercy, he wrote in 1572. "If one man hated another because of some argument or lawsuit, all he had to say was 'This man is Huguenot' and he was immediately killed. (That happened to many Catholics.)"[28] Such is civil dissension across the millennia. Hatreds and grudges often overwhelm principles and politics.

Twenty-five hundred years after Thucydides, the presiding judge at a United Nations "Prosecution of Persons Responsible for Serious Violations of International Law" invoked the Greek historian. The Guyanese judge reflected on what had occurred in the former Yugoslavia. One Duško Tadić stood accused of the torture and murder of Muslims in his hometown in Bosnia-Herzegovina. His actions exemplified a war of ethnic cleansing fueled by resentment and hatred. "Some time ago, yet not far from where the events in this case happened," something similar occurred, stated the judge in his 1999 opinion. He cited Thucydides' description of the Corcyraean civil war as one of "savage and pitiless actions." Then as today, the judge reminded us, men "were swept away into an internecine struggle" in which vengeance supplanted justice.[29]

Some observers—not many—have glimpsed an advantage in the animus of civil wars. Insofar as passion and hatreds fuel civil conflict, they find it superior to the cold violence of state-versus-state war. Chateaubriand, the nineteenth-century French writer and diplomat, was one of these. "Frankly, is it much more humane to slay a family of German peasants whom you do not know?" he asked in his memoirs. "Whatever men may say, civil wars are less unjust, less revolting, and more natural than foreign wars." For Chateaubriand civil wars were "based at least upon individual outrages. . . . If the passions do not justify the evil, they excuse it, they explain it, they give a reason for its existence."[30]

The twentieth-century Sicilian novelist Leonardo Sciascia captured this sentiment in his 1958 short story "Antimony," in which a young illiterate Italian miner naively volunteers for the forces that Mussolini sends to aid the Nationalists in the Spanish Civil War. After they take a small town from the Republican forces, he watches a throng assemble. He imagines a celebration is about to take place. Instead, the residents gather "to see the prisoners about to be shot filing past: a hundred men tied together in threes." If the Republicans reconquer the town, he knows, priests and landlords will be slain, not peasants and workers. Each side has its cause. He realizes that a civil war is not like a war in which one country invades another and soldiers attack people they don't know for reasons they don't understand. "A civil war is not a stupid thing like a war between nations, the Italians fighting the English, or the Germans against the Russians, where I, a Sicilian sulphur miner, kill an English miner." A civil war makes bitter sense to this young peasant solider. One fights for the familiar in the here and now. "A civil war is something more logical, a man starts shooting for the people and things he loves, for the things he wants and against the people he hates; and no one makes a mistake. . . . Only those who start shouting 'Peace!' are wrong."[31]

The point can be conceded, but does not justify the situation even to Sciascia's soldier, who regrets his role. ("And I think that, of all Mussolini's faults, that of having sent over thousands of Italian poor to fight the Spanish poor can never be forgiven him.") Personal stakes may make civil conflicts more "logical," but they also make them more dangerous, more terrifying, and more unpredictable than interstate wars. Sciascia's soldier finds solace with a Spanish woman "full of hate." Her husband, who had "gone to the dogs through drink and politics," joined the Republic, whose partisans had killed her father. "She wanted all those who fought for the Republic killed, in revenge for her father and to make sure her husband did not get away."[32]

Italo Calvino, Sciascia's compatriot and almost exact contemporary, wrote a two-page short story that pivots on a soldier's confusion about the impersonality of state-versus-state violence. Luigi volunteers for an unnamed war, but only to settle accounts with Alberto, "an enemy of mine." He explains to the higher-ups that Alberto is a crook; besides, he "made me make a fool of myself with a woman." The officers reply that in war one kills "only enemies of a certain type," not whomever one wants. "'So?' said Luigi. 'You think I'm dumb? This Alberto is precisely that type. . . . When I heard you were going to war against that lot, I thought, I'll go too, that way I can kill Alberto.'" Luigi does kill people in the war but doesn't come across Alberto. Only after the war is over does Luigi find and kill Alberto; he is arrested for murder and hanged. No one accepts his justification.[33]

The personal motives that infuse civil strife make the conflict palpable and the stakes obvious. These constitute its attraction and its undoing. The mix of the personal and the political leaves deep wounds that mend slowly, if at all. State-versus-state wars are more straightforward. The dead can be buried, the wounded healed or helped, and few doubt the war's justness. The enemy lies across the border or the sea, which facilitates the observances. Foreigners do not interrupt the ceremonies. But in civil wars victims and victimizers hail from the same neighborhood. For these reasons, civil wars prove difficult for their participants to discuss, much less commemorate. Typically, nations do not celebrate a civil war—or do so with hesitation and misgivings. What is there to celebrate? That neighbors killed neighbors? That citizens defiled citizens? Old wounds fester.

The United States celebrates its War of Independence with July 4 and Veterans Day honors the end of World War I, but no national day salutes the American Civil War. Memorial Day, which honors the war dead, dates from after the Civil War but originally excluded the southerners. The day commemorated those "who died in defense of their country during the late rebellion" as the commander in chief of the Grand Army of the Republic stated in 1868.[34] It was not till 1897 that President McKinley proposed that the national government take responsibility for Confederate graves. The display of Confederate flags within those cemeteries, however, became a contentious issue that was not resolved until a 2002 court decision that forbade it.[35] The Confederate flag and other Confederate insignia remain volatile symbols, evidence that the war still smolders. The governor of Virginia proclaimed April 2010 Confederate History Month, igniting a national controversy.[36] Inasmuch as race remains an issue in the United States, few can doubt the long-term impact of the American Civil War.

The story is the same elsewhere. Greece celebrates its war of independence, and Ochi Day (for όχι, or "no") honors the Greek refusal to accede to an Axis demand to billet its troops on Greek soil in World War II, but only stray monuments commemorate the Greek Civil War of 1944–49. The issue of how to honor its civil war dead has roiled Greece almost to the present. Even the name of the war proved contentious; for years the government spurned the term *civil war* as dignifying the conflict and preferred *bandit war*. Only by 1989 had passions cooled enough so that legislation ended references to the "bandit war" and to the label "bandits" for its Communist partisans. Henceforth the conflict would be officially termed the Greek Civil War.[37] Again, the reasons for this tortuous history seem obvious. The issues remain charged and divisive. Anthropologists have found that bitterness over the war's "personal and family feuds" persisted into the 1980s. At the end of that decade, a prime minister remarked that there was "scarcely a household not scarred by tragedy and pain."[38]

The brief Irish Civil War of 1922–23 gave rise to similar issues: how to celebrate a victory over good Irish patriots? The war divided Irish nationalists, those who supported a treaty with England and its conditions and those who opposed. The new Irish government—the Free State—moved quickly to mark its victory over the insurgent Republicans and commissioned a monument. With a gilt cross and an inscription ("For the glory of God and the honour of Ireland"), the bronzed monument symbolized the resolve of state and army. But the real symbolism was contained in the wood, plaster, and bronze paint that constituted the monument; within a year it started to fall apart. Official ceremonies at the site ceased. A consensus to restore or rebuild it could not be reached until 1948; even so, the new memorial was never officially unveiled and remains, in the words of one historian, "a monument to unease—an unease with a past."[39]

Decades after its end, the Spanish Civil War still troubles the Spanish. Unlike Ireland's, it affected millions; perhaps five hundred thousand fled Spain after the victory of Franco's forces. The war convulsed Spain and often sundered families. In a 2009 piece marking the seventieth anniversary of the war's end, the London *Times* reports a typical story: a husband enlisted in the Republican forces, while his wife sided with the Nationalists. After the war the husband joined the flood of exiles, and "the couple were separated for nearly 30 years until their daughter found her father in a refugee camp in southern France."[40]

To be sure, the Spanish Civil War seems to diverge from other civil wars in that it ended with a clear-cut resolution, which the victors celebrated with confidence and enthusiasm. Statues of a victorious Franco were erected throughout Spain. Franco had built a vast monument called the Valley of the Fallen to commemorate the Nationalist war dead, and for years an annual Victory Parade celebrated the defeat of the Republican forces. On church walls, those who died in action were listed—but only the Nationalist dead. The French had done this after the First World War, which inspired the Spanish Nationalists. "But that was an international war and the victims belonged to all the French," admitted one of the originators of the policy, who had a change of heart much later.[41] Yet the celebrations and monuments have not stood the test of time. Six months after Franco's death in 1975, the Victory Parade was held for the last time. A few years later it was resurrected under a new rubric, "Armed Forces Day." Even while Franco was alive, the volatile subject of the civil war proved difficult to manage. As in Greece, the authorities censored the term *civil war* and employed phrases like "the War of Spain," which seemed less divisive.[42]

The Spanish Civil War remains a fraught topic on its home ground. "A silence that was almost deafening" marked its fiftieth anniversary in 1986, writes the historian Paul Preston, who describes a "pact of oblivion" or tacit agreement to forget.[43] Twenty years later, in 2006, the Spanish government proposed a law that dealt with how the civil war should be celebrated and stipulated that tributes to Franco should cease at the Valley of the Fallen, an idea that provoked much opposition.[44] In recent years the government has been removing the Franco statues, but the recriminations and accusations on both sides have hardly slackened.[45] A *New York Times* reporter commented that "in many villages where neighbors betrayed one another, and even husbands and wives don't easily talk about the war, a common policy is still don't ask, don't tell."[46] It is an old story; neighbors who turned on neighbors want to forget. The wounds run deep and remain unhealed. In 2010 an investigation into Franco-era deaths still agitated Spain.[47]

The United States Civil War fits the general rubric at least in the scale of its violence. In its number of casualties and in its political consequences the Civil War eclipses other American conflicts. The number of war dead—more than six hundred thousand—surpasses the total American losses in all other conflicts from the

Revolutionary War to the Vietnam War, and this in a population a
fraction of today's. The rate of death in the Civil War updated for
the present American population would entail 6 million fatalities,
a barely conceivable figure.[48] Like other civil wars, the American
conflict set kin against kin. "Secession has broken up the dearest
social relations in every community of the border slave States," lamented a Missouri newspaper in 1861, "turning son against father,
brother against brother, daughter against mother, friend against
friend."[49]

Many echoed those sentiments. "We are engaged in a war, a
civil war; if you please, sir, a fratricidal war," declaimed a Republican senator in 1864. "Brother rises up in arms against brother,
son against father, and father against son."[50] "What an awful thing
is war!" wrote one soldier on the dawn of a battle. "Here lay, almost within cannon shot of one another, eighty or ninety thousand men—brothers of the same race and nation, many of them
blood relations; thousands of them believing in the same Savior,
and worshipping the same God . . . yet just waiting for the light
of the holy Sabbath that they may see how most surely to destroy
one another!"[51]

Walt Whitman, who worked as a volunteer nurse during the
war, at one time tended in the Armory Square Hospital in Washington two wounded men, Confederate and Union.

> I staid tonight a long time by the bed-side of a new patient . . .
> very feeble, right leg amputated. . . . As I was lingering, soothing
> him . . . he says to me suddenly, "I hardly think you know who I
> am . . . I am a rebel soldier." I said I did not know that but it made
> no difference. . . . In an adjoining Ward I found his brother. . . . It
> was in the same battle both were hit . . . both badly wounded. . . .
> Each died for his cause.[52]

The model of the American Civil War (and the Spanish one,
for that matter) may partially mislead, however. As Whitman
noted, "Each died for his cause": the cause of state's rights and

slavery, on one hand, and federal unity and abolition on the other. But often the causes in civil wars cannot be pinpointed; ethnic, religious, economic, and territorial grievances run together. This is especially true of contemporary civil wars. "Once upon a time civil wars were fought predominantly over ideologies," writes a political scientist referring to wars in the United States and Spain. "In most contemporary civil wars, it is hard to identify the enemy" or the ideology. Personal hatreds and vendettas drive the conflict.[53]

What "cause" divides the sides in the Congo, Somalia, or the Sudan? The clashes look like the family and blood feuds they may be. Even the Greek Civil War looked different closer up than it did from afar. Was it simply a contest between nationalists and communists? Not in the (fictional) Greek mountain town of Castello, as viewed by the writer Nikos Kazantzakis, best known for his novel *Zorba the Greek*. Here local animosity trumped political ideology. "Each had a neighbor, or a friend, or a brother, whom he had hated for years, without reason, often without realizing it," wrote Kazantzakis in his 1961 novel *The Fratricides*. His description answers the homage to civil strife by Leonardo Sciascia.

> The hatred simmered. . . . And now, suddenly, they were given rifles, and hand grenades; noble flags waved above their heads. The clergy, the army, the press urged them on—to kill their neighbor, their friend, their brother. Only in this manner, they shouted to them, can faith and country be saved! . . . And the chase began— brother hunting brother.[54]

Nor is all this mere fiction. Decades after his mother's execution during the Greek Civil War in a real mountain town, Nicholas Gage left his job as a *New York Times* reporter to investigate the circumstances of her death. In the United States, where he had fled as a child with the remainder of the family, he had heard his sister and father repeat a hundred times: " 'Tin fagane I horiani'—'It was the villagers who devoured her.' . . . It was our neighbors whom they held responsible for my mother's death." In his book *Eleni*, titled after his mother, he concludes that the guerrillas "pulled the strings," while the villagers were the "puppets."[55]

In a striking parallel to Gage's quest, Ramón Sender Barayón, the son of the Spanish novelist Ramón J. Sender, sought to understand the execution of his mother in the early years of the Spanish Civil War. After her death Barayón, like Gage, was spirited away with his sister and raised in the United States. His father always refused to tell what he knew; only after his father's death in 1982 could Barayón delve into the past. He traveled to Spain and unearthed a tragic tale not so much of politics as of family betrayal. When the war broke out, the Senders found themselves in the Nationalist zone. The husband, a well-known leftist, slipped away, while his wife, unable to accompany him with their small children, returned to her hometown of Zamora. "I'll go home where everybody loves me," she said at the time. "Where I'll be safe." She was mistaken. As is often the case, home harbors murderous hatreds and jealousies. Barayón tells the story in *A Death in Zamora,* a neglected memoir of the Spanish Civil War. With the complicity of her sister, who does not want to share the family property, her brother-in-law betrays her as a leftist. She is arrested, imprisoned, and executed in a cemetery. The man who pulls the trigger has his own motives; he is a spurned lover.[56]

In many civil wars the political motives recede or disappear altogether. "The chaos" that engulfed Sierra Leone cannot be called a guerrilla war or a civil war, concluded an observer, "for no side seriously pretends to be fighting for a cause."[57] The journalist William Finnegan, who studied the civil war in Mozambique in the late 1980s, called his book *A Complicated War.*[58] The anthropologist Stephen Lubkemann, who did field work in Mozambique, seconded this observation. He found that local and family disputes displaced the national platforms of the government and the rebels. For instance, the owner of a successful milling business was denounced to the insurgents, who executed him, by two of his brothers, who wanted the mill for themselves. "Such accounts were typical rather than exceptional," reports Lubkemann, who conducted many in-depth interviews. "The violence of the national parties" was diverted to local enmities. He dubs the Mozambique war "fragmented."[59]

Today's principal conflicts are fratricidal struggles—regional, ethnic, and religious: Iraqi Sunni versus Iraqi Shiite, Rwandan Tutsi versus Rwandan Hutu, Balkan Muslim versus Balkan Christian, Sudanese southerner against Sudanese northerner. "Nowhere in Africa has fratricidal strife torn apart communities as nearly identical as between Hutu and Tutsi," noted the French political scientist René Lemarchand. Or as a Rwandan minister declared about the genocide there, "Your neighbors killed you."[60] A reporter in northeastern Congo writes that in seven months of fighting there, several thousand have been killed and more than a hundred thousand driven from their homes. He comments, "Like ethnic conflicts around the globe, this is fundamentally a fight between brothers: the two tribes—the Hema and the Lendu—speak the same language, marry each other and compete for the same remote and thickly populated land."[61]

Somalia is perhaps the signal example of this unending fratricidal strife. As a Somalian-American academic observed, Somalia can claim a "homogeneity rarely known elsewhere in Africa." The Somalian people "share a common language (Somali), a religion (Islam), physical characteristics, and pastoral and agropastoral customs and traditions."[62] This has not hampered violence. On the contrary. "The Green Line in Mogadishu, a blasted-out boulevard with blackened buildings on each side," reports *The New York Times*, "is a monument to fratricide." It is the dividing line between two clans, the Haber Gedir and the Abgal, "which are actually part of the same family."[63]

In Sudan too, kindred groups are slaughtering one another, though the antagonists are often characterized as exclusively Arab Muslims and black non-Muslims. A reporter visited a combat zone and discovered that both sides came from the same group, the Nuer tribe, who were not Muslims. "The battlefield had seen

Nuer fight Nuer before: Among the still-bleeding corpses were scattered vertebrae and clean-picked skulls. . . . Every bone had once belonged to a Nuer."[64] An archbishop in Southern Sudan asserts that the Arab militias, the outsiders, have not been the only guilty party. "It is we who are killing ourselves," he told the journalist Bill Berkeley, who was in Juba in Southern Sudan reporting on the war. Berkeley found that the Southern Sudanese rebels, split between the Nuer and Dinka tribes, frequently attacked one another as well as the civilian population.[65]

To be sure, fraternal violence is nothing new in Southern Sudan. As in Spain or Russia, enmity derives from propinquity. Some seventy years ago the English anthropologist E. E. Evans-Pritchard wrote up his findings about Southern Sudan and remarked on the similarity of the neighboring peoples, the Nuer and Dinka. "They are alike in cultures and social systems," he wrote. Individuals from "one people are easily assimilated to the other." At the same time, he stumbled on a paradox: the Nuer "show greater hostility towards, and more persistently attack, the Dinka, who are in every respect most akin to themselves, than any other foreign people." This led him to the observation that "Nuer make war against a people who have a culture like their own rather than among themselves or against peoples with a culture very different from their own."[66]

The Israeli-Palestinian conflict also is waged not between strangers but rather between kindred peoples. In the heady years after World War I, when the Arabs and the Jews sensed the possibility of independent states, the principals emphasized the kinship of their peoples. That was a moment when a defeated Ottoman Empire gave the victorious Europeans the power to divvy up the Middle East and to create new countries both for diasporan Jews and for the Arabs, who had been dominated by the Turks. Faisal Ibn Husain, who would become king of Iraq, met with Chaim Weizmann, who would become the first president of Israel. In the aftermath of the encounter, Faisal declared that "the two main branches of the Semitic family, Arabs and Jews, understood one another." He called the Jews our "nearest relations" and "our cousins."[67] Of course this could be a problem.

"We Israelis resemble our Arab enemies in more ways than we care to know," writes Avner Falk, an Israeli psychologist, in a book titled *Fratricide in the Holy Land.* Falk refers to character traits, customs, food, and dress. He reminds us that Jews and Arabs believe they descend from two biblical half brothers, Isaac and Ishmael. "From the psychological viewpoint, the Israeli Jews and Palestinian Arabs think, feel and act like rival brothers who are involved in a fratricidal struggle."[68] He notes also that "almost half of the Israeli Jewish population came from Arab or Muslim countries" and that "many of them are culturally and linguistically Arab."[69] This does not mean that this population appreciated their Arab counterparts more than the European Jews might. Closeness has bred contempt. Sephardic Jews—at least those from the Middle East—are generally much more anti-Arab than the Ashkenazi from Europe and Russia. The assassin of Israeli prime minister Yitzhak Rabin came from a family of Yemenite Jews and believed Rabin to be too conciliatory toward Arabs. He declared after his arrest in 1995, "I was afraid an Arab might kill him [Rabin]. I wanted Heaven to see that a Jew had done this."[70]

Moreover, the internal divisions within both Palestinian and Israeli society cannot be ignored, as Matt Rees, a journalist, emphasizes in his 2004 book on the Middle East, *Cain's Field.* In Palestine the militias of Hamas and Arafat's PLO gun each other down. Israel attempts to project a picture of unity but, in Rees's words, suffers from a "skein of fraternal hostility." The ultra-Orthodox "refuse to acknowledge kinship" with the less religious majority. West Bank settlers flout the laws in their pursuit of "holy" colonization. Rees meditates on Cain and Abel, pointing out how Palestinians and Israelis alike identify with Abel's innocence and ignore how they partake of Cain's aggression. They look for opponents across the border, but the foe is also on their own turf. The final fate of Cain may be instructive, Rees tells us. In the end he did not escape a violent death; a kinsman, his own great-

great-great-grandson, killed him. This may be the fate of Israel and Palestine, devoured by mutual hatred.[71]

The enmity that has long beset the Protestants and Catholics in Ireland is a classic case of kin against kin. What distinguishes the two groups? Each sees the other as the enemy, but how much do they differ? The Canadian-Irish scholar Donald Harman Akenson, in a book titled *Small Differences,* concludes that very little separates them. "Despite a mass of folk beliefs about the differences between Protestants and Catholics" in Ireland, he writes, "neither in family structure, nor in economic behavior, nor in the treatment of women was there any compelling evidence for major differences, and, in some instances, there was positive evidence of fundamental similarities."[72]

Indeed, what separated Irish Catholic from Irish Catholic in the Irish Civil War of 1922–23? One study of the conflict in Cork, the most violent of the Irish counties, showed that personal loyalties overshadowed politics. Some years ago Peter Hart, a historian of Ireland, located veterans of that civil war. "Twelve of the thirteen veterans I interviewed had fought on the republican side," he writes. "None could remember making a specific choice to do so. 'I hadn't a clue'; 'It was very confused altogether.'" He asked one Corkman "why he and his brother wound up on opposite sides of the struggle." The man explained that it was owing to loyalty to opposing leaders.[73] In his autobiography, the writer Seán Ó Faoláin, who was from Cork, ponders why he joined the Republican insurgents in the Irish Civil War—a conflict in which "every man's eye is against his brother." He could not say precisely. "If I were asked what exactly the Republican ideal could do for this old, beloved Ireland and for these poor that could not be done under the constitution of the Irish Free State, I would not have quite known how to say it." He states that he had "nothing to guide me" but ideas of "pride and honor" and "those flickering lights before the golden ikons of the past."[74]

Nenad Miscevic, a Croatian philosopher who left Croatia in 1993 because of harassment by nationalists, invokes the Irish situation as analogous to that of the Balkans. Like the Irish Catholics and Irish Protestants, the Croats, largely Roman Catholic, and the Serbs, largely Serbian Orthodox, share much, including mutual disdain. Miscevic questions the conventional notion that nationalism directs itself against foreigners. More often "close neighbors" give rise to resentment. "Croatian nationalists have nothing against Plácido Domingo singing Spanish music in Zagreb: they don't want Serbian singers from Serbia and above all Serbian singers from Croatia itself." He notes that "culturally," Croats and Serbs were "extremely close, sharing (what is linguistically one) language, customs (including folk-songs, traditions, superstitions), moral values, as documented in literature, art, cinema or folk traditions." The only real differences stem from religion, the split in Christianity between the Eastern and Western churches. But the religious fissure exists in societies that today are "predominantly atheist."[75]

In the same year in which Miscevic was forced from his homeland, the Canadian historian and politician Michael Ignatieff reported on the fighting between Croatia and Serbia and asked himself the same question: what divides these people? Bunkered with some Serb soldiers, he ventures to ask one of them, How do you tell the difference between a Serb and a Croat? The soldier looks "scornful and takes a cigarette out of his khaki jacket. 'See this? These are Serbian cigarettes. Over there . . . they smoke Croatian cigarettes.'" This answer dissatisfied even the soldier, and a bit later he amended it. "'Those Croats, they think they're better than us. They want to be gentlemen. Think they're fancy Europeans. I'll tell you something. We're all just Balkan shit.'"[76]

Vamik Volkan, a Turkish-American psychiatrist, echoes Ignatieff's observations in his remarks about the Greeks and Turks in Cyprus before the island's 1974 division. To a tourist out for a summer stroll in Nicosia, the Cypriot Greek and Cypriot Turk crowds appeared to be "a homogenous group of Mediterranean people dressed alike and taking pleasure in the cool evening air." But to inhabitants the "minor differences" jumped out as "obvi-

ous and important." For instance "at a glance" the Cypriots identified one another by the cigarettes they smoked. "Greeks usually
preferred those packaged in blue and white, the Greek national
colors. . . . Turks smoked brands packaged in red and white, the
Turkish colors."[77]

Like others who reported from the scene of the recent fighting in the Balkans, the journalist Chris Hedges concluded that
the strife stemmed from all-but-invisible differences, the preferred
brand of cigarettes notwithstanding. "The warring sides invented
national myths and histories designed to mask the fact that Croats,
Muslims, and Serbs are nearly indistinguishable." Perhaps for this
reason, "bloody disputes take place over tiny, almost imperceptible
nuances within the society." Hedges witnessed arguments over the
origin of heart-shaped gingerbread cookies that almost devolved
into violence. "The Croats insisted that the cookies were Croatian.
The Serbs angrily countered that the cookies were Serbian." Serbs,
Muslims, and Croats "struggled, like ants on a small hill, to carve
out separate, antagonistic identities," he writes. "One defined oneself mostly by what the other was not."[78]

The Balkans remain a classic case of similarities that breed
enmities. The Carnegie Endowment, which had published the
inquiry into the Balkan wars of 1912–13, republished the same
report in 1993 during the wars that wracked the former Yugoslavia. Too little had changed to require anything more than a new
introduction to the old text. The diplomat and historian George
Kennan noted in the new introduction that the "revolution in
weaponry" was chiefly what set the new conflict apart from the
earlier one, which had proceeded without air power and almost
without motor vehicles. By contemporary standards, the earlier
atrocities lacked technological know-how, depending as they did
on "the bayonet, the rifle butt, the cudgel and the whiplash." Apart
from progress in the technology of murder, Kennan was struck
by "the many and depressing evidences of similarity" between the
violence of 1913 and that of the 1990s.[79]

The Yugoslavian writer Milovan Djilas hailed from Montenegro, a small mountainous patch of the Balkans that (like the rest of Yugoslavia) has become an independent nation. A man of the left, he dedicated his life to communism, first aligned with the official Communist Party and then against it. During the war he fought the fascists, and after the war he moved into the top reaches of the government, but by the 1950s he had concluded that bureaucrats and reactionaries ran the Communist Party of Yugoslavia. For his outspokenness he was jailed repeatedly. He exemplified the classic, if scarce, twentieth-century dissident intellectual, who swam against the current, the repressive orthodoxies of his day. In his memoirs, however, he recalls that "in one respect" his family's history is "typical" of Montenegro. Many members of his family died in bloody disputes with other Montenegrins, not in battle against foreign invaders or ideologies.

> The men of several generations have died at the hands of Montenegrins, men of the same faith and name. My father's grandfather, my own two grandfathers, my father, and my uncle were killed as though a dread curse lay upon them. My father and his brother and my brothers were killed even though all of them yearned to die peacefully in their beds beside their wives. Generation after generation, and the bloody chain was not broken.

Djilas adds a sentence that bespeaks the acrimony of kin through the centuries. He refers to the historic antagonism between Balkan Christians like his family and the Muslims of the Ottoman Empire, the despised outsiders: "The inherited fear and hatred of feuding clans was mightier than fear and hatred of the enemy, the Turks."[80]

Fratricide informs the founding texts of Western culture. The Hebrew Bible opens with brothers killing brothers. Rome originates in a fratricide. For Hannah Arendt the omnipresence of these stories suggests their potency. "Cain slew Abel, and Romulus slew

Remus. . . . The first recorded deeds in our biblical and secular tradition . . . have travelled through the centuries" and have given us
"cogent metaphors or universally applicable tales." For Arendt the
tales spoke clearly: "Whatever brotherhood human beings may be
capable of has grown out of fratricide, whatever political organization men may have achieved has its origin in crime."[81]

Fratricide and enemy brothers appear in writings of the ancient Greeks as well. The first kings of Sparta were twins who,
Herodotus tells us, "being brothers, were, as long as they lived, in
discord with each other." That is, they fought not despite but because they were brothers. For the Greeks, brothers were often the
least, not the most, trustworthy of men.[82] Hesiod advised, "Even
with your brother, smile and get a witness."[83]

No ancient story has elicited more study than that of Oedipus.
Arendt could have added the Oedipus tale to the "legendary beginnings of our history" that pivot on fratricide. While Oedipus
and his misdeeds have garnered the most attention, the tale encompasses the fate of his children. In most accounts of the myth,
Oedipus, who has unknowingly killed his father and married his
mother to become king of Thebes, departs from the city when
he discovers his transgressions. Humiliated and self-blinded, he
wanders the countryside. In his hour of need, however, his sons
fail to minister to him and Oedipus curses them. The sons, heirs to
the Theban throne, quarrel over who will assume the kingship and
they slay each other. Parricide passes into fratricide.

The sons "should not divide their patrimony in friendship,"
runs the *Thebaid,* an ancient Greek epic poem that exists only
in fragments, "but the two of them [should divide] ever in battle and strife."[84] Sophocles and Aeschylus pursued the theme. In
Sophocles' *Oedipus at Colonus,* Oedipus damns his sons, Polyneices
and Eteocles, because they abandoned him. "They saw me sent
forth homeless, they heard my doom of exile cried aloud" and did
nothing. Oedipus decries their efforts to wrest the throne from
each other. He wishes that they may die by a "kindred hand." As
Ismene, one of Oedipus' daughters, says of the brothers, "an evil

rivalry has seized them."[85] In Aeschylus' *Seven Against Thebes* Polyneices raises an army to attack Thebes and seize the kingdom from
Eteocles. The brothers meet at the seventh gate. Eteocles seems
almost to relish the inevitable, mutual destruction. "I'll match him,
brother to brother, enemy to enemy." The chorus laments,

> *When men die by a kinsman's hand,*
> *When brother is murdered by brother,*
> *And the dust of the earth drinks in*
> *The crimson blood that blackens and dries,*
> *Who then can provide the cleansing?*
> *Who can wash it away?* [86]

Roman poets too wrote at length about the sons of Oedipus
and their "fraternal strife."[87] But Rome did not need Greece for
tales of fratricide, since in its lore, the city originated with murder
of a brother by a brother.[88] The story in its outline resembles other
foundation myths in which the hero, cast off at birth by a distinguished family, is saved by strangers who raise him. Later the son
returns to avenge his honor.[89] The Roman story differs in that the
hero is plural, brothers.

In the Roman version of this foundation myth, the infant
twins, left to perish in the wilderness, wash up on a riverbank, and
in a scene that has inspired painters and sculptors, a she-wolf finds
and suckles them. A shepherd stumbles upon the boys, names
them Romulus and Remus, and raises them as his own. The boys
grow up, restore the throne to their grandfather, who had been
deposed, and resolve to "build a city in the same place where they
were in their infancy brought up." This place becomes Rome on
the Tiber River. If the story seems unlikely, argues Plutarch, the
reader should "consider that the Roman power would hardly have
reached so high a pitch without a divinely ordered origin, attended
with great and extraordinary circumstances."[90]

However, the brothers quarrel over what the new town should
be called—and where it should be located and how it should be

ruled. "Unhappily the brothers' plan for the future was marred by the same source which had divided their grandfather and Amulius [his brother]—jealousy and ambition," writes the Roman historian Livy. They seek to resolve the dispute by an augury, but this does not succeed. "Angry words ensued," Livy writes, "followed all too soon by blows, and in the course of the affray Remus was killed." For Livy this is how Romulus obtained "sole power" and how Rome was founded and named.[91] Here too, fratricide succeeds parricide, since after their triumphant return Romulus and Remus had killed the tyrant, their granduncle, who had seized power from their grandfather (more enemy brothers!).

As Rome in later centuries descended into civil wars, its writers invoked its fratricidal beginnings. In a youthful poem Horace asks with bitterness whether too little Latin blood has been spilled in foreign wars, since now Romans bleed Romans. "This is not the way with wolves or the lions; / they turn only on other beasts." Why do Romans kill Romans? "This is the answer: a harsh fate haunts the Romans, / and the evil of fratricide, / since the innocent blood of Remus stained the earth, / a curse on all his descendants."[92]

And Adam knew Eve his wife; and she conceived, and bare Cain, and said, I have gotten a man from the Lord.

And she again bare his brother Abel. And Abel was a keeper of sheep, but Cain was a tiller of the ground.

And in process of time it came to pass, that Cain brought of the fruit of the ground an offering unto the Lord.

And Abel, he also brought of the firstlings of his flock and of the fat thereof. And the Lord had respect unto Abel and to his offering:

But unto Cain and to his offering he had not respect. And Cain was very wroth, and his countenance fell.

And the Lord said unto Cain, Why art thou wroth? and why is thy countenance fallen?

If thou doest well, shalt thou not be accepted? and if thou

doest not well, sin lieth at the door: and unto thee shall be his desire, and thou shalt rule over him.

And Cain talked with Abel his brother: and it came to pass, when they were in the field, that Cain rose up against Abel his brother, and slew him.

And the Lord said unto Cain, Where is Abel thy brother? And he said, I know not: am I my brother's keeper?

The literature inspired by Cain and Abel in Genesis 4 towers above that provoked by Romulus and Remus. To list authors who use or dedicate whole works to the Cain and Abel story would amount to a roll call of the great writers, from the Anglo-Saxon author of *Beowulf* to Byron, from Dante to Shakespeare, from Melville to Unamuno.[93]

Every facet of the first biblical murder remains murky—the occasion for centuries of commentary. "Two stories have haunted us . . . the story of original sin and the story of Cain and Abel. And I don't understand either of them," notes a character in John Steinbeck's novel *East of Eden*.[94] "No other Biblical situation contains so many questions or arouses so many uncertainties," concludes Elie Wiesel.[95] The motive, the place, and even the instrument of death is unclear. Why did the offerings of Cain earn less respect than those of Abel? Is there significance to the fact that Abel was a herder and proffered sheep to the Lord, and Cain, a farmer, vegetables and fruit? Why exactly did Cain murder his brother—and how?

More questions follow. Cain, condemned to be a fugitive and vagabond, is paradoxically saved by the Lord, who "set a mark upon Cain, lest any finding him should kill him." His punishment is not to be slain but to be branded. What is that mark? Cain "talked" with Abel—and then killed him. What did the brothers say to each other? Herein may lie a lesson for a world that makes a fetish of communication. Talk does not suffice.

Enmity marks the relationship of brothers throughout the Hebrew Bible. Esau considered killing Jacob; Joseph's brothers contemplated killing Joseph.[96] "Am I my brother's keeper?" rings out as the great rhetorical question of Western culture. Brothers should "keep" each other, but what about strangers? The relationships between brothers can be understood only in reference to strangers. Who was a brother and who was a stranger? This was a question of some moment.

The biblical strictures about usury raised this very issue and proved critical in abetting the hostility between two fraternal religions, Christianity and Judaism. The relevant biblical passages depended on defining who was and was not a brother. The key statement, Deuteronomy 23:20, prohibits the charging of interest to brothers. "Unto a stranger thou mayest lend upon usury; but unto thy brother thou shalt not lend upon usury." This might appear to be a simple injunction, but it raises the question of how to distinguish a stranger from a brother. Learned rabbis spent long nights cracking this nut. Who was your brother to whom you could not loan with interest and who was the stranger to whom you could?[97] These questions assumed increasing importance as a modern economic society that required loans and capital took shape in fifteenth-century Italy. For some critics Judaism never overcame the spirit of Deuteronomy that established the sharp demarcation between Jew and stranger. Jews could advance money with interest to strangers, whereas Christianity breathed the spirit of universal brotherhood: everyone was a brother, which disallowed usury in every case.[98]

But Christianity could not escape the conflict between a universal brotherhood that proscribed usury and an economic society that required loans and where the line between loans and usury turned blurry. In the process of coming to terms with charging interest, some brothers became strangers. *From Tribal Brotherhood to Universal Otherhood* runs the subtitle of Benjamin Nelson's study of the history of usury.[99] The early Church authorities such as Ambrose took the hard line: "The Law forbids you under any circumstances to exact usury from your brother." This meant, however, that over the centuries pawnbroking and lending devolved upon Jews and on a class of disreputable Christians, mainly Lombards.

As a commercial society emerged in the Renaissance, some theologians and priests objected to the dependence on these outcasts to fund the new economy and sought to remedy the situation. In mid-fifteenth-century Italy, Franciscan monks formed church-based financial societies and pawnshops called *monti di pietà*, charitable economic institutions that allowed Christians to loan money at interest to Christians.[100] As one Franciscan explained in his history of these outfits, the problem was that Jews and Lombards advanced money in order to enrich themselves and not to serve their "fellow-men" out of "Christian charity."[101] However, the establishment of the *monti di pietà* drew upon anti-Semitic sentiments and led to anti-Semitic edicts. Brotherhood engendered enmity. As the *monti di pietà* took shape, Christians began to contemplate ostracizing or expelling the Jews. They declared the Jews infidels.[102] In 1463 Florentine authorities required Jews to wear yellow badges and limited their numbers in the city. A popular Renaissance morality play had two Jewish moneylenders talking:

> *I have heard one Brother Picciuolo preach.*
> *He has said—I tell you the truth—*
> *That loans will be ended, and a monte di pietà built . . .*
> *He says and reaffirms that it would be good*
> *To send us out right away from this land.*[103]

The reaffirmation of brotherhood entailed defining its limits. Brotherhood was announced and the gates went up. As the *monti* spread, so did the plan to remove the Jews.[104] As Nelson puts it, "The Brotherhood of Man was the banner under which anti-Semitic friars, especially of the Franciscan Observants, cloaked their demagogic appeals to expel the Jewish pawnbrokers."[105]

Romulus founded a city, but it is frequently forgotten that so did Cain. He established the first city mentioned in the Hebrew Bible. ("And Cain went out from the presence of the Lord, and dwelt in the land of Nod, on the east of Eden. And Cain knew his wife; and she conceived, and bare Enoch: and he builded a city, and called the name of the city, after the name of his son, Enoch.") In the West, urban civilization, perhaps politics itself, originates in fraternal violence. "A connection exists between murder and the founding of [Cain's] city," writes a historian of antiquity.[106] Or, as the late theologian and philosopher Jacques Ellul put it, the city "is the direct consequence of Cain's murderous act."[107]

This is myth, not fact, but may capture a truth. "The city is founded in fear of violent death, but first in fratricide," writes one student of Judaism. "This taint, one must believe, is, from the Bible's point of view, inherent in civilization as such."[108] The psychoanalytically minded classicist Norman O. Brown has speculated that every city "carries the guilt" of earlier violence.[109]

Indeed, the history of the city—at least in some versions—testifies to violence. "By the time the archaeologist's spade unearths a recognizable city," writes Lewis Mumford in *The City in History*, "he finds a walled precinct, a citadel, made of durable materials."[110] The wall protects but also allows for attacks. It defends and offends. Romulus kills his brother when Remus jumps over a wall of the new settlement. "So perish whoever else shall overleap my battlements," he cried, according to Livy.[111] It is an old story—and a new story, as Mumford indicates. From the Kremlin to the Pentagon, the citadel exudes absolutism and violence.

To be sure, the fratricidal origins of the city were not news to the Christian theologians. They saw the cities as dens of iniquity. "See what was Cain's choice, after he had forsaken God," wrote Matthew Henry in his classic eighteenth-century Bible commentary. Cain pitched a settlement in this world: he and his "cursed race dwell in a city, while Adam and his blessed family dwell in tents."[112] In this theory Henry followed early Church thinkers such as Augustine, who distinguished the city of men from the "City of God." Augustine's thousand-page tome, *The City of God,* separated the impure city of man—Rome itself—and the pure spiritual city. Cain belonged to the city of man, but Christlike Abel belonged to the City of God. "The first founder of the earthly city, then, was a fratricide," Augustine wrote.

Augustine also made a fateful association that continued to resonate through the millennia. He identified Cain as a Jew and, implicitly, Abel as the Christian. "Cain received God's admonition like the criminal he was. . . . He lay in wait for his brother and slew him. Such was the founder of the earthly city. He also prefigures the Jews by whom Christ was slain."[113] Here, some sixteen hundred years ago, the basic precepts of anti-Semitism can be found. Cain the wanderer and primal Jew murders a Christian and founds the first city. The notion sticks together the city, sin, rootlessness, and Jews—a constellation of images that would resurface throughout the centuries.

For Augustine, the murder that founded the first earthly city prefigured another misdeed, the founding of Rome. The crime of Cain constituted an archetype, and Romulus's crime "mirrored" it by "a kind of image of itself." Fratricide defined both crimes, but they differed in that one murder represented a split between the City of God and the city of men, and the other represented a fissure within the city of men. "The strife that arose between Remus and Romulus," wrote Augustine, "showed the extent to which the earthly city is divided against itself."[114]

The depravity and licentiousness of the earthly city prompted Augustine's *The City of God*. He wanted to defend Christianity from the charge that it had led to the sack of Rome. Of course the woes of Rome were not new. Augustine refers to the Roman poet Lucan, who had also linked the crime of Romulus with civil wars. "Rome's first walls were drenched with a brother's blood," the poet declared. Lucan wrote of Rome's civil wars, which had started when Julius Caesar, violating ancient Roman law, crossed the Rubicon and entered Italy proper with his forces. He depicts the endless savagery of these wars. "I sing," he begins, "of a mighty people attacking its own guts . . . of kin facing kin." Lucan noted a primal truth of civil wars—that they are more ruthless than the conventional kind. "No foreign sword has ever penetrated so: it is wounds inflicted by the hand of fellow-citizen that have sunk so deep."[115]

The antinomies of brotherhood surface in the Bible, and fraternal violence may lie at the origin of the city or of political organization itself, which Hannah Arendt suggests. However, Arendt neglected one point: if politics begins with fratricide, politics may also end with it. This progression is most visible in the not-so-distant past, when the call for fraternity included its opposite, "Kill your brother." In the French Revolution fraternity and fratricide converge.

The demand for fraternity resonated little among American political thinkers, but when it appeared as a revolutionary slogan in France, murder of Frenchmen accompanied it.[116] Talk of fratricide in the French Revolution usually summons up images of Paris, the Terror, and the guillotine. Innumerable books reproduce the engraving of the head of Louis XVI, who was guillotined in Paris's Place de la Concorde. In fact the violence outside Paris during the Terror far surpassed the bloodletting in the capital. "In the light of the number of victims, Paris is dwarfed by the provinces," writes a historian, and among the provinces, one area—the Vendée, a region in western France—outstripped the rest. Paris accounts for less than a sixth of the deaths in the Terror, the Vendée more than half.[117] Moreover, deaths in the Terror comprise a tiny fraction of the losses in the Vendée, the site of a civil war (1793–96) that set Frenchman against Frenchman. Those losses run as high as 250,000 of the inhabitants, perhaps a fifth of the region's population.[118]

The Vendée proved recalcitrant to revolution. It rose up to defend its young men, who refused conscription in the Revolutionary armies, and to defend its priests, who refused to swear loyalty to the new government. In the name of king and Church the rebellion became an assault on the Revolution itself. As France fought against a European coalition in a traditional conflict, it also embarked on a civil war in the Vendée that, as the historian David Bell puts it, "set a new European standard in atrocities." Complete "physical extermination" of enemies took place in the war years, continues Bell. "The enemies in question, however, were not English or Austrian or Prussian, and the fields of battle were not in Belgium or the Rhineland." The enemies were French and the battlefields in France.[119]

Paris sought to put down the rebellion, but the Vendéens savaged the army that had been sent to subdue them. The Vendée declared invalid the Revolutionary laws and even issued its own money and instituted tithing to the Catholic Church. For a moment—and this has become the ultimate justification for the vengeance wreaked upon it—the Vendée seemed to offer a beachhead to England, an enemy of France and the Revolution.

The barely organized peasant army of the Vendée practiced its own bloodletting. In one town the insurgents—or Whites, as they became known—butchered scores of inhabitants. As in much civil strife, what exactly happened in this locale—Machecoul, a village outside of Nantes—has provoked controversy that continues into the present. The town fell to insurgents, who imprisoned several hundred local "patriots," the supporters of the Paris-based revolution. To avenge losses elsewhere, the Vendéens shot 160 of the imprisoned in a cemetery. That is the best-case scenario. They may have tortured, castrated, and mutilated prisoners, which seems "plausible," according to a recent assessment of the events by the historian Edward Woell. He adds that such atrocities would not be surprising in "a highly divisive civil war in which bitter partisans not only knew each other but lived side by side in the same community."[120] Woell nods to a truth. Atrocities arise when the combatants are neighbors.

Others had a different explanation: religion. Republicans often claimed that it was religious fervor that led the Whites to maim and torture. The nineteenth-century French writer Alexandre Dumas interviewed a witness to the events in the Vendée. Dumas offered no excuse for the Revolution's violence. "But it must be admitted," he wrote in his memoirs, that the Vendéens had themselves set an "abominable example" and he noted that "wars conducted by priests"—as was the case in the Vendée—"are apt to be barbarous wars."[121]

If the Vendéens spilled blood in vengeance, they suffered the same and more. The loose Vendée army could not withstand the power of the central state. In late 1793, Revolutionary Paris gave a Jacobin, Jean-Baptiste Carrier, unlimited authority to reestablish order and end the rebellion. *Paris Against the Province!* reads the title of a recent book on the Vendée war.[122] In Nantes, a wealthy Vendéen port city of eighty thousand, Carrier initiated a reign of wanton killings. The full extent of the violence will never be known, since truth and rumor have become inextricably entangled. Reports of his misconduct horrified even the Parisian Revolutionaries. After the fall of Robespierre, Carrier was brought to trial, accused of barbarism. "In all the pages of history, even in the centuries of barbarism, one can hardly find deeds with which to compare the horrors committed by the accused," read the indictment.[123]

In early 1794, to finish off the weakened rebellion, the French government gave General Louis-Marie Turreau supreme command. Turreau proposed a series of columns, which became known as the infernal or hell columns, to sweep through the area. He ordered the officers who led the columns "to burn down all the towns, villages, and hamlets of the Vendée." No one was to be spared, including women and children. "Everyone will be bayoneted," read his orders.[124] His officers instructed their troops accordingly. The leader of the first column directed his men "to put to the torch everything that can be burned and to put to the bayonet every inhabitant you encounter on your way," a secular version of the "Kill them all" command of the papal envoy at the thirteenth-century massacre at Béziers. "I know that there may be some patriots in this country; no matter, we must sacrifice them all."[125] Or as a partisan of total extermination put it, "It is necessary to kill them all or they will kill us."[126]

This was a civil war of unusual ferocity, which included mass executions. Firing squads and even the guillotine could not keep up, and Carrier in Nantes instituted what has passed into history as "vertical executions"—that is, mass drownings. A citizen explained: "Because shooting [the captured rebels] takes too long and would use up powder and bullets, we've decided to put a certain number in large ships, take them to the middle of the river . . . and . . . sink the ship. This operation is carried out daily."[127] The result was annihilation or extermination, words that crop up frequently in the contemporary reports. A commander exulted:

There is no more Vendée, Republican citizens. It died beneath our free sword, with its women and children. I have just buried it in the swamps and woods. . . . Following orders . . . I crushed the children beneath the horses' hooves, massacred the women who, those at least, will birth no more brigands. I have not a single prisoner to reproach myself with. I exterminated them all. . . . The roads are strewn with cadavers. There are so many that in some locations they form a pyramid.[128]

The war of French against French was, as another commander noted, much worse than the war of French against Prussians or Austrians. The duc de Lauzun, who had fought against the English in the American Revolution and against the Austrians in the French Revolutionary wars, knew that the Vendéen war differed. It could not be "considered under the same point of view as external wars. . . . Here, Frenchmen fall under the blows of other Frenchmen; the villages which we devastate are ours; the harvests that we destroy belong to us; and all the blood that runs is ours as well."[129] General Turreau himself called the civil war in the Vendée "more cruel" and "more bloody" than the war against the Prussians and Austrians that he had just fought in. He wondered whether it was "the most horrid war that ever existed."[130]

At his trial, Carrier admitted to many of the atrocities but justified them by explaining that they took place in a civil war. He charged that his accusers had forgotten about the violence of civil wars. He asked whether anyone had ever calculated what the Roman civil wars cost humanity "in misfortunes, tears, deaths and calamities." Or how many men died in the English Civil War of the seventeenth century, or how many "massacres" that war occasioned. "There are," he said in his defense, "misfortunes inseparable from revolutions; and here it is not simply a question of revolution, but a civil war, the longest, the most disastrous war that has ever existed."[131]

Amid the accusations and recriminations, the terms *barbarism* and *cannibalism* made a comeback. As the historian Bronislaw Baczko has indicated, the violence of the Vendée forced the issue for all who could see: the barbarians were not "exterior" to the Revolution. "From all the evidence, the presence of 'barbarians amongst us' was an established fact."[132] Those who organized mass drownings, for instance, were charged with being cannibals and barbarians. The government, demanded a representative, "should, if it were possible, invent new punishments for these cannibals."[133] The enemy had proved to be inside, not outside.

As he ordered his lieutenants "to put to the bayonet" all they encountered, including women and children, General Turreau scribbled a Revolutionary motto that ended with "Fraternity or Death."[134] This was a paradoxical slogan. The French Revolution championed "Liberty, Equality, Fraternity." Of the three terms, "Fraternity" seemed the least stable and most revealing in its "Fraternity or Death" version. The phrase cropped up sporadically. In Paris a revolutionary group declared, "For a free people, there should be no neutrality. There are only brothers or enemies." Paris authorities occasionally ordered that "Liberty, Equality, Fraternity or Death" be inscribed on buildings during the Revolution. A rare print of the Jacobin Club in Paris displays the slogan "Society of Jacobins . . . Fraternity or Death."[135]

Yet as the Revolution slowed, the phrase receded.[136] With Thermidor, or the end of Revolutionary Terror, newspapers and local governments urged citizens to remove it. "In one of our last issues," reported a newspaper, "we have invited citizens to erase from the frontispiece of their homes this inscription dictated by the terror: 'Fraternity or Death.'" The newspaper observed that one Parisian neighborhood had already done that.[137] A contemporary journalist, Jean-Sebastian Mercier, remarked on the changing fate of the phrase. He noted the appearance of "Brotherhood or death" on "all our walls" and added that half the phrase had already vanished. "The words 'or death' have since been effaced."[138]

When Chateaubriand returned to France from exile in 1800 he also took note of the truncated slogan. As he entered Paris the motto appeared to have been covered over. "Daubed on the walls, and already old, was the Republican inscription: LIBERTY, EQUALITY, FRATERNITY OR DEATH. Sometimes there had been an attempt to erase the word DEATH, but the red or black letters still appeared under a layer of whitewash."[139] The nineteenth-century French historian Alphonse Aulard reported that he saw the phrase "or Death" on the Parisian Faculty of Law on September 4, 1870—the day the empire collapsed—but it was soon covered up again.[140] Today a plaque on the mayoral building of Troyes, a commune southeast of Paris, may be the only place where it can still be viewed in public.

Chateaubriand's formulation seems psychological, almost psychoanalytic: the phrase gets repressed but keeps surfacing. "Or Death" peeks out from under the whitewash. Perhaps an inner tension besets the motto; perhaps it should read not "Fraternity or Death" but "Fraternity and Death." Does the Revolutionary slogan betray a fratricidal intent? A contemporary of Chateaubriand, the writer Nicolas Chamfort, wondered about this. He is remembered today, if at all, for his aphorisms, which have been admired by thinkers from Nietzsche to Camus. Like much about Chamfort, even his name was invented. Born out of wedlock to an aristocratic mother and raised by commoners, he developed a mordant wit. To the suggestion that he become a priest, he supposedly replied, "I'll never be a priest. I'm too fond of sleep, philosophy, women, honor and real fame; and not fond enough of quarrels, hypocrisy, honors and money."

Chamfort supported the Revolution but associated with the moderate faction. As the Revolution's pace intensified, suspicion fell on those who questioned or seemed to question the Terror. Revolutionaries smelled counterrevolutionaries everywhere. Chamfort worked as a director of the Bibliothèque Nationale when he was first arrested and locked up in a horrific prison. He was released after two days, and he swore he would not again be imprisoned. A few months later, the authorities came back to arrest him again. He asked and was given a moment to change his clothes. He retired to his dressing room, where he committed suicide—or tried to. First he shot himself in the head. When he discovered himself alive, he proceeded to slit his throat and wrists. Even this did not work, and he clung to life. "This is what it means to be clumsy," he remarked. "You don't succeed in anything, not even killing yourself."[141] He lived for some months but succumbed to the infection caused by his wounds.

Chamfort had tried his hand at many writing forms, including the theater. He often took up the theme of fraternal friendship, about which he wrote a play.[142] He noted, however, that "a cordial relationship between brothers is so unusual" that in classical mythology only Castor and Pollux appear as an example; moreover, they are "shown as never meeting."[143] As Frenchman turned upon Frenchman in the Revolution, Chamfort translated the slogan "Fraternity or Death" into "Be my brother or I will kill you." He added that "the fraternity of those people is that of Cain and Abel." According to his loyal friend and editor Pierre-Louis Ginguené, he often made this remark—too often. When criticized for repeating himself, he substituted Eteocles and Polyneices for Cain and Abel. His iterations probably helped seal the case of the Terror against him.[144]

The French Revolution hardly invented fratricide, although it almost invented fraternity as a political plank. The term never received the same attention as "liberty" and "equality." Moreover, a fog covers its inception—or its eruption. Prior to the French Revolution, "fraternity" had made little impression, either as a political or moral claim. In the "treasure trove of words" supplied by the French Revolution, writes the historian Mona Ozouf, "the relative absence of the word *fraternity*" is "striking."[145] The classic text of the Enlightenment, the twenty-eight volume *Encyclopedia* of the mid-eighteenth century, bestowed four sentences on "fraternity" and none hinted of a political consequence. ("Fraternity is the bond that connects together brothers, or brother and sister. . . .") The listing for "liberty," by comparison, filled fourteen pages.[146]

Fraternity as a political mandate may have first surfaced, at least obliquely, in the opening events of the French Revolution.[147] To recall the ABCs of those years: In 1788 a bankrupt monarchy dredged up a parliamentary institution, the Estates General, to solve the fiscal crisis. The selection of representatives for this outfit set in motion a series of events that proved incendiary. The Estates General wrangled over its role, and how it should internally conduct its voting inasmuch as it was divided into three separate sections or Estates—nobility, clergy, and everyone else. The bickering came to a halt on June 20, 1789, when the deputies discovered that the king had closed the hall in which they had been meeting. It was nine in the morning and raining.

Uncertain how to proceed, the delegates of the largest group, the Third Estate, milled about outside the hall and pondered the next move. They decided to meet elsewhere.[148] Where? A professor of anatomy, who would soon gain fame for his invention of a simple machine that ended life quickly, knew of a large space that could be used. Dr. Guillotin suggested a nearby indoor tennis court, which the throng commandeered. Six hundred delegates crowded into the plain and high-ceilinged room and swore they would remain together until France had a constitution—a decisive and revolutionary act. The delegates claimed in effect to be France herself.

The scene has come down to us as *The Tennis Court Oath*, an unfinished painting by Jacques-Louis David. The soon-to-be mayor of Paris, Jean Bailly, stands center stage; others are gathered around with their arms stretched out toward him.[149] Some delegates are hugging each other. The emotional lines of the scene flow horizontally. A month later the Bastille, a symbol of the old regime, fell to surging crowds. In the celebrations of those events a year later, speakers often invoked fraternity. Not only are we free but "we are brothers," proclaimed the municipality of Paris in its address to all of France.[150]

One need not be a Freudian to register the Oedipal dimensions. The sons bond together as they overthrow the father. One psychoanalyst dubs the Tennis Court Oath meeting the "assembly of brothers."[151] Bailly in his memoirs referred often to the "fraternal" spirit among the delegates.[152] The idea that the delegates constituted a brotherhood or family grouping came up frequently. "If we should see ourselves as a united family," stated a delegate, "it is because the king calls us his children."[153] Yet the father has angered the children, who kill him. The sons suffer not only from guilt but also from resentment. To subvert the father is also to subvert the lines of inheritance. The spoils have to be shared. How? The Vendée and the Terror lie in the near future. Bailly himself succumbed to the machine named after the doctor. First the brothers swear fidelity to one another, then they unsheathe the knives. History recapitulates myth. Parricide turns into fratricide.

3

GENOCIDE IN HISTORY: KILL THY NEIGHBOR

How can friend be distinguished from foe? It may be a simple enough matter among soldiers on the battlefield; it is another matter among neighbors at home. Sometimes overt differences have disappeared. Sometimes they never existed. The issue defines fraternal strife—the imperative to identify, and the difficulty of identifying, neighbor-turned-enemy. Your neighbor looks like you. "The worst of these wars," commented Michel de Montaigne of the sixteenth-century conflict between Catholics and Huguenots, "is that the cards are so mixed up." The enemy is "indistinguishable from you by any clear indication of language or deportment, being brought up under the same laws, manners and climate."

Montaigne's reflections were prompted by meeting on the road a gentleman of "good appearance" who was "on the other side from us"—that is, a Huguenot—but who pretended to be a Catholic. Montaigne journeyed along with the fellow, whose periodic anxiety was all that suggested where his allegiances lay. "I noticed he almost died every time" they passed a Catholic town. His misgivings about his deception almost gave him away. "It seemed . . . you could read right into the very secret thoughts of his mind through his mask."

Yet misgivings rarely serve to identify a foe, as Montaigne admitted. Although he traveled along with this "man of mine" for some time without divining his religion, Montaigne feared the reverse situation as well, in which a clear conscience amounts to little. He worried that he might encounter "our own troops" on the road and that he would be unable to prove his identity. Indeed, that "mishap" had occurred "on another occasion." Montaigne offers few details, but presumably he had been attacked by Catholic forces. His party suffered loss of life, including a young Italian page, "beautiful and full of great promise."[1] These fatal mistakes bedevil civil wars and hostilities. How do you know whether your neighbor is friend or enemy?

In English the Hebrew word *shibboleth* now sometimes refers to clichés or tired slogans. "I know the old shibboleth about there being no such thing as bad publicity" runs a typical usage. However, the term first connoted a way to distinguish friends and enemies who otherwise appear indistinguishable. In the Hebrew Bible the good sons of Israel, the men of Gilead, fought and defeated the not-so-good men of Ephraim. The Gileadites commanded the Jordan River, which the Ephraimites sought to ford in order to escape. Except for his accent or dialect, an Ephraimite could pass as a Gileadite. The victors forced each Ephraimite attempting to cross the river to take a linguistic test. The price for failure was death. "Then said they unto him, Say now Shibboleth: and he said Sibboleth: for he could not frame to pronounce it right. Then they took him, and slew him at the passages of Jordan: and there fell at that time of the Ephraimites forty and two thousand" (Judges 12:6). So unfolded an early fratricidal massacre. The difference between the two groups rested on the pronunciation of *sh*.

Shibboleths or linguistic markers to ferret out an enemy have often been employed. A fourteenth-century peasant revolt in England targeted local Flemish, who were resented for their wealth and entrepreneurial success. Indeed the English denizens viewed them as Jews, who had already been banished. But who were they? The Flemish looked like the English. The angry crowds employed a linguistic test, "a *Shibboleth* to discover" the enemy. Again the price for mispronunciation was high. "He who pronounced *Brot* and *Kase* for *Bread* and *Cheese* had his head lopt off," stated a chronicle of the events. The crowd chased the mispronouncers as "sport" and hacked them to death.[2]

Linguistic tests seldom work in fratricidal struggles, however; brothers speak the same language. Catholics and Protestants in Northern Ireland may detest each other, but like French Catholics and Huguenots or Rwandan Tutsis and Hutus, they do not differ in their language. To determine who is who requires other markers since differences do not jump out. A University of Ulster psychologist notes that Protestants and Catholics use various "cues" to identify each other, such as "school attended, first name, and area of residence." When this information is lacking, he reports, "we may fall back on less reliable cues such as surname, facial appearance or even type of swear words used."[3] A survivor of Nazi genocide in Poland recalls that a former schoolmate helped the occupier identify the Jews in a breadline. "He is a Jew! He is a Jew!" the school chum pronounced as residents lined up for bread.[4] The point is obvious, the implications less so. The Nazis needed help because Polish Jews sometimes looked like Polish Christians.

Nazi propaganda often addressed the difficulty of how to identify the Jews who might resemble non-Jews. A 1938 Nazi textbook for schoolchildren compared Jews to poisonous mushrooms that appeared edible. *The Poisonous Mushroom* opens with a mother and son in the forest gathering mushrooms. She instructs him about the "poisonous mushrooms of humanity," the Jews. Just as a single mushroom can kill a whole family, "a solitary Jew can destroy a whole village, a whole city, even an entire Volk." But a dangerous toadstool can look just like a delectable one. "To see the difference between edible and poisonous mushrooms is often as difficult as to recognize Jews as swindlers and criminals," reads the caption to an illustration. One chapter of the book summarizes the lessons the schoolchildren have learned on how to identify a Jew. Not only the nose, but the gait, size, ears, and lips are significant. "The eyelids are mostly thicker and more fleshy than ours," recites a student to the approbation of the teacher. "The Jewish look is wary and piercing."[5]

The Nazi propaganda film *The Eternal Jew* took up this issue for adults. It shows Eastern European Jews wearing the traditional caftans, beards, and earlocks. The Jews appear exactly as who they are and thus can be avoided. The film then shows clips of the same individuals in Western garb, clean shaven in suits and ties. Once the Jews shed their ghetto clothes, the film intones, only the "sharp-eyed" can pick them out. The Nazi experts underestimated the problem, however; the film denounces for his decadent work the "Jew" Charlie Chaplin, who was not Jewish.

The same problem arises in present-day civil strife, for example, that between Shiites and Sunnis in Iraq. "There is no way to physically tell Sunni Arabs from Shiite Arabs," reports a journalist, "so militiamen and insurgents are increasingly killing people based on small, telltale signs—whether the owner of a car or a house has posters or stickers of Shiite martyrs, for instance, or whether a driver has a car with a license plate from a Sunni-dominated province." The account notes that "stories abound" of militiamen, insurgents, or uniformed men stopping Iraqi civilians at checkpoints to inspect their identification cards. "If they have a suspect name or a hometown dominated by the rival sect" they are executed on the spot. In July 2006 Shiite gunmen set up fake checkpoints in the al-Jihad neighborhood of Baghdad and shot people after examining their identification cards.[6]

Many argue about what constitutes genocide, but a related issue is rarely addressed: how do you identify the persecuted? In the words of the 1948 United Nations Convention on the Prevention and Punishment of the Crime of Genocide, its perpetrators target "a national, ethnical [sic], racial or religious group." Of course, this leaves open several questions. How extensive or planned must the killing be? Does the destruction of Native Americans constitute genocide? The murder of Armenians by the Ottoman Turks during and just after World War I? "What mattered," writes Samantha Power in *A Problem from Hell*, which examined America's reluctance to interfere in genocides, "was that one set of individuals intended to destroy the members of [a] group not because of anything they did but because of who they were."[7]

This definition seems clear enough, but in fact the perpetrators frequently cannot pick out the targeted individuals. The group may be hated, but who are its members? How can they be identified? Moreover, if the group displays no obvious identifying characteristics, then what is the meaning of the hatred? It is easy to reify the categories—German and Jew, Hutu and Tutsi, Turk and Armenian, Catholic Irish and Protestant Irish—but difficult to flesh them out. "Because Rwandans all speak the same language," writes an anthropologist, "live in the same face-to-face communities, dress similarly, share the same names, it is not possible to deduce a person's ethnicity" in everyday situations.[8] To be sure, Tutsis are generally taller and have longer noses than Hutus, but such markers prove unreliable. "With the increase in mixed marriages in recent decades," reports an analysis of the origins of the Rwandan genocide, "it has become more difficult to know a person's group affiliation simply by looking at him or her." This report notes that "during the genocide some persons who were legally Hutu were killed as Tutsi because they looked Tutsi."[9] The Rwandan government, which had long asked for ethnic affiliation in surveys, discovered in follow-up studies that over a quarter of the population misrepresented itself. "Tutsi have a tendency to declare themselves Hutu," it concluded.[10]

As with all historical cataclysms, genocide prompts reexamination of the past. We search for reasons—for causes. Not only thoughtful citizens but also scholars read the present into the past. We have a chronology of the events, but we look for the "causes" of the French or Russian Revolution: economic collapse, political ineptitude, angry citizens. This approach is valid but remakes history into a determinist schema: what happened had to happen. Counterforces get short shrift. After all, the conservatives who sought to save the old regime failed. Yet in playing to the victors—here the revolutionaries—we distort history by discounting antithetical groups or currents. We look for lessons, but we may not draw the right ones. We attend to what jumps out and neglect what stays back.

Just so with genocide. In recent years genocide and Holocaust studies have emerged, complete with their own journals and conferences. We want to uncover the mainspring for mass murder. Although it is unsettling to admit, the Nazis might be called victors, since they largely achieved their goal of a *Judenrein* Europe. The Jewish population of Germany fell from a half million before 1933 to fewer than fifty thousand after the war; that of Poland from more than 3 million to also fewer than fifty thousand. When we look for the "causes" of this Jewish extermination, we often distort history. We believe that the group hatred—the anti-Semitism—that turned murderous in the 1930s developed out of the anti-Semitism of the previous century, even of the previous millennium; that the Jews of the twentieth century existed as a maligned and ostracized group. Their annihilation makes insane sense in that it constituted the last step in a diabolical sequence. But the opposite vantage point should be considered as well. The Jews of twentieth-century Germany were not shunned or excluded; they were not outsiders but insiders. Genocide may feed off resemblance, not difference.

The killing of the Jews in Germany in particular, and the anti-Semitism that sustained it, may be the paradigmatic case of fraternal genocide. After all, Jews and Christians share a great deal. Jesus himself was a Jew. An account of early Christian anti-Judaism bears the title *Faith and Fratricide*. Its author, Rosemary Ruether, explains that whereas pagan anti-Judaism emerged from a world distant from the Jews and found monotheism incomprehensible, Christian belief overlapped with Jewish belief. "The special virulence of Christian anti-Semitism" can only be understood as a form of "sibling rivalry." It derives from a "religious fraternity" in which Christians and Jews partook of the same religious symbols.[11]

The long history of Christian attitudes toward Jews encompasses many issues, and only a few can be addressed here. Inasmuch as Jews and Christians inhabit the same milieu and honor some of the same texts, how are they to be distinguished? This is an elementary as well as a complex question, since it contains numerous issues: What is a Christian to a Christian? What is a Christian to a non-Christian? What is a Jew to a Jew? And what is a Jew to a non-Jew? It is the last question that is pertinent here. Anti-Semitism rests on the notion that Jews can be identified by outsiders.

George Montandon, one of the "race" experts in Vichy France, assumed that. He published a little book in 1940 that sought to provide scientific backing for what he believed was the invariable sixth sense among Christians that enabled them to sniff out Jews. His book *How to Recognize the Jew* opened with a little vignette. You are sitting in a Parisian café and a person with Jewish features sits down near you, and you say to yourself, "There is a Jew!" However, if you were to ask yourself how you recognized him, it would be difficult to be precise. Then a companion of this individual, very different in appearance, comes and sits down next to him. "A second Jew!" you say to yourself, but this time it is even more difficult to explain your identification. Montandon purports to show how Jews, although they differ among themselves, are nevertheless "recognizable."[12]

The term *anti-Semitism* derives from the late nineteenth century, and research into ancient anti-Judaic sentiment dates from the same period. The terrain has proved a minefield among scholars.[13] What sets Jews apart? Not only anti-Semites but Jews themselves have argued that something separates Jews from others. The "inner

quality" of anti-Semitism arose from the Jews themselves, concludes one Jewish historian of antiquity. The Jews were "an alien
body" within the nation. "The alien character of the Jews is the
central cause of the origins of anti-Semitism, and this alien character has two aspects: The Jews are alien to other peoples because
they are foreigners . . . and they are alien because of their foreign
customs which are strange and outlandish in the eyes of the local
inhabitants."[14] Other historians, however, argue with great vigor
that nothing in the ancient world set Jews apart from Gentiles.

But the Christian world did develop a notion of Jewish dis-
tinctiveness, although centuries passed before it cohered. The story
of Cain and Abel looms over this history. Christians read this episode as prefiguring the relationship between Jews and Christians.
Cain the Jew slew Abel the Christian, and God marked him as
a consequence. The Jew bears the mark of Cain. In retelling the
Cain-Abel story, Elie Wiesel, the Holocaust survivor and writer,
calls the killing of Abel by Cain the first genocide: half of mankind kills the other half.[15] Wiesel does not mention that if this be
genocide, it represents a reversal with the Christian, not the Jew, as
victim; at least this is how many Christians understood it.

Textually and historically, that interpretation makes no sense—
Christians did not exist at the time—but popular ideas, ratified
by artistic representations and learned theologians, equated Cain
with the Jew and Abel with the Christian. Saint Ambrose in the
fourth century stated, "These two brothers, Cain and Abel, have
furnished us with the prototype of the Synagogue and the Church.
In Cain we perceive the parricidal people of the Jews, who were
stained with the blood of their Lord, their Creator. . . . By Abel we
understand the Christian who cleaves to God."[16]

As noted in chapter 2, Saint Augustine, too, frequently drew
the parallels. Cain received God's admonition "like the criminal he
was." Augustine continues, in the *The City of God:* "He also prefigures the Jews by whom Christ was slain, the Shepherd of the flock
of men, who was foreshadowed in Abel, the shepherd of the flock
of sheep."[17] Elsewhere he states,

Who now knows what each people in the Roman empire was, when all are made Romans, and all are called Romans? But the Jews remain with their distinguishing mark: they have not been so conquered as to be absorbed by the conquerors. Not without cause, when Cain killed his brother, did God place a mark on him, so that no-one should kill him. This is the mark which the Jews have.[18]

From the most sophisticated thinkers like Augustine to the most common, this notion persisted and developed through the centuries. Christian writers reiterated that Cain's fate anticipates the fate of the Jews.[19] Popular medieval texts that commented on biblical verses frequently identified Cain as the Jew. "Cain who killed Abel his brother, signified the Jews who crucified the Lord Jesus Christ," ran a typical commentary. Another offered, "God cursing Cain signifies Jesus Christ who curses the Jews."[20]

The translation of the Cain-Abel story into the Jewish-Christian conflict stumbled on a critical problem. An angry God "set a mark upon Cain, lest any finding him should kill him." The Lord wanted him marked but not killed (Genesis 4:15). God seemed to be playing a Talmudic joke, since the text offers no clue as to the nature of this mark. Philo, an Alexandrian Jew, in his commentary puzzles about the obscurity. The Lord, Moses tells us, puts a mark upon Cain, "but what his mark is, he has not shown, although he is in the habit of explaining the nature of everything by a sign."[21] How is Cain to be identified? What is the mark? How do we know who is the Cain among us? After all, Cain is your brother and looks like everyone else, which is the problem. The door opened wide for commentators to argue about what marks Cain and, by extension, what marks a Jew: a tattoo? horns? trembling? rootlessness?[22]

The answer to this question tapped folk traditions, myths, and holy writings. The story of the wandering or eternal Jew itself addressed this question. It is a tale with a thousand versions that took off from Cain's fate and stayed alive right into the Nazi period. The

Jews are "just like rats," pronounces an "authority" in *The Eternal Jew*. They decamp from the Middle East to Spain, France, and Germany. The film presents maps with arrows showing the movements of the "wandering" Jews as they depart Palestine for Egypt, Europe, and America.[23] While the National Socialists scarcely cared about biblical precedent, they followed it.

The Lord damned Cain to "be a fugitive and a vagabond in the earth."[24] This was the fate of the wandering Jew. While the tale showed up in oral chronicles, only in the early seventeenth century was it written down and published. In an early printed version a Jew witnesses Jesus, who is dragging the wood for his cross, as he stops for a moment to rest. The Jew goads him to move on, and Jesus replies, "I shall go and I shall rest; but you will walk and will not rest; you will walk as long as the world is the world."[25] Thus the Jew became forever homeless and nomadic. Popular woodcuts and prints represented the wandering Jew with a walking stick, travel-worn, bearded, and poor.

Another feature was added to this basic image. The Septuagint, or Greek version of the Hebrew Bible, translated the curse of Cain as trembling and groaning. Early Christian writings adopted this interpretation, and shaking also became a mark of Cain. In a Christian text from the sixth century called *The Conflict of Adam and Eve*, Cain trembles from fear as he buries Abel in the earth. An angry God condemns Cain to perpetual trembling. "Then Cain trembled and became terrified; and through this sign did God make him an example before all the creation, as the murderer of his brother."[26] This idea has persisted virtually to the present, for instance in a twentieth-century Catholic Bible, which reprises an earlier commentary: "The more common opinion of the interpreters of holy writ supposes this mark [of Cain] to have been a trembling of the body."[27] The mark of Cain, then, consisted of two components, trembling and wandering.

From there it was only a short step to identify Jews as those who trembled and wandered. Augustine made that step—and was followed by others. In his *Contra Faustum* he pinned the fate of

Cain on the Jews: "'Groaning and trembling shalt thou be on the earth.' Here no one can fail to see that in every land where the Jews are scattered they mourn for the loss of their kingdom, and are in terrified subjection to the immensely superior number of Christians."[28] In the thirteenth century Pope Innocent III, the pope who called for the crusade against the Cathars, tied together Cain, Jews, nomads, and trembling:

> The Lord made Cain a wanderer and a fugitive over the earth, but set a mark upon him, making his head to shake, lest any finding him should slay him. Thus the Jews, against whom the blood of Jesus Christ calls out, although they ought not to be killed . . . yet as wanderers ought they to remain upon the earth, until their countenance be filled with shame.[29]

The French abbot Peter the Venerable, an ally of Innocent III, expressed similar sentiments. God did not want Cain to die but to suffer and wander; just so with "the damned and damnable" Jews. "Since they spilled the blood of Christ—their brother in the flesh—they are enslaved, afflicted, anxious, suffering, and wanderers on the earth, until . . . the miserable remnants of this people . . . will be converted to God."[30]

These images of the anxious, shaking, wandering Jews formed a mainstay of anti-Semitic ideas. They allowed for the identification of Jews and implied a link to their supposed favorite activity— busyness or business. In the modern period science stepped in to give a progressive allure to these characteristics. The old shaking Jew became the new hysterical Jew. In the age of psychology the Jew became a patient, the prime neurotic.[31] Hysteria and neuroses served to mark Jews.

Both anti-Semites and Jews themselves advanced the idea of the anxious Jew. Edouard Drumont, a Frenchman who authored in 1886 a popular anti-Semitic book, *La France juive* (*Jewish France*), viewed the Jews as unique by virtue of their nervousness. Neurosis, he stated, is the "inevitable disease of Jews." Inasmuch as they plot incessantly, speculate in money, take up the professions that prize intellect, and hardly exercise, "their nervous system collapses."[32] Doctors in the late nineteenth century concurred and regularly identified Jews as a "neurotic race." Specialists in nerves yoked together the faster pace of urban life and the anxiety of Jews. A German pathologist offered statistical evidence that Jews suffered from hysteria at twice the rate of non-Jews. An American doctor studied the "Hebrew insane" at a New York hospital in 1902 and concluded, "The Hebrews as a race are hysterical and neurasthenic."[33] A British doctor who investigated "the insane Jew" at a London asylum in 1900 found that the male Jew is typically "neurotic," the woman "hysterical," and both suffer from "neurasthenia." He knew why. The "mental strain" from the "excessive zeal in acquiring riches" led to "the mental breakdown of these people."[34]

Jews themselves frequently advanced similar ideas. In his 1911 study *The Jews,* Maurice Fishberg, a Jewish anthropologist and doctor, noted, "In most monographs on hysteria and neurasthenia the authors never omit to state that these diseased conditions are most frequently observed among the Jews." This is accurate, according to Fishberg. All the major capitals are filled with neurotic and hysterical Jews. The Jewish population of Warsaw alone offers an "inexhaustible source" of hysterics. "In London and New York City the clinics of nervous diseases can be seen daily to be overcrowded with Jews."[35]

In accordance with the medical materialism of the time, it was believed that the Jewish body itself gave rise to nervousness. This too could be another mark of Cain the Jew—bodily weakness or defective structure. "In the case of the Jew," wrote French historian Anatole Leroy-Beaulieu in 1895, "the development of the mind has outstripped that of the body," which lacks muscles and strength. "In his feeble frame there reside frequently a lucid mind and a strong will." However, the imbalance renders the Jew neurotic and hysterical. All researchers have "verified" that the Jew is "particularly liable to the disease of our age, neurosis," since "nerves, not muscles, constitute the Jewish body." For Leroy-Beaulieu,

The Jew is distinguished by the predominance of his nervous, over his muscular, system. . . . He is far less muscular than nervous; he is all nerves, if we may be permitted this expression. . . . The Jew is the most nervous of men, perhaps because he is the most cerebral, because he has lived most by his brain. All his vital sap seems to rise from his limbs, or his trunk, to his head. . . . His over-strained nervous system is often apt, in the end, to become disordered or to collapse entirely.[36]

The notion of the overdeveloped Jewish intellect and the underdeveloped body shows up frequently in the works of fin de siècle commentators.[37] But as early as the late eighteenth century, Jewish writers lamented the corporal weakness of their brethren. Jewish young men spent too much time studying, complained one doctor. "Is this not the reason why we see so few well-formed men within our race?" He compared Jewish youth to hothouse fruits that lack vigor. When they leave the protected environment, they wither. This is David Friedländer, a student of the philosopher Moses Mendelssohn, both of whom fought for an enlightened Judaism and sought equality for Jews from the Prussian government. Friedländer offered an unusual argument that reflected a belief in sickly but brainy Jews. With equality, he believed, Jews would join the mainstream and no longer stick out. However, success would come at a price. Once accepted into society, Jews would become "more stupid and more strong."[38]

The stray remarks on Jewish nervousness and bodily weakness get turned into a program by turn-of-the-century Zionism. As promoted by Max Nordau, Theodor Herzl's confederate, Zionism took up the idea of the febrile Jew and ran with it. Nordau believed that "degeneration," a nervous disorder that beset the modern age, especially enfeebled Jews. He championed a "muscular Jewry" in opposition to the image (and he believed, the reality) of the puny and hysterical Jew. His Jews no longer bore the mark of Cain but stood tall and strong like their Gentile confreres. The long-noted irony is that turn-of-the-century exponents of Zionism like

Nordau and Herzl were thoroughly assimilated Jews. For years Nordau hid his Jewish past. He changed his name from Simon Maximilian Südfeld to Max Simon Nordau. He claimed to have been raised by a "Baltic mother" and "Prussian" father who identified with all things German. "I have never known or felt that I am a Jew," confessed Nordau.[39] He and Herzl wanted to be accepted as good Western European citizens. They sought not to be different but to be the same. They were not primarily Jews but ordinary nationalists.[40]

This was the point—and the reason the "cultural" Jews, who wanted to cultivate the unique elements of their religion, objected to Herzl's Zionism. His Jews seemed like Christians. When Martin Buber, an exponent of cultural Judaism, visited the Zionist office in Vienna, Herzl boasted of the technological future of Palestine. "How much horsepower has Niagara?" he asked. "Eight million? We shall have ten million!" This future horrified Buber since he believed that it amounted to a surrendering of the unique Judaic identity.[41] The Jew would become like everyone else.

This was almost Herzl's goal: to replicate, not diverge. His Jewish utopia resembled a prosperous Europe without anti-Semitism. Jews no longer looked and acted as if they stood apart. They spoke German and French and went to the opera. Jewish youth would become robust and athletic. Jews would have rifle and athletic clubs as in Switzerland, David, the host in Herzl's utopia, reports with enthusiasm to the visitor—and cricket and football teams. "Once, Jewish children were weak, pale, cowed. Look at them today! . . . We brought these children from dank cellars and slums into the light of day!"[42]

Nordau all but copyrighted the term *degeneration*, the title of his best-selling book.[43] Degeneration for Nordau designated irrational and romantic ideas in culture, a decay of reason. But he was a physician, and the bodily manifestations of degeneration, such as exhaustion and hysteria, figured often in his text. He dedicated *Degeneration* to the Italian Jewish physician Cesare Lombroso, who pioneered a criminal anthropology in which bodily deformations or so-called atavisms—big jaws, low brows, even tattoos—identified the delinquent. Psychology textbooks today sometimes feature Lombroso's photographs to illustrate a faulty biological determinism. Nordau believed that intellectual degeneration paralleled or surpassed physical degeneration—and that it carried its own stigmata. "It is not necessary to measure the cranium of an author, or to see the lobe of a painter's ear, in order to recognize that he belongs to the class of degenerates."[44]

Not until Nordau encountered Herzl did Jews figure into his broadside. Herzl converted him, if incompletely. Thenceforth degeneration encompassed Jews, at least in the physical department.[45] Nordau tapped into the Zeitgeist—or into one of its chambers—since the idea of the physical degeneracy of Jews became a mainstay of Zionist thought. To be sure, the discussion did not broach Cain or his mark; however, these Jews sought to remove the physical stigmata associated with Judaism. They wanted to create what historian Paul Breines has called "tough Jews."[46] The international Zionist conferences regularly featured doctors who bemoaned the "narrow chests," the flabby constitution, and the nervousness of Jews. Jews suffer from "weak muscles, badly developed respiratory organs, weak bone structure, [and] slight physical strength," argued one Zionist doctor. Only the "cranial capacity of the Jew is on average greater than that of the non-Jewish population."[47]

At the same time the (German) Jewish Gymnastic Association emerged, dedicated to furthering Jewish goals by "corporeal means." Its program called for restoring "the elasticity" to the Jewish body—"to make it fresh and vigorous, agile and strong." The group complained of a "one-sided education" that led to "our nervousness and mental fatigue."[48] Nordau himself addressed the gymnasts and wrote for their periodical. He called upon Jews to become "deep-chested," "sturdy," and "sharp-eyed."[49] Members of the Jewish Gymnastic Association performed for an audience that included Nordau and Herzl at the Sixth Zionist Congress at Basle in 1903. They demonstrated, at least according to their own report, that Jews did not have "pale faces, hunched-over backs, and broken hearts and chests." Their magazine regularly praised muscles as the answer to nervousness. "The Jews shall become muscle men instead of nervous men."[50]

Of course, the weak musculature, trembling, and hysteria that the Zionists wanted to overcome did not constitute a fail-safe marker of Jews—if indeed these were the marks of Cain. They would hardly suffice to pick out a Jew on a city street. Numerous nineteenth-century anthropologists and social Darwinists took another tack and sought to identify inheritable signs of Jewishness. As one nineteenth-century scholar of race put it, "the psychological traits of Jews" cannot be approached with any precision. "Nowadays science is measurement accurately calculated," which means taking into account the physical and racial characteristics of Jews, what he called "their anthropometry or bodily measurements."[51] These scientists—Jews and non-Jews—zeroed in on body types and bodily features such as noses, feet, stature, eyes, and chest sizes.

Francis Galton, the founder of British eugenics and a cousin of Darwin, sought to nail down the physical and inheritable Jewish traits. He made composite photographs of boys from a Hebrew school for the poor in order to distill out common characteristics. He found that the boys shared a piercing "look." "Every one of them was coolly appraising me at market value." Apparently Jews scrutinize the world in a certain way, which Galton confirmed just outside the school grounds. "The feature that struck me the most as I drove through the adjacent Jewish quarter," he noted, "was the cool scanning gaze."[52] Joseph Jacobs, an Australian Jewish scholar who commissioned the photos from Galton, also had no doubts. "Photographic science" applied to Jewish boys from widely different backgrounds confirmed the reality of "the Jewish expression," which seemed defined by a "peculiar intensity."[53] A small army of scientists joined in this enterprise of tabulating Jewish facial and bodily features. The physiognomists plotted Jewish noses, ears, and mouths.[54] The anthropologists measured stature, chest sizes, head shapes, girth, and body mass. Fishberg, the Jewish anthropologist, worked with a tape measure and joined what appears to have been an impassioned controversy about the circumference of the Jewish chest. "Discussions on the girth of the Jewish chest," comments Fishberg before entering the fray, "occupy many pages of the anthropological literature of the Jews." Fishberg boldly advances but concludes that chest size cannot be considered a "stable" Jewish marker.[55]

Zionists often believed that bodily features defined Jews.[56] Arthur Ruppin, a sociologist and the "father" of Jewish settlements in Israel, subscribed to a racial idea of Jews and feared Jewish degeneration. He offered a taxonomy of Jewish noses as a way to study the race.[57] Shneor Bychowski, a Polish physician and Zionist, put it all together: nervousness, wandering, racial types, and eugenics. For years he studied Jewish nervous diseases and degeneration. ("It interests me as a doctor; it irritates me as a Jew, and it torments me as a Zionist.") Persecution and miserable work conditions had led to Jewish weakness, he believed. In a 1918 essay "Nervous Diseases and Eugenics in Jews," he wrote that the Bolshevik Revolution would emancipate the Jews and spell the end of the nervous wandering Jew, who would "remain only in the world of stories and fantasies." However, he feared that Jews would now flow even more into their traditional professions of law and medicine. From a "eugenic perspective" this would be undesirable; for the sake of Jewish "nerves" he would prefer that the young people "strengthen" their "physical powers" and enter agricultural and technical schools.[58]

In Vienna some of those who had not taken up gymnastics or entered technical schools visited a young doctor who specialized in nervous disorders. Sigmund Freud's early work, such as his *Studies in Hysteria,* analyzed hysteria by drawing on an almost exclusively Jewish clientele. Moreover, Freud had trained in Paris at the Salpêtrière sanitarium with Jean-Martin Charcot, who frequently showcased hysterics and emphasized their Jewishness. In his popular lectures, Charcot brought forth his patients and discussed their ailments. With a Jewish patient at hand, he remarked "how in the [Jewish] race, nervous symptoms of all sorts . . . are incomparably more frequent than elsewhere." On another occasion he stated, "The Semites have the privilege of presenting in an extremely accentuated degree all that . . . can be imagined in the area of neuropathic afflictions."[59]

In 1893 Henry Meige, one of Charcot's students, systematized the master's comments in a booklet titled *Le juif-errant à la Salpêtrière* (*The Wandering Jew at Salpêtrière*). "It is remarkable," observed Meige, "the great frequency of nervous disorders in the Jewish race." He noted that the patients who came a great distance to seek help from Charcot were exclusively Jews. "In that there is surely something more than a plain coincidence." Meige put together old stereotypes and new science. He claimed that the contemporary Jewish hysteric represented nothing more than the old wandering Jew, who invariably suffered from overexcitedness. Meige presented profiles, photographs, and diagrams of "Moses B.," "Siegmund S.," and other hysterics. His pamphlet included a photograph of "Gottlieb M.," a shabby and bearded traveler, over the title "Israelite, Neuropathic Wanderer." Meige believed he had rediscovered the archetype. "The wandering Jew still exists today. . . . His face, dress and gestures remain the same over the ages."[60]

Be that as it may, wandering, narrow chests, and nervousness could not immediately identify Jews. If these were marks of Cain, they did not always announce themselves as such. Perhaps for this reason, pictorial representations of wandering Jews often depicted them as externally branded. In a woodcut by the nineteenth-century French illustrator Gustave Doré, the wandering Jew bears a cross on his forehead. Brands or badges served as more effective means of identification than trembling or facial features. In their function and history, badges join tattooing, branding, and the other markings that traditionally served to identify slaves, prisoners, and criminals.[61] When religious or state officials require a group to wear badges, they admit in effect that group peculiarities do not suffice to identify its members. The paradox is so common it almost escapes comment. The badge testifies that the badged could pass unnoticed.

The situation that gives rise to badges might be set against the situation in which badges are superfluous. In the antebellum United States, blackness connoted slavery. "The black color is presumptive proof of slavery," ruled a New Jersey court in 1826. In South Carolina, if a dispute arose as to a claim to citizenship, what a judge dubbed "the mark which nature has put upon" the individual will decide. If she or he is black, the claim is denied.[62] This basic supposition meant that free blacks needed to carry certificates at all times to prove that they were legally free.[63] Before the Civil War, summarizes one historian, "almost every state forced free Negroes to register and carry freedom papers."[64]

The "presumptive proof" loses its meaning in the absence of presumption or visible cues. Or, to put it differently, brothers look like one another. Scholars might argue about what constitutes the "mark" of Cain, but the very argument proves the point: the mark was not obvious. French Huguenots and French Catholics looked like each other, as do Iraqi Sunni and Shia. Even if he trembled and wandered, the Jew could not be easily identified by visible or audible signs. A requirement that possible Jews carry papers to prove that they were non-Jews would make little sense, since they could not be readily identified as Jews in the first place.

But situations did arise when non-Jews needed to carry proof of their Gentile status. In the Nazi period Vichy France not only issued a raft of laws and edicts to define who was a Jew, it also issued "Certificates of Non-Adherence to the Jewish Race" (*Certificats de Non-Appartenance à la Race Juive*).[65] These attested that the bearer "should not be considered a Jew by terms of the law of June 2, 1941."[66] That law considered a Jew to be a citizen who had three Jewish grandparents, but it left ambiguous the significance of conversions and baptisms. The uncertainties meant that a Christian with Jewish grandparents could be taken as a Jew and therefore might seek a certificate to prove otherwise. For instance, the state restricted the number of Jewish doctors to 2 percent (but who exactly were the Jews?), and some of the targeted applied for certificates to prove they were kosher, as it were—that is, nonkosher or Christian.[67] Fiction caught up with reality in Joseph Losey's 1976 film *Monsieur Klein,* set in occupied Paris, in which the life of the Catholic Robert Klein gets conflated with that of the hunted Jew Robert Klein. The Christian Klein has a rude awakening when notices meant for the Jewish Klein find their way to his door.

In any case, the language of the certificate waffled. It did not say that the bearer was not a Jew—only that he or she was not a Jew according to the law of June 2, 1941, which was constantly being amended. According to Carmen Callil in her book on Vichy France, the Commissariat for Jewish Affairs issued at least "eighteen executive orders, sixty-seven texts and 397 articles" setting out what constitutes a Jew.[68] In some disputes, the authorities availed themselves of a simple criterion: they checked for circumcision. The Vichy authorities caught up with one Marcel Weiller, a merchant, who had two Jewish grandparents. They claimed he was of the "Jewish race" because, among other things, he was circumcised.[69]

Other countries of Occupied Europe occasionally used this method. The invading Nazi soldiers in Poland rounded up the population, including young Solomon Perel, and tried to identify the Jews, who were slated for immediate murder. "While I was waiting," recalls Perel, "I heard the clang of the shovels digging graves for my Jewish brothers and I heard the machine-gun salvos close by." Perel, who had already fled from Germany and spoke perfect German, claimed to be an ethnic German. Inexplicably, the Nazis believed him, but spared only him. He passed the shibboleth test. Others, who lacked impeccable German, claimed to be Ukrainian or Lithuanian, not Jewish. Whenever the soldiers had doubts about a man, "they ordered him to drop his trousers. If he were circumcised, they cursed at him" and sent him to be machine-gunned.[70]

On occasion circumcision proved a virtue. At the war's end Jacov Lind, a young Austrian Jew who managed to survive in Nazi Germany by posing as a Dutch Gentile, sought to pass into France. The French Army arrested him at the border and took him for a fleeing German soldier or SS man. Lind became "furious," he writes in his autobiography. He had eluded the Gestapo during the war but could not explain his situation in French to the French Army. "I was pushed through a door marked 'Intelligence' and had to lower my trousers." The investigator "must have had considerable experience with cocks. . . . He could tell right away. . . . This man has a little bit of his foreskin missing, ergo this man is a Jew."[71] Lind was released.

The Nazis were hardly the first to use circumcision to identify Jews, although they may have been the first to turn it into a death sentence.[72] Jewish tradition (the Midrash) expanded on the account of the Queen of Sheba and King Solomon in the Hebrew Bible, which tells how the Queen came to Jerusalem to challenge the King. She wanted to test with "hard questions" his vaunted wisdom. But the Bible gives no details on the questions. The Jewish commentators filled in the blanks with riddles that the Queen posed. After asking Solomon to distinguish between a group of male and female children of the same height and attire, which he did, she brought before him some men. "Distinguish between the circumcised and the uncircumcised." Solomon signaled the high priest to open the Ark of the Covenant. Immediately the circumcised, not the uncircumcised, bowed down before it and "their faces were lit with God's radiance."[73] Faith rendered a hidden mark visible.

In the first century CE the Roman government instituted special taxes for Jews, but not all Jews advertised or admitted their identity. Who were they? "Jews and gentiles in antiquity," writes a historian of early Judaism, "were corporeally, visually, linguistically, and socially indistinguishable" from Gentiles. The Roman historian Suetonius reported that the authorities levied the tax with the "utmost vigor" and flushed out shirkers. Those "who lived a Jewish life without registering (themselves as Jews), as well as those who concealed their origin" were prosecuted. "I recall being present in my youth," stated Suetonius, "when a ninety-year-old man was examined by the procurator before a very crowded court to see whether he was circumcised."[74]

Yet obvious problems beset ferreting out Jews by circumcision. King Solomon's method might not work for everyone. An Ark of the Covenant might not always be available. To drop trousers proves awkward, if not unworkable, in everyday life. Besides Jews, other peoples circumcise their sons—for instance, Muslims. Moreover, the method leaves out the female half of the Jewish population. Finally, even for many anti-Semites, circumcision did not in itself loom large. For those who subscribed to a racial idea of Judaism, circumcision played no role. They wanted to identify inherited, not acquired, Jewish features. George Montandon's *How to Recognize the Jew* addresses noses and lips, not penises.

For these reasons, in the early medieval period Church and state sought a better system for identifying Jews. It may have been the Muslim world that took the lead. Muslim viziers commanded Jews to wear special badges, hats, or other distinctive clothing. Early Islamic authorities employed so-called neck sealing—a form of quasi-permanent necklace—to mark groups such as the Jews who had to pay special taxes.[75] A manuscript from the early twelfth century reports that the caliph of Baghdad ordered that each male Jew "should wear a yellow badge on his headgear" as well as a special necklace. "Each woman had to have a small brass bell on her neck or shoe, which would tinkle and thus announce the separation of Jewish from Gentile women." The account notes that as a result "the Gentile population used to mock at the Jews," and the mobs and their children "beat up the Jews" in the streets of Baghdad.[76]

In the West the badges commence a bit later. Louis IX in the thirteenth century ordered Jews of both sexes to wear a felt circle or yellow badge so that "they could be recognized and distinguished from Christians." To avoid any confusion, the regulation prescribed that the badge should be worn at chest height on both front and back. In this way one could see a Jew coming or going.[77] No need to drop breeches.

Louis' promulgation followed that of papal authorities. Pope Innocent III, who linked Cain, Jews, and trembling, called into being the Fourth Lateran Council (1215), usually considered the most important of the papal councils and sometimes called the Great Council. It included some four hundred bishops and nine hundred abbots and priors, as well as envoys from secular powers.[78] The council approved seventy decrees or canons that the pope presented to them, a grab bag of very large and very small issues. The last canon called for a new crusade to "liberate the Holy Land from the hands of the ungodly." Another specified that abbots can bring no more than six horses to ecclesiastic meetings.

Four canons took up the Jews. One decried the "excessive interest" or usury that Jews exacted and enjoined Christians to "abstain from commerce with them." Another prohibited Jews from holding public office. A third forbade Jews who converted to Christianity to practice old rites. A fourth addressed how and when Jews should appear in public. "They shall not go forth in public at all" on the three days before Easter. On every other day Jews in public must wear distinctive clothing.

> In some provinces a difference in dress distinguishes the Jews or Saracens from the Christians, but in certain others such a confusion has grown up that they cannot be distinguished by any difference. Thus it happens at times that through error Christians have relations with the women of Jews or Saracens, and Jews and Saracens with Christian women. Therefore, that they may not, under pretext of error of this sort, excuse themselves in the future for the excesses of such prohibited intercourse, we decree that such Jews and Saracens of both sexes in every Christian province and at all times shall be marked off in the eyes of the public from other peoples through the character of their dress.[79]

The "confusion" that arose because Jews "cannot be distinguished by any difference" motivated the decree for distinct clothing. In other words, Jews looked liked Christians. The council did not specify what Jews should wear, and its directives included Saracens, or Muslims. Except for in Spain, however, Muslims were not an issue for the Western Church—or only an issue at or beyond its borders, not as an internal population that might pass as Christians. In the wake of the council, local churches adopted regulations that addressed what Jews—not Muslims—should wear, an omission reflecting that fact. For instance, soon after the council, the church of Narbonne ruled, "That Jews may be distinguished from others, we decree and emphatically command that in the center of the breast (of their garments) they shall wear an oval badge, the measure of one finger in width and one half a palm in height."[80]

Over the next years, indeed centuries, the effort to mark Jews in public with badges or distinct clothing waxed and waned. Authorities commanded hats, insignia, and ribbons, sometimes in red, usually in yellow, and sometimes bells. The motive always remained the same, to mark those who seem unremarkable so there would be no confusion. The citizens of Spain in 1371 petitioned the king to decree such a measure. Since he had not yet expelled the Jews, they asked that he order that Jews "be marked and separated from the Christians as God has commanded . . . and . . . that they wear signs as they do in other kingdoms, so that they might be recognized among the Christians and be less inclined to cause so much evil."[81]

It is possible to follow these laws through the centuries. An edict of the archduke of Austria in 1551 complained of the reprehensible activities of the Jews: "These scandalous evil actions are said to flow in good part from the fact that the Jews in numerous localities dwell and move about among the Christians without any distinguishing marks and without any difference in clothes and costume and thus cannot be distinguished from Christians nor recognized as Jews." For this reason Archduke Ferdinand decreed that all Jews "wear publicly and uncovered a sign by which they are to be distinguished and recognizable from Christians, namely, on the outer coat or dress over the left breast a yellow ring . . . made of yellow cloth."[82]

In Italy authorities seemed to prefer red or yellow hats to badges.[83] The Jews wear yellow hats, reported a seventeenth-century traveler to a papal-run city, "to distinguish them from Christians."[84] A seventeenth-century English visitor to Venice and Rome also observed that the Jews wore red or yellow hats "for notice sake to distinguish them from others." This traveler made a further revealing comment, which pointed to the issue of distinguishing another undistinguishable population, Catholics. "Would to God" that this "custom" of hat wearing were "enjoined to all the Papists here in England, so should we easily discern them from the true Christians."[85]

The use of badges and hats to mark the Cains among us died a slow death. By the late eighteenth century, the impact of the Enlightenment and the French Revolution had ended these requirements across Europe. Still, as late as 1826 a traveler reported that in Rome Jews were "obliged to wear a yellow ribbon as a mark of distinction when they mix with Christians."[86]

History progresses and regresses. In the twentieth century badges returned with a vengeance. In 1939 first in the occupied territories of Poland, and then in Germany itself, and finally in the occupied regions to the west, Nazi authorities commanded Jews to wear badges. At a Paris meeting in the spring of 1942, Nazi "specialists on the Jewish question" gathered and decided that Jews in Occupied Western Europe should wear a yellow Jewish star, about ten centimeters square (four inches), with the word *Jew* in the national language. In Belgium they thoughtfully allowed a bilingual star in Flemish and French.[87]

Both Jews and anti-Semites understood that the Nazis were reviving a venerable tradition. "We are returning to the Middle Ages," wrote a fifteen-year-old Dawid Sierakowiak in his diary of the Lodz Ghetto in Poland. "The yellow patch once again becomes a part of Jewish dress."[88] Lucien Rebatet, a French anti-Semite who flourished in Vichy France (and was imprisoned after the war), made a similar observation with a different goal. He addressed Catholic disquiet at the appearance of the yellow stars. It is "easy to salve their conscience," he wrote. "The yellow star connects up to the most strict Christian tradition," centuries of "true and solid faith, of pure Catholic civilization" when hats and badges marked Jews.[89] The arguments that invoked the kings and popes of the Middle Ages who ordered distinct marking for Jews pleased the German authorities. They reported to Berlin that the Paris press made "additional propaganda" promoting the Jewish star unnecessary.[90]

Xavier Vallat, the first commissioner for Jewish affairs in Vichy France, struck the same note. A militant Catholic and anti-Semite who also was imprisoned after the war, he argued that the expulsion of Jews from public life followed a venerable Church tradition. Twenty-nine popes, he declared, issued fifty-seven bulls that addressed "the Jewish question." He followed precedent, he believed. To be sure, inasmuch as he did not recognize conversions or baptisms of Jews, he may have diverged from Church teachings, but no matter. As two historians of Vichy remark, for Vallat "heredity was stronger than holy water."[91]

Nevertheless, Vallat believed he was upholding Christianity. He told the court after the war that he had not complied with the racist Germans but with the Church. The Jew was an "unassimilable foreigner" who had been condemned "to wander across the world." To protect society, the Church had instituted the yellow star in the thirteenth century and set up curfews for Jews in the sixteenth century.[92] Vallat cited chapter and verse from Catholic teachings in his defense of his policies. He did this not to take "Rome as a shield" but to show that he adhered to Church dogma.[93]

The edicts on badge wearing in early modern Europe can be documented, but we have for that period virtually no record of what responses they elicited from Jews or non-Jews. For the Nazi era, however, we do know the reactions of some who wore badges and some who saw them. The regulations created a zone where unremarkable neighbors suddenly surfaced as remarkable. For a number of Frenchmen the law that ordered Jews to wear badges proved salutary. Invisible Jews became visible. Now we will know whom we are dealing with, exulted a reporter. "Henceforth Levy, Blum or Cohen, even if they call themselves Dubois, Dupont or Durand, will no longer be able to gain our confidence or good faith."[94]

In accord with the edict that Jews wear the yellow star in Occupied Western Europe, Parisian officials spelled out the details for France. They issued an ordinance on May 31, 1942, that required Jews over the age of six to identify themselves in public by wearing a palm-sized yellow six-pointed star lettered *Juif* in black. It specified that the star "should be worn clearly visible on the left side of the chest, securely sewn to the garment." The order would take effect in one week and gave Jews five days to report alphabetically by last names (A–B on Tuesday, June 2, through S–Z on Saturday, June 6) to their local commissariat to collect their badges.[95] On June 8, the day after the regulations came into effect, *Le Petit Parisien*, a collaborationist newspaper, noted that Parisians were "astonished" at the "considerable number" of Jews who showed up in the streets. The paper hoped that its readers might reflect on the fact that Frenchmen had barely "suspected" the existence of so many Jews—not only in certain quartiers known to be Jewish but in "chic" arrondissements as well.[96] Another newspaper concurred. "One only has to spend a quarter of an hour on a Sunday strolling between the Madeleine and the Place de la République," offered this journal, to convince oneself of the "Jewish peril." Last Sunday "one of our reporters" counted 268 people wearing yellow stars. "The proportion of passers-by marked with a yellow star surpasses anything one might have imagined."[97] Before its imposition, Frenchmen might have been innocently nodding or chatting with individuals who were Jews.

Louis Rebatet defended the law with enviable lucidity. Indeed his words cannot be improved upon. They describe a world in which enemies look like brothers—a world in which badges are required to set off neighbor from neighbor, a world where the Cains are unmarked.

> I don't know any longer which politician once said, "If the Jews were black or blue, there would be no Jewish question. Everyone would recognize them and avoid them." The yellow star rectifies this strange situation in which one human group that is radically opposed to the people of white blood and which for eternity is unassimilable to this blood, cannot be identified at first glance.[98]

For Jews themselves the order was catastrophic. Now at "first glance" they could be identified. "Integrated Jews who had long thought of themselves as French above all else were suddenly not only subjected to discriminatory laws but forced to look physically different at all times," writes a historian of French Jewry.[99] Of course they responded in varied ways. The fourteen-year-old Maurice Rajsfus, the son of Polish Jews, dreaded the walk to school. He always rushed home. All the world seemed against him. He never grew accustomed to wearing the badge. He suffered from nightmares in which the yellow star became "enormous and brilliant like the full moon."[100]

"Yesterday the regulations came into effect," wrote Hélène Berr in her memoirs, as she struggled over how to react the first time she wore the star. "This morning I went out with Maman. In the street two boys pointed at us and said: 'Eh? You seen that? Jew.'" At the bus stop a young woman "pointed me out to her companion. Then they exchanged some remarks." With her student friends, she felt like an outsider. "I suffered there, in the sunlit Sorbonne courtyard, among my comrades," wrote Berr. "I suddenly felt I was no longer myself, that everything had changed, that I had become a foreigner." She felt as if "my forehead had been seared by a branding iron."[101] She had become Cain.

Berr sometimes wondered whether she should refuse to wear the yellow star. Some Jews didn't wear it, or not all the time. "I had long ago stopped wearing the yellow star," wrote a seventeen-year-old Paul Steinberg, in his memoirs. "I figured it was a trap for suckers."[102] Steinberg, a professional survivor, stood at the furthest remove from the gullible. Betrayed, he was arrested in Paris and deported to Auschwitz. He shows up in Primo Levi's *Survival in Auschwitz* as Henri, a young man totally manipulative and totally committed to life. He "fights to live without distraction and with all the resources" of his quick mind and refined education, observes Levi.[103] Indeed, Steinberg survived Auschwitz.

That Steinberg did not wear a star suggests that some Jews could "pass." They were Jews but few knew. The records of the office that enforced anti-Semitic policy in France (*Commissariat Général aux Questions Juives*) include an account of the arrest in August 1943 of Mlle. Marguerite Gleidmann, a dressmaker. The report notes that she did not have "Jewish features." She ran afoul of the authorities because her star was only pinned on and regularly fell off.[104] She was sent to Drancy, an internment camp. A list of interns of convoy 59—the authorities carefully typed out registers—who left Drancy for Auschwitz the following month includes a Marguerite Gleidmann. Unlike Steinberg, she did not return.[105]

The reaction of non-Jews to seeing their neighbors branded was mixed. Not everyone cheered with the anti-Semites, of course; some resisted and demonstrated their solidarity. A number of non-Jewish Parisians parodied the yellow star. These included Michel Ravet, a salesman, who wore a false star with the inscription *Goy,* and Marie Lang, a newspaper vendor, who put a Jewish star on her dog.[106] Such individuals were detained but usually released after a short time. Others made small but significant gestures. One Frenchwoman recalls that when she arrived at school hesitant and humiliated with her star plastered on her chest, the teacher made an announcement. "You see here Jeannette. She has earned the right to this star because of the excellence of her work. Those of you who are capable of doing as well will also in your turn earn one."[107]

Berr writes that she was wearing the star and strolling down the Avenue de la Bourdonnais "thinking, I believe, about my shoes" and became aware of a man who approached her. He offered his hand and proclaimed loudly, "A French Catholic shakes your hand . . . and when it's over, we'll let them have it!"[108] The gesture buoyed Berr, but for her there was no "over." She died aged twenty-four at Bergen-Belsen concentration camp in 1945.

Anti-Semitic sentiment appears to be a perfect case of "othering." The standard interpretation posits Jews as alien people with strange practices. As Bernard Lazare put it in his *Antisemitism: Its History and Causes* (1894), "To the antisemite, the Jew is an individual of a foreign race, incapable of adapting himself, hostile to Christian civilization and religion; immoral, antisocial, of an intellectuality different from the Aryan intellectuality, and, to cap it all, a deprecator and wrongdoer." The Jew is "strange, noxious, disturbing and inferior."[109]

With varied emphases, this characterization runs through anti-Semitism—and the interpretation of anti-Semitism. Joshua Trachtenberg's book on medieval anti-Semitism, *The Devil and the Jews*, has on its cover a seventeenth-century graphic of a Jew with horns, which was one interpretation of the mark of Cain. For the anti-Semite, Trachtenberg writes, the Jew is "alien in his habits, his pursuits, his interests, his character, his very blood."[110] A recent volume on racism and anti-Semitism captures the tendency in its title, *Demonizing the Other*. In the programmatic essay we are told that anti-Semitism presents the perfect case of demonization. To "demonize a human" is to ascribe to him or her "all immoral and evil attributes existing in society."[111]

However, the standard interpretation of the Jew as the other, a strange being, may eclipse a deeper truth. In much of Europe, especially in the modern period, the Jew was not foreign and unadaptable but familiar and integrated. He or she did not wear horns or a yellow hat but looked like everyone else. The Jew was your neighbor, acquaintance, and sometimes your lover, husband, or wife. Consider Wilhelm Marr, the German journalist, who coined in 1879 the term *anti-Semitism*. He sought an expression that sounded more scientific than Jew hating or hatred of the Jews. The coinage enjoyed immediate success. Marr himself penned many anti-Semitic pamphlets and founded the Anti-Semitic League, which sought to preserve Germany from "complete Judification."[112]

However, to Marr Jews were hardly alien beings with exotic practices. "I came to know the Semitic race in a thorough manner, in its most intimate details," he wrote in his memoirs. This is an understatement. Three of Marr's four wives were Jewish. He declared that he found with his second wife, whom he called a "pure Jewess" and whose maiden name was Israel, great happiness and tranquility. "My life with her was happy."[113] Alas, she died in childbirth, and Marr proceeded to marry another Jewish woman. This man launched the word *anti-Semitism*.

To be sure, the stranger, often the Polish or Russian coreligionist who in garb and customs preserved the old traditions, haunted the assimilated Jew too. For the German Jewish burgher, Eastern Jews represented the "other," a weird tribe, if not Asian, at least half-Asian—which was the title of a popular collection of short stories (*Aus Halb-Asien*) by Karl Franzos, an Austrian Jewish writer. Franzos saw the Eastern Jews as partaking of a world that was neither purely civilized as in Germany nor purely barbaric as in Turkestan; rather they lived in a strange twilight, a mixture of Europe and Asia.[114]

Within the Jewish world the stranger emerges and gives rise to the same paradoxes. He or she is different but also close, and must be kept at a distance. The exotic Eastern Jew threatened the integration of the Western European Jew into society. The more the Reform German Jews identified themselves as good German citizens, the more they rejected their Eastern brethren, who dressed in peculiar clothes and spoke a peculiar jargon, Yiddish. For many years the German Jewish poet Ernst Lissauer saw himself as a full-throated German nationalist. During World War I he wrote a jingoist poem ("Hymn of Hate against England") that swept Germany. "He was the most Prussian, or Prussian-assimilated, Jew I had ever known," recalls Stefan Zweig.[115] Lissauer's family disdained Eastern European Jews and in fact reproved use of the word *Jew*, for which they substituted *Armenian* or *Abyssinian*.[116] Lissauer believed that German Jews shared nothing with Eastern European Jews. "We German Jews" do not speak Yiddish or wear caftans. He recalled that once "as I stood with some fellow Jewish students at the door of my Berlin high school, a man with a Jewish caftan and *peyes* who had come from the train station asked, 'Are there any Jews in Berlin?' Instinctively I answered to myself, 'No,' for he meant something else by the word than we did." Lissauer concludes, "We are not their compatriots."[117]

The rejection of the outsider with whom a relationship nevertheless exists reinforces the insider. This is an old story with many variations. Among Jews it persisted into the New World, where the rituals of the Orthodox also triggered the anxiety of the assimilated. Philip Roth's short story "Eli, the Fanatic" captures the disquiet when an ultra-Orthodox Jewish school opens in a "progressive suburban community." The black coat and wide-brimmed Talmudic hat of the teacher upset the assimilated American Jews, who settled in the suburbs and want only to be invisible. The old Jew dresses funny; he looks funny. The assimilated threaten legal action. They suggest that at least the teacher wear "clothing usually associated with American life in the 20th century." They give him a green suit.[118]

Roth's story echoes the account by the Czech Jewish playwright František Langer of his brother's peregrinations decades earlier, in pre–World War I Prague. Jiří Langer, an acquaintance of Franz Kafka, decamped from their home of assimilated Jews to embrace the Hasidim of Eastern Europe. In František's words, he moved five hundred kilometers east and five hundred years back in time. Jiří's reappearance in the garb of the ultra-Orthodox frightened the family. "Father told me with a note of horror in his voice that Jiří had returned. I understood what filled him with dread as soon as I saw my brother." He had a full beard and earlocks and dressed in an old black overcoat with a black velvet hat. František notes that Jews "in our part of the world" did not look "different in their outward appearance from other citizens." Just as in Roth's story, the Jewish outsider—here an insider who becomes an outsider—caused discomfort. When Jiří left the house, his attire, hair, and shuffling gait "drew people's attention to him and made him the laughing-stock of the street, the effects of which were felt by our entire family."[119]

Yet as this vignette suggests, some assimilated Jews like Jiří Langer embraced the unassimilated. The stranger becomes the brother. A history of the relationship of German and Eastern European Jews by Steven Ascheim bears the title *Brothers and Strangers*.[120] The category of the "other" gets flipped to become something desirable. In a small countermovement to the main drive of assimilation, some assimilated Jews regarded the Eastern Jew—and the East in general—as more soulful and genuine than the Western Jew and the West. Lissauer with his ardent German nationalism represented one extreme, but a number of contemporaries celebrated the Eastern European Jews and their "Asian" world. A Jewish journal in Berlin, *East and West*, sought sometimes to mediate the differences and sometimes to romanticize the Eastern Jews.[121] "I am not exaggerating," wrote the great Jewish historian Gershom Scholem in his autobiography, "when I say that in those years there was something like a cult of Eastern Jews."[122]

As evidence of this cult Scholem mentions the early work of Martin Buber such as *The Tales of Rabbi Nachman*, which romanticized the Hasidim of Eastern Europe. The idolization of the Eastern Jew passed into the idolization of the East itself—into a positive Jewish Orientalism. A collection of essays by Buber's protégés celebrated the Orientalism of Jews; its opening essays are titled "The Jew as Oriental" and "The Spirit of the Orient." A contributor called upon Jews to reconnect with their deepest Oriental roots.[123] Scholem's own assimilated German family evinced this Orientalism. On the occasion of a family wedding, his mother wrote for her small sons a playlet that reveled in it. Called "Ex Oriente Lux" or "Light Comes from the East," it has the four Scholem boys dressed up in Eastern garb—Arab, Chinese, Jewish, and Hindu.[124]

If the categories can be reversed, perhaps the individual can be as well, which also suggests the malleability of the "foreign" and the "familiar." Many an individual has transformed himself or herself to become what earlier had been the stranger. This is an old story—and a new one. *The New York Times* recently ran an account of a Polish neo-Nazi "skinhead" who became an ultra-Orthodox Jew after he discovered that he had two Jewish grandparents. Yesterday he defaced Jewish cemeteries. Today he davens at the synagogue. He did not want his last name used in the paper "for fear that his old neo-Nazi friends could harm him or his family."[125]

In the 1920s a few assimilated Jews like Jiří Langer abandoned their environs and joined the Hasidic world.[126] Others made the personal leap into the East itself. Friedrich Arndt, a teacher and architect, converted to Islam and showed up in Munich in a red fez and flowing robes as Omar al-Rashid Bey to teach about the wisdom of the East.[127] Leopold Weiss, as he tells us in his autobiography, *The Road to Mecca*, left the Viennese cafés, where he had spent many "intoxicating" evenings listening to "the early pioneers of psychoanalysis," to visit an uncle in Palestine.[128] So began a journey that ended with his conversion to Islam. As Muhammad Asad he became a respected translator and diplomat, who represented Pakistan at the United Nations.[129] Lev Nussimbaum converted to Islam and reinvented himself as Kurban Said, a Muslim prince and writer.

The story of Nussimbaum has recently been told in Tom Reiss's biography, *The Orientalist*. Nussimbaum made a career as a popular author who wrote romantic thrillers and nonfiction, usually set in the East. "While most Jews in Germany after the First World War tried as hard as they could to assimilate," Reiss comments, "Lev did everything he could to make himself stand out as an ethnic outsider, sporting flowing robes and a turban in the cafés of Berlin and Vienna."[130] Nor was this just pretense. One of his books is titled *Allah Is Great*. In this 1936 volume, subtitled *The Decline and Rise of the Islamic World,* Nussimbaum announces that the energy and spiritual strength of the East may soon overwhelm the West. "The defeat of European power in the Orient will not be the result of technological, but exclusively the spiritual weakness of Europe, which stands facing the incomparable spiritual strength of Islam," he writes.[131]

The cult of the Eastern Jews, and the full embrace of the East and what it represented, suggest that the categories of stranger and other mutate. Individuals can pass from one identity to another. However, both the leap into and the recoil from Eastern Jewishness depend on proximity. The Eastern Jew and the Western Jew shared a religion and a past, since virtually all the European Jews had their roots in Eastern European villages and ghettos. The assimilated sought to leave this history behind. The fright they felt, as in František Langer's family, rested on recognition. As František put it, Jiří's presence aroused in their father "memories of stories, long since forgotten" of the misery of ghetto life. "It disturbed his feelings of security and permanence. . . . It was a spectre from the past that had come among us."[132]

Yet the Eastern Jew, with his visible religious affiliation, proved less alarming to the anti-Semites than the Western Jew without obvious markings. It was similarity more than dissimilarity that troubled the Jew haters.[133] The Eastern Jews advertised their allegiance and could be avoided. The German Jews, who hid theirs, presented a greater threat inasmuch as they could slip undetected into the sanctums of power or privilege. German Jews themselves noted this. A mid-nineteenth-century commentator in the main German Jewish newspaper observed that as Jews became more educated and successful, hatred of them increased. "The more the old Jew with his diverse and ridiculous aspects fades away, the more the hatred of Jews increases," declared this writer. "To be sure, one disdained the Jew who made one laugh, but tolerated him, but one hates the

Jew in equal position and with equal rights."[134] Wilhelm Marr, the
inventor of the word *anti-Semitism*, agreed. With the assimilated or
Reform Jew, he wrote, "One never knows where the Jew begins and
where he ends." He prayed that God would save Germany from the
assimilated Jew. "Better the most orthodox Polish rabbi!"[135] Some
seventy years later in the wake of World War II, Carl Schmitt, the
unrepentant Nazi political theorist, concurred. The communist may
change, he wrote, but the Jew remains the same. "Exactly the assimilated Jew is the true enemy."[136]

No simple or single account can comprehend the history of Jews,
anti-Semitism, or genocide. Yet a facile emphasis on the Jew as
the "other," the alien, the threatening stranger always finds a ready
reception. We want to believe that the persecuted are outsiders.
How else can we explain what happens to them? We find it difficult to accept that the persecuted are insiders or neighbors; this
makes the story more uncomfortable. Recently Daniel Goldhagen
tapped into this notion of Jews as outsiders whom most Germans
wanted eliminated. His book, *Germany's Willing Executioners,* became an international best seller. Why? It is rare for an academic
book to get snapped up by the larger public. Despite a gloss of heresy, Goldhagen seconded a conventional outlook about the fear-
some "other." In his judgment, Germans had always despised the
Jewish outsiders. Germans had always sought to rid their nation
of these hateful creatures.[137] This is a consoling notion inasmuch
as we can understand and accept hatred for outsiders. A hatred for
insiders, however, unsettles us.

The attack-the-foreigner explanation apprehends with ease
other genocides. Why did the Serbs murder the Bosnians? Or the
Rwandan Hutus murder the Rwandan Tutsis? No need to ask. Mutual hatred, we say. Yet the opposite may be closer to the truth. The
Serbs and Bosnians, and the Tutsis and Hutus lived together naively,
without really knowing or caring who was who—for centuries. In
the same way Jews lived in Germany with minimal fuss or notice.

However, we prefer the notion of a primal hatred for primal strangers. This is psychologically easier to grasp and requires no introspection. The message from Goldhagen that the image of the Jew as "poisonous, evil, eternally strange" was "deeply embedded" in German society renders their destruction understandable.[138] We now comprehend the genocide of the Jews, but do we? As the late Amos Elon put it in *The Pity of It All: A History of Jews in Germany, 1743–1933*, "The history of Jewish assimilation, not only in Germany, has long been a subversive subject, which the assimilated have suppressed so as not to draw attention to themselves, and the Zionists, for equally self-interested reasons, have distorted."[139]

Hundreds, perhaps thousands, of memoirs and testimonies give evidence that German Jews before the onset of Hitler saw themselves—and were seen—as fully integrated into society. Many had converted to Christianity. These were not sham acts. Moreover, conversion often meant that the children did not identify with Judaism or even know about their family's connection with it. The historian Fritz Stern recalls that as a boy shortly after Hitler became chancellor in 1933, he squabbled with his sister and uttered an anti-Semitic insult. "Instantly, I was summoned to my father's study, a rare event in itself." Not simply his parents—his father was a successful doctor—but his grandparents on both sides had become Christian. One set had converted; the other considered themselves Christian and had their children baptized. Stern believed he was Christian. He said his evening prayers, and the family celebrated Christian holidays. At Christmas they sang traditional carols around the tree and enjoyed a classic German Christmas goose dinner. So successful was the family's assimilation that the children knew nothing of their Jewish roots. On that day in 1933 with a Nazi chancellor in power, young Stern received in his father's office "an astounding revelation" of the family's Jewish origins. "The full significance of this dawned on me only in the following weeks."[140] In 1938 the Stern family fled Germany for the United States.

The Stern family's thorough assimilation may have been extreme but was not atypical. German Jews frequently buried their past so completely that the children knew nothing of it. In the family of the philosopher and journalist Theodor Lessing, Jewish practices, much less talk of Jews, never surfaced. He grew up believing that Jews meant something evil: after all, they had killed "our beloved Lord Jesus." One day he called a classmate, whom he was tormenting, a Jew. The classmate responded, "'You are one also.' I said indignantly, 'It is not true.'" But Lessing inquired of his mother. "She laughed and gave an evasive answer."[141]

Jewish families often celebrated Christian holidays. "Our festivals," recalled Sigmund Freud's son of family holidays, "were Christmas, with presents under a candle-lit tree, and Easter, with gaily painted Easter eggs."[142] Gershom Scholem remembers the same. "Since the days of my grandparents . . . Christmas was celebrated in our family—with roast goose or hare, a decorated Christmas tree . . . and the big distribution of presents."[143] A trajectory from pious Jew to successfully integrated—and often Christian—German citizen marked many German Jewish and Austrian Jewish families. The Mendelssohns offer a prime example in Germany, the Wittgensteins (to whom they were distantly related) in Austria.[144]

The Wittgensteins—descended from Hermann Wittgenstein, who died in 1878—were perhaps the most wealthy as well as the most philanthropic family in turn-of-the-century Vienna. Hermann and his wife had converted to Protestantism, and for good measure Hermann had adopted "Christian" as his middle name. He forbade his many children to marry Jews. His very successful son Karl, father of the philosopher Ludwig Wittgenstein, raised his children as Catholics. "In matters of honor," Karl reportedly said, "one does not consult a Jew."[145] With its lawyers, musicians, and industrialists, the Wittgenstein family partook of all sectors of Austrian society. Their integration was so successful that some members knew nothing of their Jewish past. One daughter inquired of an uncle, a Christian evangelist, whether the rumors of their Jewish origins were true. *"Pur sang,"* she was informed.[146]

Moses Mendelssohn, the son of a poor Jewish scribe, became one of the lions of the eighteenth-century German Enlightenment and a celebrated liberal Jew toasted throughout Germany. The incarnation of an open and tolerant Judaism, he translated the Hebrew Bible into German, in part for his sons. He called upon them, and upon Jews in general, to adapt "to the land to which you have been removed, but hold fast to the religion of your fathers too." No matter the burden, he wrote in his *Jerusalem*, "no wiser advice than this can be given." We are permitted to reflect upon Judaic law, but we cannot abandon it. "Persevere, remain unflinchingly at the post."[147]

The story of the Mendelssohn family over the next generations, which includes Moses's grandson the composer Felix Mendelssohn, fills many books, but this is clear: they were astonishingly successful and none remained unflinchingly at the Jewish post. The family spawned prosperous bankers, burghers, and diplomats who abandoned Judaism and moved into the top strata of German society. Of the patriarch's six children, four gave up Judaism. Two of his daughters converted to Catholicism. One became strident and lamented that the rest of the family did not join the new faith. Both sons—Philipp and Jonas Veit—of the other daughter became Catholic religious painters who specialized in New Testament themes. A number of their offspring became nuns.

Two sons of Moses Mendelssohn became successful bankers. The younger, Abraham, had his children baptized, and afterward he and his wife converted to Christianity. He wrote to his son Felix that Judaism was "antiquated, distorted, and self-defeating" and that Christianity was "accepted by the majority of civilized people." Abraham also changed his last name to Mendelssohn Bartholdy. He explained to Felix that "a Christian Mendelssohn is an impossibility."[148] Another son also converted. If there was a split in the family, it was between the Catholic and Protestant branches. By the middle of the century, the fifty-odd living members of the Mendelssohns, either descended directly or married into the family, included only four Jews. In 1880 the last Jewish member of the family died.[149]

By the twentieth century the family was flourishing in all domains of German society; it yielded industrialists, bankers, diplomats, musicians, and professors. Consider the offspring of Felix alone: One of his sons, Paul, pioneered the development of dyes and cofounded Agfa, a firm that became one of Germany's largest chemical companies and remains famous for its photographic products. One of Paul's sons, Otto von Mendelssohn Bartholdy, became a banker so successful that he was raised to nobility by the Kaiser.[150] To bring this story of assimilation almost to the present, one of Felix's great-grandchildren married Hans-Joachim Schoeps, a historian of religion and a German Jew. Schoeps, who died in Erlangen in 1980, so identified with German society that in 1933 he founded a Jewish group that worked—to no avail—to find its place in the Nazi state. "The world significance of National Socialism," he wrote in 1933, "is that it has conquered Bolshevism in Germany." He lauded National Socialism for finding a "third way" between Moscow and the Western democracies; it had saved Germany from "ruin." He called upon Jews to be prepared to play their role. "Today Germany experiences a popular renewal." Schoeps stood with the few deluded Jews who endorsed the Nazi "national revolution," which tapped, he wrote appreciatively, "the primal grounds of blood and race."[151]

His affection for Nazism went unrequited and Schoeps fled Germany for Sweden, where he survived the war. His parents did not have the same luck. Their deaths in concentration camps hardly affected his thinking. To the end he considered himself a good Prussian conservative, even a monarchist. In fact, his thought drew upon a modern font of Christian conservatism, Friedrich Julius Stahl, himself a converted Jew. In 1955 the Hohenzollern royal family, overthrown in 1918 by the founding of the German republic, honored Schoeps for his efforts on their behalf.[152]

Schoeps may be an exception in his embrace of Nazism, but not inasmuch as he exemplified the larger Mendelssohn family and the integration of German Jewry into mainstream society. In 1929—the two-hundredth anniversary of Moses Mendelssohn's birth—celebrations and exhibits took place across Germany, which included popular lectures and radio programs. In the Berlin State Library two government ministers inaugurated a vast exhibition of Mendelssohniana. The mayor of Berlin gave an address, after which Leo Baeck, the respected leader of the German Jews, took the podium and honored Moses Mendelssohn for his achievements.[153] For the first time, he said, a Jew had emerged who in his body and soul was European and who, without renouncing his Judaism, could proudly stand up in the new Europe. Moses Mendelssohn "tied together" German and Jewish history. He was a pathbreaking and true Berliner—a sort of American, able to mix the old and the new. Generations of Jews followed him and enlivened the spirit and culture of the city. "Berlin without Jews?" asked Baeck. "Surely, how very much Berlin would miss if its Jewish population disappeared!"[154]

Baeck stood on firm ground, or so it seemed. In 1929 a Berlin without Jews did not seem possible. In the course of two centuries European Jews had moved from the margins to the center. While statistics provide only part of the story, by most indexes Jews in modern Europe enjoyed astounding success. They constituted an extremely disproportionate number of bankers, journalists, doctors, merchants, lawyers, writers, musicians, and scientists, even though Jews made up just a small fraction of the population in European countries: not more than 5 percent and usually closer to 1 percent, as in Germany. Compared to their numbers in the population, Jews were greatly overrepresented in cities and urban professions. In Berlin before World War I, about a third of the taxes came from Jews. In Frankfurt Jews paid four times the amount of taxes than did Protestants, eight times more than Catholics.[155] In the later nineteenth century Germany's Jews accounted for one-fifth of the country's wholesalers and bankers. In 1871, of 580 banking houses in Prussia, 23 percent were Jewish and another 37 percent "mixed"—again in a population of which Jews made up 1 percent. Similar numbers show up in a survey of retail outfits and journalism.[156] Of the three big houses in newspaper publishing, two (Mosse and Ullstein) were run by Jews. In mainstream book publishing, in addition to Mosse and Ullstein, Samuel Fischer played a leading role.[157] When the Nazis came to power, almost one-third of those in the natural sciences, more than one-third of the medical faculties, and almost half the mathematicians were forced out. These were largely Jews.[158]

Elsewhere in Western Europe, such as Austria-Hungary, even higher percentages of bankers and professionals were Jewish. In the Austro-Hungarian Empire, more than three-quarters of the leading bankers were Jewish. "In turn-of-the-century Vienna, 62 percent of the lawyers, half the doctors and dentists, 45 percent of the medical faculty, and one-fourth of the total faculty were Jews," summarizes Yuri Slezkine in *The Jewish Century*, "as were between 51.5 and 63.2 percent of professional journalists. In 1920, 59.9 percent of Hungarian doctors, 50.6 percent of lawyers, 39.25 percent of all privately employed engineers and chemists, 34.3 percent of editors and journalists, and 28.6 percent of musicians identified themselves as Jews by religion." Nor was this unusual. "In large parts of Eastern Europe, virtually the whole middle class was Jewish."[159] These were societies in which Jews constituted a small fraction of the population.

Economic and social success does not mean successful acceptance; this is evident and has provoked much debate. Yet economic and social success does not mean rejection either. In regard to German Jews, and other West European Jews, the notion of the alien, the "other," often prevails and distorts history. Those who hold this view look at events through the wrong end of the telescope. They turn history into a determinist chain of events; they look back to find a cause and leap to the conclusion, "Aha! German Jews were outsiders and foreigners." This conclusion may reassure us by its clarity, but it evades harder truths. The destruction of European Jewry seems both predestined and comprehensible, but it was neither.

In 1933, as the Nazis came to power, a few German Jews decided to publish a substantial one-volume encyclopedia to demonstrate their contribution and successful integration into the establishment. The book proceeds field by field, from literature and physics to social welfare and sports. It surveys Jewish accomplishment and provides thumbnail biographies, from heroic humanist Moses Mendelssohn in the eighteenth century to winning tennis player Daniel Prenn in the twentieth. It encompasses the great, like Albert Einstein, and the not-so-great, like Moritz Goldschmidt, a botanist who wrote on the flora of the Rhön mountains.[160]

Jews succeeded so well in integrating themselves in German society that the volume included a fifteen-page appendix listing non-Jews who were commonly considered Jews, such as Berthold Brecht and Igor Stravinsky.[161] In fact, anti-Semites made mistakes in both directions and celebrated numerous Jews as pure Germans.[162] Their frequent errors suggest the success as well as the successful assimilation of the German Jews. Even the anti-Semites did not know who they were. That was the problem. The encyclopedia's projected publication date—year two of the Nazi regime—did not bode well. The government prohibited its publication. The editors fled. The book was published only in 1959. Its fate merits only a footnote in the history of the Third Reich, yet the volume illustrates the real achievements of German Jewry within Germany, its success and, above all, its assimilation. Jews in Germany were far from outsiders; they were consummate and accomplished insiders. Like the French Huguenots, they were neighbors. So much the worse.

4

FEARFUL SYMMETRIES

If Cain and Abel were the first brothers in the Hebrew Bible, Esau and Jacob were the first twins. They fight even in the womb. Rebekah conceived twins, who "struggled together within her." She asks the Lord, Why is this happening? He informs her, "Two nations are in thy womb and two manner of people shall be separated from thy bowels" (Genesis 25:22–23). This is as unpromising as it sounds. Jacob is born grasping the heel of Esau—a token of either closeness or competition—and they divide over everything. Jacob cheats Esau of their dying father's benediction. For this Esau plans revenge. "The days of mourning for my father are at hand; then will I slay my brother Jacob" (Genesis 27:41).

Brothers can be contentious. Jeremiah advises, "Do not trust your brothers. For every brother is a deceiver" (Jeremiah 9:4). But twins can be worse, and here twins will encompass the phenomenon of doubles, or doppelgängers. There are many stories of twins who are devoted to each other, of course, but rancor often marks the relationship. The birth of twins prompts fear in many societies. Something about twins is unsettling. What?

Violence tends to be fratricidal and pivots on similarities more than on differences, as I have emphasized in previous chapters, or it pivots on differences that rest on similarities. The proposition that likeness breeds malice runs counter to common understanding. We live in a culture that reifies and fears the "other." The stranger threatens us, or so we think. The gates get higher to keep out the unfamiliar; the familiar—of course, the word derives from *family*—reassures us. However, violence often emerges inside the gates, within the family itself, which the hostility of brothers exemplifies. Twins represent a heightened case of brothers. To consider twins and doubles is to contemplate the menace that arises from likeness, or what Freud called "the narcissism of minor differences"—hostility engendered by small disparities.

"There is always a sense of something uncanny," observed the nineteenth-century traveler Mary Kingsley of twins in West Africa. "The terror with which twins are regarded in the Niger Delta is extremely strange and real." Often the mother is killed along with her newborns.[1] This practice upset a number of nineteenth-century missionaries, who sought to end the custom.[2] "It is a fact that this people idolize their children," recorded a missionary about a Nigerian Ibo-speaking society, but "when God . . . gives them two," they "murder" them.[3] A contemporary scholar summarizes, "Stark terror surrounds the birth of twins in aboriginal and archaic societies."[4] An Italian medical researcher recently visited several marginal African societies and found the situation still bleak for twins. "All twins are killed here," a priest in southern Ethiopia told her. "I was stunned," she writes, ". . . having thought this occurred only in the past." In southern Madagascar she found that the villagers believed that the arrival of twins spelled bad luck; this often meant death for the infants. Some escaped, however; she discovered almost one hundred pairs of twins who had been placed in orphanages.[5]

As a literary theme the double appears in numerous forms, such as a shadow, a reflection, or a twin. The situation is sometimes played for laughs but most often evokes unease. Why? The replica menaces the self because it might be the real self, or a version of it. The copy challenges the original. Two implies that one is fraudulent. The copy mirrors and stands in judgment. "I feared him," says William Wilson in Edgar Allan Poe's story when he meets his namesake, who resembles him in every way. When he steals toward the sleeping doppelgänger, Wilson is struck by "intolerable horror." The "detestable coincidence" of "his accent, his air, and general appearance" recalls something of his earliest infancy, "wild, confused and thronging memories." The double plagues Wilson throughout the rest of his life. "Impostor! . . . You *shall not* dog me unto death!" Wilson cries out. When he finally attacks his double with a sword, a mirror shows him that he has pierced himself. "As I stepped up to it [the mirror] in extremity of terror, mine own image, but with features all pale and dabbled in blood, advanced to meet me with a feeble and tottering gait."[6]

Much the same tale unfolds in Dostoevsky's story "The Double." When Mr. Golyadkin encountered the second Mr. Golyadkin, he "wanted to scream. . . . His hair stood on end, and he almost fell down with horror." Tormented by his double, whose success taunts the inept Golyadkin, he addresses him: "Either you or I, but both together is out of the question!" He demands that his double leave him alone or duel with pistols. But nothing stops the descent of the original Golyadkin into madness.[7] So too in Oscar Wilde's story of Dorian Gray, who is mocked by his portrait, which fills him with such "terror" that he is driven to kill the painter. This does not suffice, and he destroys his likeness, "this monstrous soul-life," and in so doing destroys himself.[8]

Many fiction writers have dealt with doubles. Only a few nonfiction writers, such as the nineteenth-century Englishman Thomas De Quincey, have directly addressed them. De Quincey wrote not only about opium addiction—in a book that made him famous—but frequently about murder. In a lighthearted treatise on homicide, "Considered as One of the Fine Arts," De Quincey honored Cain as "the inventor of murder"—possibly a "first-rate genius," although by contemporary standards his "performance" was just "so so."[9] De Quincey also pondered doubles. He wondered whether a second Archimedes or Milton could ever appear. "Nature does not repeat itself," he concluded, and noted that if it did, the replicas would cause widespread alarm. "Any of us would be jealous of his own duplicate," he remarked. "If I had a doppelganger, who went about personating me, copying me, and pirating me, philosopher as I am, I might (if the Court of Chancery would not grant an injunction against him) be so far carried away by jealousy as to attempt the crime of murder upon his carcass."[10]

What do twins or doubles signify? The linguistic link between duplication and duplicity suggests fraud. "Duplication involves not only duplicity but instability," comments the British social anthropologist A. E. Crawley.[11] A second raises doubt about the authenticity of the first. Twins are not always blessings; they may connote danger—two fathers, perhaps, or two competing souls. When the anthropologist Bronislaw Malinowski remarked on the similarity of two brothers in the Trobriand Islands, this was taken as a great insult. "What astonished me," he writes, ". . . was, that in spite of the striking resemblance between the two brothers, my informants refused to admit it" and became quite angry. "The incident taught me never to hint at such a resemblance."[12]

The double evokes doubt about which is the original. It frightens by its eerie similitude. It is the self as a stranger—an "other" who seems to be oneself. The double also portends death. To see oneself as an other is to feel that one's own self is dead. For this reason, the sighting of a double connotes disaster. Tales of doubles that presage death fill popular lore.[13]

Even in real life the encounter with a double often prompts a feeling of strangeness. "I was sitting alone in my sleeping compartment" on a railroad journey, reported an aging doctor in 1919, "when the train lurched violently. The door of the adjacent toilet swung open and an elderly gentleman in a dressing gown and traveling cap entered my compartment. I assumed that on leaving the toilet, which was located between the two compartments, he had turned the wrong way. I jumped up to put him right, but soon realized to my astonishment that the intruder was my own image, reflected in the mirror on the connecting door."

This is Freud, who saw his double and found the experience "thoroughly unpleasant," even "uncanny." He recounted this "adventure" in the final footnote to his three-part essay on "The Uncanny," which the foreword to a recent edition has called one of his "weirdest" writings.[14] For Freud the uncanny was inextricably connected to the double. He noted in the essay that virtually nothing existed on the topic of the uncanny. It is a common enough phenomenon, but what makes something "uncanny"? He trolled through dictionaries and short stories by German romantics to apprehend it.

"The uncanny" is something both strange and familiar that prompts an unsettling recognition. Uncanniness depends on both dimensions, the foreign and the close. In unpacking the topic, Freud finds clues in the German language. In English, the words *uncanny* and *canny* reveal little. In German, however, *unheimlich* (uncanny) stands opposite to *heimlich* (familiar; belonging to the house, homey). The linguistic link between the opposites suggests to Freud an inner connection and a psychological truth. What is uncanny is something oddly familiar; nothing is more familiar than the self, and nothing is stranger than the self in a foreign guise.

In the Greek myth, Narcissus falls in love with himself—his own reflection—and dies contemplating it. The constellation of self, its reflection, and death informs the Freudian idea of the double. The double attracts—Narcissus cannot tear himself away from his image—but also frightens inasmuch as it presages death. The nymph who gives birth to Narcissus asks a prophet whether the handsome boy will live a long life. "Yes, if he never knows himself," she is told. What did this mean? "For many years his words seemed meaningless; / but then what happened in the end confirmed / their truth." Narcissus comes to know or recognize himself and dies because of it.[15]

For Freudians, the double can reassure, as a baby doll reassures an infant. But when the infantile stage passes, the meaning of the double changes. It becomes a rival, an authority, and an "uncanny harbinger of death."[16] Oscar Wilde's Dorian Gray keeps his youth as his portrait ages. "Once, in boyish mockery of Narcissus, he had kissed, or feigned to kiss, those painted lips."[17] But the picture now taunts him by showing him as the old Dorian, who must die. As Otto Rank, Freud's erstwhile student, stated, the narcissistic desire to "remain forever young" represents a fear of death.[18]

To be sure, the news of one's coming death might not prove startling. Or as Freud drily put it, "It is true that in textbooks on logic the statement that 'all men must die' passes for an exemplary general proposition, but it is obvious to no one."[19] The fear of death informs much of life and includes fear of doubles and replicas. Superstitions about portraits and mirrors draw on these misgivings and can be found throughout the world. Some peoples shun photographers as soul stealers. In German folk traditions, to break a mirror signifies an imminent death. To this day religious Jews cover mirrors during the period of mourning. Reflections cause anxiety.

To contemplate twins and doubles and what they evoke means to consider sameness, not difference, which is a more alluring topic.[20] Of course, categories of sameness and difference are not— to use academic argot—binary opposites. Things can be both different and similar—and usually are. A common phrase that rejects a comparison of two situations as "comparing apples and oranges" can just as easily be reversed. Inasmuch as apples and oranges are both fruits, they indeed can be compared. The usual inclination, however, is to reify, sometimes magnify, differences, especially when we consider culture and violence. Perhaps this tendency has always marked popular talk, but in recent years it has swept the academic world as well. Professors discuss "the other" and how the world divides into "strangers" and "friends." This is a more tantalizing viewpoint than seeing the world's people as more or less the same, as a population nuanced but not divided. We are "merchants of the exotic," comments one anthropologist. His discipline is "immersed in the study of difference, of the Other."[21]

Edward Said's influential *Orientalism* (1979) turned on this distinction between us and them. It was a book-length argument on how the West had fashioned Orientalism, a foreign entity: "Orientalism was ultimately a political vision of reality whose structure promoted the difference between the familiar (Europe, the West, 'us') and the strange (the Orient, the East, 'them')." Said found "Orientalism" throughout the world of scholarship and politics. "This vision in a sense created and then served the two worlds thus conceived. Orientals live in their world, 'we' live in ours." To be sure, Said attacked this binary opposition of friend and stranger. "When one uses categories like Oriental and Western," he wrote, ". . . the result is usually to polarize the distinction." For Said Orientalism leads to the "regrettable tendency" to "channel thought into a West or an East compartment."[22]

So far, so good. Yet a damaging criticism turns Said's argument against its author and maintains that Said contrived an Orientalism that rarely existed. In his learned critique, Robert Irwin of the London School of Oriental and African Studies charges Said with stereotyping. According to Irwin, Said does not simply denounce Orientalism, he constructs it. "Orientalism has become a reified 'Other,'" writes Irwin of Said. "At first sight, this might seem plausible," he admits, but the evidence does not support it. "If one considers, for example, how medieval churchmen misrepresented Islam, they tended to portray it as a Christian heresy (usually Arianism), rather than as something exotic and alien." The writings of the academic Orientalists also do not confirm Said's thesis. Said can make his argument only by ignoring much of their scholarship, especially that written in German and Latin. German Orientalists, for instance, writes Irwin, "argued that Islam was, together with Eastern Christendom and Byzantium, the joint heir of classical antiquity."[23]

No matter these objections. The exotic or alien resonates. A thousand books and ten thousand articles pursue "Orientalism" or its analog, the Other. In the same spirit contemporary political thinkers often embrace the idea of the "clash of civilizations" to fathom the violence that besets the world. The notion of colliding worlds is more appealing than the opposite—conflicts hinging on small differences. A "clash" implies that fundamental principles about human rights and life are at risk.

Samuel Huntington took the phrase "clash of civilizations" from the Princeton University Islamicist Bernard Lewis, who was referring to a threat from the Islamic world. "We are facing a mood and a movement far transcending the level of issues and policies," Lewis wrote in 1990. "This is no less than a clash of civilizations" and a challenge to "our Judeo-Christian heritage."[24] "The underlying problem for the West," writes Huntington, "is not Islamic fundamentalism. It is Islam, a different civilization."[25] Huntington, a conservative foreign policy adviser, and the late Said, a leftist English professor and Palestinian activist, probably agreed on little or nothing. Nonetheless, they both posited a bifurcated world.

If one turns to the principals themselves, much evidence for a primal contest can be found. The mullahs, the priests, and the shamans as well as presidents, prime ministers, and their experts often view the conflict in stark terms; it is us or them. Populations pour into the street, or stream to the ballot boxes, to defend their culture, religion, or way of life, when they perceive those things to be threatened. The wrath of the humble and the not-so-humble gets unleashed when central cultural symbols seem under attack. Within impoverished societies, reports of a desecrated Qur'an provoke thousands to protest. Twelve cartoons published by a provincial Danish newspaper that lampooned the Prophet Muhammad led to riots and hundreds dead in Nigeria, Libya, and Pakistan.[26] Meanwhile corruption, daily violence, pollution, and collapsed economies elicit shrugged shoulders.

When asked about the "clash of civilizations" by an interviewer, Osama bin Laden resolutely affirmed it. "I say that there is no doubt about this. This is a very clear matter, proven in the Qur'an and the traditions of the Prophet, and any true believer . . . shouldn't doubt these truths." For Bin Laden, "the battle is between us and the enemies of Islam."[27]

Or consider the words of a Hindu nationalist who addressed the conflict with Indian Muslims. How is unity to come about? she asks.

> The Hindu faces this way, the Muslim the other. The Hindu writes from left to right, the Muslim from right to left. The Hindu prays to the rising sun, the Muslim faces the setting sun when praying. If the Hindu eats with the right hand, the Muslim with the left. . . . The Hindu worships the cow, the Muslim attains paradise by eating beef. The Hindu keeps a mustache, the Muslim always shaves the upper lip.

She concludes, "Whatever the Hindu does, it is the Muslim's religion to do its opposite."[28]

The principals in the field offer versions of the clash of civilizations. French Catholics believed that French Protestants incarnated the devil—and vice versa. This is an old story, but it retains its appeal. The pulse quickens when one is confronted with presumed threats to one's sacred identity. To argue the reverse, that differences are minor—of degree, not of kind—does not stir people.

Some three centuries ago, Jonathan Swift deflated talk of primal clashes. In *Gulliver's Travels* he questioned what divided Catholics and Protestants, whose disputes at the time centered on several interlocking issues such as the nature of bread and wine in the Eucharist. "Differences in opinion," he wrote, "hath cost many millions of lives: for instance, whether *flesh* be *bread*, or *bread* be *flesh*," and whether the juice of a certain berry "be *blood* or *wine*." Swift would have none of it. "Neither are any wars so furious and bloody, or of long continuance" when "differences in opinion" are small. Swift satirized the conflict between the Protestants and Catholics in his account of this "most obstinate war" between "two great empires" of Lilliput (England) and Blefuscu (France). What was the issue? How to break open a soft-boiled egg. The traditional (read Catholic) way cracks the big end. But as a boy, the "present Majesty's grandfather" had cut his finger while cracking the big end, whereupon his father commanded his subjects to crack the egg in a new (read Protestant or Anglican) way at the small end. This led to many rebellions, even a regicide, and to much loss of life. "It is computed that eleven thousand persons have, at several times, suffered death, rather than submit to break their eggs at the smaller end." The struggle between the Little-Endians and Big-Endians, Swift wrote, was far from over. "Many hundred large volumes" had been written about the controversy, which turned on interpreting a line from the holy book that reads, *"That all true believers shall break their eggs at the convenient end."* This had caused endless controversy. Which was the convenient end? The books by the Big-Endians, who were barred from public employment, were forbidden. But the Big-Endians found support from Blefuscu and that led to war in which many vessels and "thirty thousand of our best seamen and soldiers" were lost.[29]

Though Swift's satire hit home, it may be too psychologically simple. Why *do* minor differences explode into bloody conflicts? In fact, Swift's satire does not quite apprehend Swift himself, a frequent partisan of Anglicanism who did not believe that religious differences could be reduced to how to crack open eggs.[30] For all his acuteness, he missed a psychological dimension that turns small differences into major conflagrations. Nor do the ideas about clashing civilizations and Orientalism help. They dramatize differences when the issue may be the reverse, the menace of similarities. An appointment with the doctor in Vienna is called for.

Freud took up the "narcissism of minor differences" three times and alluded to it once more.[31] The notion addressed why hostility arises between groups that are close by virtue of history or culture. Small differences seem to elicit more anger than large differences.

Why? Freud never elaborated upon the idea at length and even discounted it in a later work. Each time he discussed the notion he pared it down, and in the end it may have left him dissatisfied. Nevertheless, the idea remains provocative. Despite Freud's reservation (and perhaps against Freud), pursuing the logic of the narcissism of minor differences may offer an understanding of how similarities, not disparities, engender violence. It may illuminate fratricidal violence.

Because Freud simplified the notion as he continued to employ it, a reverse chronological examination may be justified in that it can peel back the layers to reveal the core. The issue is not allegiance to Freud but allegiance to the issue of fratricidal violence. To surpass or reject Freud requires at first fidelity to his logic; it means also attending to his aperçus, which he often tucked away in footnotes.

Freud's final reference to the narcissism of minor differences came in *Moses and Monotheism,* which he wrote in three parts. He published as separate essays parts one and two in 1937. But he "held back" part three, the largest section, which rounded out the book. When the book appeared, the last part included two prefaces, one written in Vienna in March 1938 and one written three months later in London. The prefaces reflect the political tumult of the day: the spread of Nazism and the consolidation of Stalinism.

Freud notes in the first preface that "we are living in a specially remarkable period. . . . Progress has allied itself with barbarism." Soviet Russia has improved living conditions for millions, but it has subjected its people "to the most cruel coercion and robbed them of any possibility of the freedom of thought." Italy, "with similar violence," trains people for "orderliness" and "duty." Only in Germany has "a relapse" into "barbarism" taken place uncontaminated with "progressive ideas." Freud noted the irony that he was writing from Vienna, the capital of a Catholic and conservative democracy that protected him. It is "precisely the institution of the Catholic Church which puts up a defense against the spread" of this barbarism.[32]

Not exactly. Within days of the completion of his first preface, the Nazis marched into Austria to thunderous acclaim. "Amidst scenes of the wildest enthusiasm and through dense crowds of hundreds of thousands of jubilant supporters," *The New York Times* reported, "Chancellor Hitler . . . made his triumphant entry into Vienna."[33] Three months later the eighty-two-year-old Freud boarded the Orient Express for Paris and life in exile. He proceeded to England, where he wrote his second preface. He observed that the two prefaces "contradict each other." In the short interval between writing them, his circumstances had "radically changed." The Church, far from having afforded protection, proved to be a "broken reed." He had fled Austria and "the city which, from my early childhood, had been my home for seventy-eight years" to escape certain persecution for his ideas and his "race," which he put in scare quotes. Freud died fifteen months later.

In the third part of *Moses and Monotheism* Freud addresses the anti-Semitism that afflicted "the poor Jewish people" and drove him from Vienna. While many things fueled it, the "reproach" that Jews were "aliens" [*"der Vorwurf der Landfremdheit"*] could not be sustained, he believed. "In many places dominated by anti-Semitism today," he wrote, "the Jews were among the oldest portions of the population." Freud gave Cologne as an example and by implication suggested that this was true for much of Germany. Jews came to Cologne with the Romans, even before the Germans.

Yet Jews differed "in some respects" from their European hosts. They were not "fundamentally different" since they did not constitute a "foreign race"; nonetheless, they differed "often in an indefinable way." This sufficed, however. "Strangely enough," wrote Freud, "the intolerance of groups" expresses itself "more strongly against small differences than against fundamental ones."[34] This reference to small differences does not take us very far, though Freud indicated that German Jews were hardly foreigners in Germany and that hostility seemed to have been triggered by something close, not distant. The passage suggests that Freud would concur with the idea that assimilation spurred anti-Semitism. Not the strangeness of Jews but their nearness prompted rancor.

Nazism also colored the previous reference to minor differences that appeared eight years earlier, in *Civilization and Its Discontents*. Freud closed this little book with a comment that peoples nowadays control such destructive forces that they "would have no difficulty in exterminating one another." Against this possibility, Freud hoped that the forces of life—Eros—would assert themselves against the forces of violence. He harbored doubts, however, and added in a final sentence, "But who can foresee with what success and with what result?"

Much of *Civilization and Its Discontents* considers how the aggressive urges can be tamed. Freud noted that by attacking outsiders, a group can control violence that might turn upon its own members. Nearby foreigners can serve that purpose. "It is precisely communities with adjoining territories, and related to each other in other ways," who are engaged in "constant feuds." Freud offers the examples of the Spaniards and the Portuguese, the northern and southern Germans, and the English and the Scots. "I gave this phenomenon the name of 'the narcissism of minor differences,'" he wrote, and added that "the name" does little to explain it. Freud observed that the Jews, "scattered everywhere," have played this role of an external enemy that secures the internal cohesion of a group. It is hardly surprising that anti-Semitism accompanies "the dream of a German world-dominion."[35]

An earlier reference to minor differences appears in Freud's *Group Psychology and the Analysis of the Ego* (1921). Here he challenged the sharp break between the individual and society and a corresponding rupture between individual psychology and social psychology. He sought to fathom how crowds act, both in their enthusiasms and their hatreds. The "evidence of psychoanalysis," he argued, showed that a "sediment" of "aversion and hostility" marks virtually all emotional relations between two people, including intimate relations. This animus stamps relations between groups as well. "Closely related races keep one another at arm's length," stated Freud. "Every little canton looks down upon the others with contempt." In this antipathy Freud finds self-love or narcissism. "This self-love . . . behaves as though the occurrence of any divergence from its own particular lines of development involved a criticism of them and a demand for their alteration."[36] In other words, a narrow divergence elicits aggression.

In his observation that "no one can tolerate a too intimate" relationship, Freud referred to Arthur Schopenhauer's parable on porcupines. Freud prized porcupines perhaps because they appeared to incarnate intrinsic hostility. He kept a small metal porcupine on his desk, and he claimed that he visited the United States to catch sight of a real one.[37] Standard commentaries on Freud's passage usually provide a partial translation of Schopenhauer's parable in which porcupines on a frigid day crowd together for warmth. However, their quills force them to separate. They shift back and forth until they find a "mean distance" at which they can best survive. The full parable, which came last in Schopenhauer's collection, drew an explicit moral: "Out of inner emptiness and monotony, men are forced together, but because of their many distasteful qualities and insufferable defects they knock against each other." The middling distance that results as people pull back and forth is called politeness or civility. In England those who cannot maintain this space are upbraided with "Keep your distance!"[38]

Freud pursued the idea of the narcissism of small differences most thoroughly the first time he introduced it, in a 1918 essay titled "The Taboo of Virginity," which was part of a series on the psychology of love. Unlike his later uses, where he informally used the phrase, Freud here placed it within a tangle of suggestive ideas. The early work or first formulation of a writer is often the boldest. This is the case with Freud on the narcissism of minor differences. Though he doesn't discuss it at length, he opens up several avenues that go some way in unpacking similitude and its discontents and help to get at a source of fraternal violence.

In this essay, as was his wont, Freud drew upon anthropological literature, here the writings of A. E. Crawley, in order to make points about sexual behavior. In *The Mystic Rose,* a 1902 study of "primitive" and modern marriage, Crawley posited a universal need for physical contact, evidenced in friendship, love, and sex. "Throughout the world, the greeting of a friend is expressed by contact, whether it be nose-rubbing or the kiss, the embrace or the clasp of hands." But Crawley also noted the existence of the opposite tendency. The "avoidance of contact, whether consciously or subconsciously presented, is no less the universal characteristic of human relations." Crawley called the desire to keep others distant "the taboo of personal isolation" that surrounds every individual.

In his 1918 essay Freud discusses the manner in which both "primitive" tribes and modern society honor "the taboo of virginity," although in divergent ways. Like Crawley, Freud puzzled over this taboo. Both authors subsumed it under the myriad restrictions that regulate sexual relations. A universal desire for contact—for sex—exists among men for women. At the same time a million prohibitions keep women separate from men. Anthropologists like Crawley filled tomes with descriptions of practices of puberty, hunting, and eating in which sexual segregation dominated. Obviously men have sex with women, but they do so governed by codes and customs. Crawley summarized his tour of "primitive" practices. "Two remarkable facts" have emerged, he states. "First, that it is dangerous, and later wrong, for men to have anything to do with women." Second, sexual intercourse especially endangers men.[39]

For Freud the "taboo of virginity"—the high value placed on a woman's being sexually untouched by a man—turns out to be just a particular case of a wider taboo. The word *taboo* enters European languages from Captain Cook's writings about the Pacific island peoples. But Freud, as he develops the idea in *Totem and Taboo,* does not restrict the phenomenon to primitive peoples. Rather taboos infuse all societies, which the subtitle of Freud's book, *Some Points of Agreement Between the Mental Lives of Savages and Neurotics,* suggests. In Freud's reading, taboos unfold in "two contrary directions." They signify something forbidden as well as consecrated.[40] Only something that is keenly desired needs to be forcefully prohibited.

Does the taboo of virginity partake of these contradictory characteristics? Freud considers several possibilities but follows Crawley in placing the taboo under the general rubric of prohibitions curbing sexual life. In this respect not only is the first act of coitus with a woman taboo but so is "sexual intercourse in general; it might almost be said that woman is altogether taboo." It is an illusion, Freud believes, that primitive men enjoy sexual freedom. On special occasions, such as a hunt, a man must abstain from sex, "otherwise his strength will be paralyzed." In daily life as well, sexual contact is strictly limited. Women, although desired, seem almost forbidden.

From here, Freud edges toward the narcissism of minor differences. But it appears with a twist. In his later mentions, Freud referred to close-lying communities, but here, in his first and freshest formulation, he links the narcissism of minor differences to the taboo of virginity—or, more generally, to the taboo of woman. Surprisingly, the paradigmatic "minor differences" are those between men and women. "It cannot be disputed that the general principle underlying all these regulations and avoidances," writes the Viennese doctor of the sexual taboos, "is a dread of woman."

What does man dread in woman? "Perhaps," Freud hazards, the dread is "founded on the difference of woman from man." More precisely, "man fears that his strength will be taken from him by woman, dreads becoming infected with her femininity" and that he will show himself to be a "weakling." Sexual relations may be the prototype of this dread. Man fears he will become feminine or soft. The fear is hardly confined to preindustrial peoples. "There is nothing in all of this which is extinct, which is not still alive in the heart of man to-day."

Freud returns to Crawley. He notes that Crawley believed that "each individual is separated from others by a 'taboo of personal isolation.'" Freud concurs—remember the porcupines!—but seems to attribute to Crawley something that was not there. For

Crawley the taboo of personal isolation stands as a given; he did not break it down further. Freud writes as if summarizing Crawley but puts on the table another idea. "It is precisely the minor differences [*die kleinen Unterschiede*] in persons who are otherwise alike that arouses feelings of strangeness and enmity between them." Freud adds that "it would be tempting to follow up this idea" and attribute the "antagonism" that overwhelms the biblical edict to love all humanity to this "narcissism of minor differences."[41]

This is a critical step by Freud and turns the "narcissism of minor differences" into something more than an interesting phrase. It follows on the heels of his use of the "dread of woman." The two ideas stand inextricably linked. Indeed, they may be different names for the same phenomenon. Or one might be a subset of the other. In this case the dread of woman—who could be more familiar?—as "strange and hostile" epitomizes the narcissism of minor differences. Yet the ties between the two ideas seem murky. Few psychoanalysts have pursued the phrase "dread of woman," and none has done so in conjunction with the narcissism of minor differences. The dread of woman suggests that while men love women, they fear them. They fear they will be stripped of their manliness; they worry about becoming effeminate. Again Freud: "Man fears that his strength will be taken from him by woman, dreads becoming infected with her femininity and then proving himself a weakling."[42]

The thousand rules, usually religiously based, that keep women apart from men—and sometimes keep them totally covered or hidden from men—bespeak this anxiety. If these regulations are defended on rational grounds (and not on grounds of tradition or sacred texts), they usually are said to protect women from men's sexual aggressiveness. The opposite is closer to the truth, however: the rules are meant to protect men from women and from male unease at the prospect of becoming unmanned. A 1932 essay by Karen Horney, a revisionist psychoanalyst, stands almost alone in addressing the "dread of woman." Horney reminds us that this anxiety informs all of literature and mythology. Man is drawn to

woman but fears that "he might die and be undone" by her. In fairy
tales the "heads of suitors" fill the royal palace, the remains of those
who sought the king's daughter. The Hindu goddess "dances on
the corpses of slain men." The biblical Judith beheads the Assyr-
ian general Holofernes. Delilah conquers Samson. The list is long.
"Is it not remarkable (we ask ourselves in amazement)," Horney
writes, "when one considers the overwhelming mass of this trans-
parent material, that so little recognition and attention are paid to
the fact of men's secret dread of women?"[43] Indeed.

To write the history of the dread of woman would entail, as
Horney indicated, a thousand volumes and a ramble down ten
thousand paths. The premier poem of Western literature, the
Odyssey, testifies to this fear. Not long after Freud's death, two ex-
iled philosophers signaled its importance as an allegory of Western
progress and its discontents. T. W. Adorno and Max Horkheimer
highlighted the encounter of Odysseus with the Sirens, which are
usually portrayed as female and birdlike enchanters, as the critical
episode in this tale.[44] The goddess Circe warns Odysseus to avoid
"the enchanting song" of the Sirens and "their meadow starred
with flowers." To succumb and follow the song is certain death,
and no one who hears it can resist. To bypass the Sirens in his ves-
sel without surrendering, Odysseus plugs the ears of his shipmates
with wax. He, the master, will hear the captivating song of the
women, but he will be tied to the mast. He relays Circe's advice to
the crew:

> *I alone was to hear their voices, so she said*
> *but you must bind me with tight chafing ropes*
> *so I cannot move a muscle, bound to the spot,*
> *erect at the mast-block, lashed by ropes to the mast.*
> *And if I plead, commanding you to set me free,*
> *then lash me faster, rope on pressing rope.*

All happens according to plan. As the ship approaches, Odysseus
hears "the honeyed voices":

So they sent their ravishing voices out across the air
and the heart inside me throbbed to listen longer.
I signaled the crew with frowns to set me free—
they flung themselves at the oars and rowed on harder,
Perimedes and Eurylochus springing up at once
to bind me faster with rope upon chafing rope.[45]

Here we have a short course on the danger of woman in Western culture and what she represents. The male must be tied down—to avoid the fate of effeminacy. In succumbing to the Sirens and their "viscous sweetness," writes a contemporary philosopher, "would not the man become, in effect, a woman?"[46]

In "The Taboo of Virginity," Freud added one more piece to the puzzle of the dread of woman and the narcissism of small differences. After stating that it would be "tempting" to trace back "small differences" to the "hostility" that overwhelms all love, he added this sentence: "Psychoanalysis believes that, in pointing out the castration complex and its influence on the estimation in which women are held, it has discovered one of the chief factors underlying the narcissistic rejection of women by men that is so liberally mingled with disdain."[47]

The plot thickens. While feminists may attack Freud for a theory that seems patriarchal, here we see him wrestling with the sources of male contempt for women. The primal case of the narcissism of small differences may be women and men. Women and men of the same religion, race, nation, or creed are very similar and sufficiently different. The fear of castration fuels men's widespread scorn of women. Here too lies a root of the uncanny. The male glimpses in women his mutilated double. "It is women who are *unheimlich,*" writes a feminist author.[48] In other words, the basic hostility engendered by small differences derives from men's dread of women. Men fear to be unmanned, neutered. In the dictionary of insults, "castrating bitch" ranks high (or low), but psychoanalytically all women threaten castration.

We are delving into the recesses of fratricidal violence. We have been led from the cant about the "other" to the danger of the familiar and the double. Freud has given us a purchase on the hostility that "minor differences" provoke. He has suggested that the male-female relationship might be its primal form. The conceptual drama is not over, however. In a footnote to another essay published nine years earlier than "The Taboo of Virginity," Freud introduced a character and a conceptual piece that brings us closer to a resolution. First, however, a change of scene, a flashback to six years before that.

On October 3, 1903, a young Austrian writer rented a room in Vienna in the house where Beethoven, the composer he treasured, had died. He informed the landlady that he did not want to be disturbed, as he was going to work late. He stepped out, returned, wrote a letter to his father and to his brother, and shot himself in the heart. Otto Weininger, twenty-three, had published his first book, *Sex and Character*, a few months earlier.[49] Without doubt his suicide drew attention to the book, an attention that has never slackened. Over the next twenty years his book went to press twenty-five times in Austria.[50] In fact his death sparked a small flood of publications, which has gathered strength over the decades.[51] A study about the impact of Weininger in Italy appeared not too long ago, and as a reviewer noted, a kindred study about Freud's impact there seemed inconceivable.[52] Numerous people in Vienna, where everyone apparently knew everyone, honored Weininger or were spellbound by him. The philosopher Ludwig Wittgenstein believed Weininger a genius. Nor was this just a youthful infatuation, since in the 1930s Wittgenstein was still recommending Weininger's book as "great and fantastic."[53] Freud had encountered Weininger in 1901, and after his suicide remarked that the young man had had a "touch" of genius.[54] Those outside Vienna also felt his pull, including August Strindberg, who sent a wreath to the Viennese critic Karl Kraus to be put on Weininger's tomb.

The fascination with Weininger slowly spread into the Anglo world.[55] A first English translation of *Sex and Character* appeared in 1906 with an anonymous "publisher's note": "No thoughtful man can lay down the book without being impressed by the earnestness and the honesty of the author's investigations."[56] A new English translation appeared in 2005 with an editor's introduction titled "A Book That Won't Go Away."

Perhaps it will not, but the contemporary reader may be mystified by the fuss over *Sex and Character.* The book appears to be composed of equal amounts of phony scientific theorizing, which includes a formula on what is the complete man—"$(Ia)m_\Phi + m_w =$ the ideal Man"—and zany pronouncements about women, men, sexuality, and everything in between. The biographical or historical approach to the book tempts because its content seems more symptomatic than insightful.[57] It is not Weininger's suicide but his religious and sexual manias that stand out. A hundred academic commentaries that assess Weininger's philosophical contribution cannot change that. The book navigates by the dark stars of misogyny and anti-Semitism. To follow Weininger on his journey, however, may reveal how the narcissism of minor differences sheds light on fratricidal violence.

Like Wittgenstein, Weininger struggled with his sexual identity, and like Wittgenstein, Weininger considered his Jewishness a stain. Unlike Wittgenstein, Weininger was raised Jewish, and against his father's wishes converted to Protestantism after the acceptance of his dissertation. According to Weininger's sister, "My father was highly anti-Semitic, but he thought as a Jew and was angry when Otto wrote against Judaism."[58] This sentence itself encapsulates a mind-set that warrants commentary, which will not be essayed here. In any event it connotes the contradictory world in which Weininger lived. Jewish anti-Semitism, conflicted sexual identities, and suicidal inclinations did not mark him as especially unusual in fin de siècle Vienna. Weininger often thought about murder and suicide. He remarked after the publication of *Sex and Character,* "The book means a death sentence—either for the book or its author."[59] It may be recalled that Wittgenstein often toyed with suicide and that three of his brothers killed themselves.

Sex and Character divides into two parts, a smaller "scientific" section and a larger philosophical one. Weininger set himself to resolve once and for all "the *Woman Question.*" With great vigor and confidence he presents the idea of an intrinsic bisexuality that informs all living things. Bisexuality implies that maleness and femaleness exist in a continuum; it also implies that homosexuality differs only in degree from heterosexuality. Weininger wrote with scientific ambition. "Man and Woman, then, are like two substances divided between the living individuals in different proportions, without the coefficient of one substance ever reaching zero." To hammer the point home, he provided an equation and summed up, "There are no living beings that can bluntly be described as being unisexual and of one definite sex."[60]

Consistent with this logic, Weininger offered a ringing defense of homosexuality in that sex between men differs neither philosophically nor ethically from sex between a man and a woman. "Despite all the popular drivel of today about different rights of different personalities," he wrote, "there is only one universal ethic, which is the same for all human beings." His book intended to make a "contribution" to the abolition of the "ludicrous" laws banning homosexual acts.[61]

Nevertheless, Weininger executed an about-face and posited a fixed sexual identity linked to fixed qualities. The fluid sexuality he set forth proved to be a minor note. Despite bisexual and intermediate sexual forms, psychologically "a person *must necessarily* be either *male* or *female.*" (Weininger used italics and underlines with abandon. All such markings in this and following Weininger quotations are in the original.) This duality drives the bulk of the book. Weininger wants to investigate "the meaning of this being."[62] He finds that everything soulful, imaginative, and excellent is male and everything superficial, pedestrian, and mediocre is female. He presents a catalog of virtues that all turn out to be male.

For instance, he reverses a common stereotype only to render it less acceptable. Sexuality consumes women, not men, according to Weininger. A woman's entire existence, he writes, revolves around "copulation and reproduction, i.e. her relationship with a man and with children." Man is sometimes sexual but not completely. "Woman is *only* sexual, Man is *also* sexual." From this Weininger deduces that everything in woman functions as an instrument of her sexuality, her desire to copulate and reproduce. "There have been cases of a genuine woman learning Latin," Weininger proclaims, but only so as to "help and supervise her son." In other words, learning in woman functions only in service of sexuality.[63]

Weininger's erudite book, which liberally cites Latin and Greek texts, always returns to the same point, the deficiency of woman. He holds forth on the nature of genius and ranges from the Upanishads to the Renaissance Platonists. The conclusion? "Genius is identical to *depth*. Just try to connect the words deep and *woman* as an attribute and a noun, and everybody will hear the contradiction. *A female genius, then, is a contradiction in terms.*" Weininger also determines that woman has no soul, no self, and no shame. He admits that "as my analysis has progressed, my esteem for Woman has sunk lower and lower, and I have been obliged to deny her an increasing number of lofty and noble, great and beautiful qualities." Indeed, we learn that Woman is "false," "lies, even when objectively, she is telling the truth," and is "amoral" and "alogical." We learn that "the most inferior man is still infinitely superior to the most superior woman, so much so that it seems hardly permissible to compare and rank them."[64]

When it seems that Weininger has reached yet another new high or new low—"Mathematically speaking, she has no *algebraic sign*. She has no direction. . . . *Therefore Woman is not.*"—the story takes another turn. After several hundred pages Weininger has so far restricted himself to the "pinnacles of humankind," namely, "the Aryan man and the Aryan woman." Exploring his thesis with those groups or races that have not attained the Aryan pinnacle opens up "extremely rewarding" issues. Weininger, the Christian convert, turns to the Jews because they are "the most formidable enemy" of the "standpoint" he has developed.

In the first part of the book, it appeared that Weininger would undo the frozen categories of "male" and "female." In the same manner it now appears that Weininger will undermine anti-Semitism, inasmuch as he challenges a fixed notion of Judaism. He defines Judaism not as a race or nation but as an "outlook," one that is "a possibility for *all* human beings." Once detached from actual Jews, a Jewish spirit might inhabit an Aryan. "There are Aryans who are more Jewish than many Jews." Conversely, there are Jews who are Aryans. Weininger concerns himself with any human being "insofar as he participates in the Platonic idea of Judaism."[65]

Yet, as with bisexuality, this conflation proves of little consequence, and for the same reason. Jewishness, like womanliness, is a curse, and—big surprise!—women tend to be women and Jews tend to be Jews. With some qualifications—and to the Jew's disfavor—Weininger presents Jews and women as twin creatures. Like woman, the Jew has "no personality." As there is no dignity in women, "there is no Jewish nobility." Like women, Jews value the family as a biological unit. Like women, they are soulless—and sexual. "The Jew is always more lecherous, more lustful than the Aryan man." The Jew is superficial and materialistic. "This *lack of depth* also explains why the Jews are unable to produce any really great men and why *Judaism,* like Woman, *is denied the highest degree of genius.*"

The "congruency" between Jews and women seems total, but Weininger finds a divergence. The "essential difference" is that Woman believes in "others," her man or her child, and the Jew believes in nothing outside himself. He "never regards anything as genuine, unshakable, sacred and inviolable." The Jew, writes Weininger, has no belief, doctrine, simplicity, or piety. He is not just a materialist, he is a Darwinist. He is not just a skeptic, he is a faultfinder. He stands at the greatest distance from the Christian.

In the final lines to his chapter on Judaism, Weininger's fears take wing. Humankind has "the choice" between Judaism and

Christianity and between Woman and Man. "These are the two poles: there is no third realm." In the present age he regrets that the Jews have attained "the highest peak" and "the spirit of modernity is Jewish." And worse. "Our age is not only the most Jewish, but also the most effeminate of all ages." The times lack genius and profundity. Superficiality, sexuality, and materialism reign supreme. Jews and women sing hymns to sexual intercourse. *"This age also has the distinction of being the first to have not only affirmed and worshiped sexual intercourse, but to have practically made it a duty."* It is an "age that has replaced the idea of virginity with the cult of the demivierge."[66] For Weininger, it can't get worse.

Jump to Freud's "Taboo of Virginity," which took up the cult of virginity, the dread of woman, and the narcissism of minor differences. We are on the path of fratricidal violence, pursuing how small variations between people elicit rage. Women might be a pure case of minor differences, but how are Jews relevant here? Is there a link between misogyny and anti-Semitism? Does either of them help us in figuring out the origins of fratricidal violence? In the "Taboo" essay, Freud does not mention Jews.

However, in a long footnote to a case study some years earlier, Jews and Weininger do show up, and another piece snaps into place, an inner link between misogyny and anti-Semitism. In what is known as the "Little Hans" case (1909), Freud discusses a boy who fears animals and apparently fears that he will lose his "widdler." The good doctor "interrupts" his analysis and in a long footnote broaches a series of topics barely related to Little Hans. Most psychoanalysts hardly mention, or ignore altogether, this footnote in this frequently scrutinized case.[67] As usual, the footnotes allow Freud to unwind. While there is not a single reference to Jews in the main text, in the note Freud states that the castration complex is "the deepest unconscious root of anti-Semitism" and that even little boys hear that "a Jew has something cut off his penis." This "gives them the right to despise Jews." Freud is not finished, and immediately follows with, "And there is no stronger unconscious root for the sense of superiority over women." The contempt for Jews, like that for women, derives from a fear and hatred of castration.

Freud links three elements here: the castration complex, anti-Semitism, and misogyny. To drive the point home he brings up Weininger, whom he identifies as "the highly gifted but sexually deranged" young philosopher who committed suicide after publishing a "remarkable" book.[68] In a chapter that attracted "much attention," Freud writes, Weininger "treated Jews and women with equal hostility" and "overwhelmed them with the same insults." Weininger incarnates his argument, as a representative of the linkage of misogyny and anti-Semitism by way of castration fears: "Being a neurotic, Weininger was completely under the sway of his infantile complexes." Weininger expressed in undiluted form anxieties that both women and Jews trigger. "From that standpoint what is common to Jews and women is their relation to the castration complex."[69]

Freud will not coin the "narcissism of minor differences" for another nine years, but the idea gains a footing here—a footing that Freud himself ignored or simplified in his later references. The minor-differences narcissism derives from the castration complex, which underlies the kindred phenomena of anti-Semitism and misogyny. Both express fear of small differences—the same difference. For the anti-Semite, Jews are women. They are sexual, dissolute, superficial, and materialistic. They are not real men. From the psychoanalytic vantage point—and not only the psychoanalytic—the minor differences between men and women loom large. This difference prompts fright and sometimes violence. Jews and women overlap in that both evoke the specter of castration. Both elicit dread.

Of course the (male) Jew does have a penis, but a circumcised one. As Freud wrote in a footnote—again a footnote—to his study of Leonardo da Vinci, "Circumcision is unconsciously equated with castration." He then brought up a topic unrelated to Leonardo. "The conclusion strikes me as inescapable that here we may also trace one of the roots of the anti-Semitism which appears with such elemental force . . . among the nations of the West." He surmised that "originally" circumcision may have been a "milder substitute" for castration.[70]

Freud would return to those points much later in *Moses and Monotheism,* when he grappled with "the deeper motives of anti-Semitism." He admits there that his assertion will appear "incredible." Anti-Semitism derives not only from jealousy of those who claim to be favored and first-born but also from circumcision, which elicits a repellent and "uncanny" impression. "The explanation probably is that it reminds them [the anti-Semites] of the dreaded castration idea."[71] As the psychoanalyst Otto Fenichel later explained, Jewish circumcision elicits alarm. It is a "sanguinary" operation. "The knowledge of this fact on the part of the uncircumcised," Fenichel writes, "has undoubtedly increased the feeling of uncanniness which the Jew gives them." It also gives form to "the indefinite fear" of Jewish retaliation. The Jews will castrate them, just as they do their own boys.[72]

Circumcision too has its history.[73] It was (and is) a minor procedure with a major impact. Circumcision bonds (male) Jews from Abraham to the present. It is a "sign" of the covenant between God and the Israelites as set out in the Hebrew Bible.[74] It was (and is) defended on grounds of health and sexuality—and attacked on these same grounds.[75] For critics old and new, circumcision represents something barbaric and insular. It is a sign, but a negative sign or stigma. "One thing I know," wrote nineteenth-century Italian anthropologist Paolo Mantegazza, "circumcision is a shame and an infamy." He declared that "I shall continue to shout at Hebrews, until my last breath: Cease mutilating yourselves; cease imprinting upon your flesh an odious brand to distinguish you from other men." For Mantegazza, circumcision meant that Jews "proclaim [themselves] a race apart" and do not care "to mix with ours."[76]

Beyond the biological, however, looms the psychological, perhaps phobic: how circumcision elicits anti-Semitism and awakens primal fears of castration and castrating women. A link between circumcision and castration is hardly new and can be found in the ancient world. Sometimes with humor and sometimes without, Greeks and Greek Jews considered the relationship. Horace joked about "clipped Jews" and hinted of castration. In the second century CE, Roman law both permitted circumcision and limited it to Jews. The law itself connected circumcision and castration. "The Jews are permitted to circumcise their own sons. But if they should circumcise another, they shall be punished as castrators."[77]

Two and a half centuries before Freud, Spinoza remarked that the Jews "brought resentment of all men against themselves, not only because of their external rites . . . but also by the sign of circumcision which they zealously maintain." He commented that the "sign of circumcision has such great importance as almost to persuade me that this thing alone will preserve their nation forever."[78] The Dutch Jewish lens grinder added a clause that has intrigued recent scholars. He believed that Jews might even reestablish their state if their religion had not "emasculated" them.[79] The word he used in Latin meant "to make effeminate"—*effoeminarent*.[80] Did he infer that circumcision/castration unmanned Jews?

The connections exist regardless of who posited them: circumcision = castration = Jew = woman. To be sure, in the modern period these links seem to surface most palpably on the margins of literature—in anti-Semitic tales or published psychoses. The 1893 story "The Operated Jew" by Oskar Panizza, a German writer and psychiatrist who ended up institutionalized, tells of the wealthy Itzig Faitel Stern and his effort to physically remake himself into a real "Occidental human being." The Yiddish-sputtering, fleshy, misshapen Faitel ("Faitel's customary bobbing of his upper body . . . was always accompanied by his nasal gurgling") enlists a famous anatomist to get a makeover as a good Christian. This includes not only iron braces and breaking and resetting crooked bones but replacing his Jewish blood with eight liters of Christian blood from Black Forest peasants. Faitel "wanted to shed his 'Jew-ishness' and let everything run out that could run out."

However, at the celebration of his wedding to "a blond Ger-man lass," the new Faitel, now called Dr. Freudenstern, does not last the festivities. Perhaps it was the alcohol, but to the horrified onlookers the Jew Itzig reappears. His body contorts, his mouth and eyes droop, and he lisps about copulating with Christians—Weininger's nightmare. Panizza hints that something else might have upset Faitel—namely, the knowledge that he would be found out on the wedding night. "The smart female reader will com-prehend that a wedding day is followed by a wedding night," and this entails a "wedding disrobement." Even the famous anatomist could not correct what she would see.[81]

Memoirs of My Nervous Illness by Daniel Paul Schreber, a nineteenth-century German judge who also ended up institution-alized, is a favorite of the psychoanalytically inclined—in part be-cause Freud discussed it. Schreber's book appeared the same year as Weininger's *Sex and Character* and displays some of the same obsessions. Schreber feared—and sometimes hoped—he was being turned into a woman. "My whole sense of manliness and manly honor . . . rose up against" this prospect. As with Weininger, fears about women and Jews converge. Schreber also worried that he might turn into a Jew and become "unmanned."[82] As the liter-ary critic Sander Gilman has put it, Schreber "was afraid he was turning into an effeminate Jew, a true composite of Weininger's images of the Jew and the woman."[83]

To be sure, the psychoanalytic logic does not end here. In Freud's telling, civilization begins with the revolt of the broth-ers against the father, who has forbidden sexual satisfaction and threatened castration. But guilt follows the killing of the father, and the brothers internalize his prohibitions. As Freud declares in *Totem and Taboo,* "What had up to then been prevented by his actual existence was thenceforward prohibited by the sons them-selves."[84] Circumcision becomes a reminder of the crime and of the guilt that ensued. It "not only links with the fear of femininity," writes Oxford psychology professor Stephen Frosh, "but also raises the specter of murder and guilt, reminding the non-Jews of the violence at the root of civilization."[85]

For the Christian critic, of course, circumcision signified something else. It was at best unnecessary, at worst deplorable. Faith and spirit, not a mark in the flesh, lead to salvation. In Paul's epistle to the Philippians, he advised, "Watch out for those dogs, those men who do evil, those mutilators of the flesh. For it is we who are the circumcision, we who worship by the Spirit of God, who glory in Christ Jesus, and who put no confidence in the flesh" (Philippians 3:2–3 NIV). It is possible to close the circle—at least with regard to the mark of Cain. Christians spurned the corporal circumcision of the Jew. In the primal fratricide, God marked Cain. Cain is the Jew. The Jew is circumcised. Therefore, the mark of Cain is circumcision.[86]

The idea has shown up occasionally in Christian literature. Peter Riga, a twelfth-century versifier of the Bible, wrote:

> Divine wrath gives Cain a sign so that he will not be killed.
> The Hebrew has a sign so that he cannot be killed.
> In truth, that he lives on earth in the midst of his enemies is rather amazing.
> No king, no duke, no powerful person kills him
> His skin has been cut as a sign to everyone.[87]

On July 31, 1932, the day of a German election, *The New York Times* wondered whether the Nazi Party would be successful. With "wild words," Hitler anticipated "the end" of the German republic and the establishment of a fascist dictatorship.[88] The previous day, an uneasy German physicist wrote to an Austrian psychiatrist. "Is there any way of delivering mankind from the menace of war?" wondered Albert Einstein. He explained to Freud that he was writing because of the prospect not simply of international wars but of civil wars and—probably alluding to the Jews—of "the persecution of racial minorities." Einstein admitted that his own scientific expertise afforded "no insight into the dark places of human will and feeling." He could not fathom the "lust for hatred and destruction."[89] He hoped that Freud had some answers.

Freud offered a mini-lesson in psychoanalytic thought to Einstein. The psychiatrist agreed with the physicist that an aggressive impulse facilitates war. "The countless cruelties in history and in our everyday lives vouch" for "an instinct for hatred and destruction." In the "last few years" psychoanalysts "have in fact been occupied" in studying "its manifestations." But Freud called himself an "unworldly theoretician" and mused that his ideas contained little of practical or specific value that could hinder the coming violence.[90]

Freud privately considered the exchange "tedious and sterile," perhaps rightly so.[91] He may have been admitting that on the political terrain, depth psychology lacks historical force. In reaching for the bottom, it bypasses the surface, where most of us paddle about. What, for instance, can psychoanalysis say about the advance and success of Nazism? "The instinctual structure of the average man in Germany," remarked Otto Fenichel, himself a refugee from Nazism, "was no different in 1935 from what it was in 1925."[92] Yet in those ten years the crackpots in Germany had become its rulers. The writer Otto Friedrich asked a distinguished psychoanalyst who had fled to New York and had long reflected on Nazism to explain the success of Hitler. "'That is not an easy question that you ask me.'" There follows "another long silence. Dr. Rado stares . . . thinking. . . . Finally, he decides on his answer. He speaks very slowly, very carefully. 'I don't know.'"[93]

Of course, psychoanalysts from Freud forward have addressed the social issues of the day. A sizable literature falls under the rubric of "the psychoanalysis of" fill in the blank: racism, war, colonialism, authoritarianism. As valuable as these writings may be, they often stumble when it comes to specific places and times. If psychoanalysis can explain war or hatred in general, it falls silent before this war or that hatred. We can define war "psychoanalytically," wrote one doctor, "as a criminal act, fantasized individually and consummated collectively for the purpose . . . of preserving the love object through a paranoid process."[94] Maybe, but what does this have to do with World War I or II—or current wars?

The ideas of the literary critic and philosopher René Girard may compensate for a weakness in psychoanalytic logic in that they capture a historical dynamic. His approach, in brief, registers historical change, which Freud's hardly does. Moreover, Girard's perspective may supplement Freud's in its investigation of likeness and the hostility it engenders. In the same spirit as Freud and his theory of minor differences, Girard concentrates on similarity, not difference—on brothers, not strangers. He gives us an original take on fratricidal violence and brings the topic into the twenty-first century.

The French-born Girard has lived and taught in the United States for most of his life. He is a professor of French literature and civilization, but inasmuch as he writes on philosophy, religion, and anthropology, his oeuvre resists classification. Over the course of his long career, he has earned much acclaim and many academic followers—a journal exists dedicated to his ideas—but he goes virtually unnoticed outside academic religious and literary studies.[95] The flagship intellectual journals rarely review his work.[96] Even within the humanities, he is considered "marginal" and "largely out of step with current trends."[97] This may be a blessing.

Girard is most provocative where he challenges standard ideas about desire and similarity. For Girard, likeness is the problem, not the solution. He dubs the belief that discord stems from differences a "prejudice," a "fashionable" and false "intellectual attitude." He cites an anthropologist who gives the conventional interpretation—with its usual jargon—that conflict emerges from palpable differences within a group. "Structural differentiation, both vertical and horizontal," writes this anthropologist, "is the foundation of strife and factionalism." But for Girard, the testimony of literature and anthropology demonstrates the opposite. It is not differences that give rise to conflict, but similarity. "In human relationships words like *sameness* and *similarity* evoke an image of harmony. If we have the same tastes, surely we are bound to get along. But what happens when we share the same desires?" For Girard, "a single principle" pervades religion and literature. "Order, peace and fecundity depend on cultural distinctions; it is not these distinctions but the loss of them that gives birth to fierce rivalries and sets members of the same family or social group at one another's throats."[98]

Brothers—and twins as a special case—become prime examples for Girard. While brothers share a great deal—the same mother, father, gender—twins share more. "Twins are in a sense reinforced brothers whose final objective difference, that of age, has been removed." Girard reverses the traditional attitude about fraternity: "We instinctively regard the fraternal relationship as an affectionate one." However, the record is clear from history and literature. The theme of "enemy brothers" dominates, from Cain and Abel, down through Richard the Lionheart and John Lackland, and beyond. "It is not only in myth that brothers are simultaneously drawn together and driven apart by something they both desire—a throne, a woman, or in more general terms, a paternal heritage."[99]

For Girard fraternal strife dwells at the center of life and literature. Sibling rivalry, in turn, derives from mimetic desire, a critical concept for Girard. While the term *mimesis* surfaces in numerous fields with diverse connotations, in Girard desire itself tends to be mimetic or imitative. As individuals, our desires unfold by imitating the desires of those around us. We live and grow by copying not only what people do but what they want. We emulate their language, their gestures, but also their desires. "The mimetic aspects of desire," Girard writes in *Violence and the Sacred*, "correspond to a primary impulse of most living creatures." Herein lies the problem, however. The mimetic impulse engenders rivalry, especially in a universe of limited resources, or where only one of a kind exists—one kingdom or one special mate. If you and I desire the same thing, as we inevitably do, discord arises.

The "conflictual implications" of mimesis, Girard believes, have "always been misunderstood." Freud got much wrong. The son does not desire the mother; he imitates his father and desires what his father desires. "Oedipus is essentially the rival of the father, first elbowed out, then victorious. The father and son both desire the throne and wife." Mimesis harbors strife. "Mimesis coupled with desire leads automatically to conflict."[100]

Girard is frequently obscure, but his work as a whole functions as a tonic. In challenging the fetish of opposites, he declares not only that it is misleading to believe that opposites give rise to conflict but that the reverse is true: that is, as opposites recede, tensions advance. Too much likeness threatens people. Brothers harbor violence toward each other; they are too close. Here enters a historical moment. The stuff that sets people apart—their identifying marks—reflects historical realities. Identities endure only to the extent that their historical foundation endures; and identities alter as those historical realities alter.

What does this mean in a gritty reality? Girard seldom situates his ideas in a political framework, but this should not prevent us from doing so. In the modern era, the structures that sustain differences and identifications generally shift in one direction; they undercut those identifying differences. To repeat Girard's key sentences: "Order, peace and fecundity depend on cultural distinctions; it is not these distinctions, but the loss of them that gives rise to violence and chaos. . . . This loss forces men into a perpetual confrontation."[101]

This "loss," however, is the story of the modern world, a proposition Girard does not express. People forced into the thrall of industrialization emerge more and more alike. They get stripped of their unique markings. For instance, many groups uphold their identity by virtue of their own language, yet the forces of modernization—schooling, employment, communication—undermine the existence of small language communities. The speakers lack the numbers or the economic clout to maintain their language. This is true of languages spoken by indigenous peoples of the Americas as well as of languages such as Yiddish, once spoken by millions of Eastern European Jews. The languages lose their function in a world economy and vanish or survive only in the laboratories of scholars. *Peasants into Frenchmen* runs the title of a classic book on modernization in France, which partly concerns the victory of the French language over regional dialects once spoken by rural inhabitants outside Paris.[102]

The Girardian insight here gains its force. Likeness does not necessarily lead to harmony. It may elicit jealousy and anger. Inasmuch as identity rests on what makes an individual unique, similitude threatens the self. The double evokes fear. On a social terrain the mechanism also operates. As cultural groupings get absorbed into larger or stronger collectives, they become more anxious—and more prone to defend the dwindling identity. The French Canadians amid an ocean of English speakers are more testy about their language than are the French of France. Language is, however, just one feature of cultural identification.

Assimilation becomes a threat, not a promise. It spells homogenization, not diversity. The assimilated express bitterness as they register the loss of an identity they want to retain. Their ambivalence transforms their anger into resentment. They desire what they reject and are upset with themselves as well. The resentment feeds the protest and sometimes the violence. To draw on a philosophical truism, appearance and essence diverge. The identity that feels threatened by loss—by surrendering its distinct qualities—rears up as strong. It *appears* robust and aggressive because it *is* weak and vulnerable. In the same way as we might say of an all-consuming egoist that he or she suffers from a weak ego, we could say of the aggressive in-your-face identity that it suffers from a threatened identity. In the current world the forces of globalization or Americanization—the threat of becoming like everyone else—imperils the self-identity of many societies.

In the wake of the 9/11 attack on the World Trade Center the newspaper *Le Monde* interviewed Girard and asked him whether his ideas on "mimetic rivalry" could be applied to the current international situation. He gave a cautious affirmative. We err, he said, to always look for "difference" whenever a "mimetic rivalry" between people and cultures arises. A desire to imitate drives this rivalry. "No doubt terrorism is bound to a world 'different' from ours, but what gives rise to terrorism does not live in that 'difference.' . . . To the contrary, it lies in an exacerbated desire for convergence and resemblance," Girard told the editors of *Le Monde*. What we are experiencing is "a form of mimetic rivalry on a planetary scale." In Islam we see an effort to mobilize "those frustrated . . . in their relations of mimetic rivalry with the West."[103]

In a book written just before 9/11, Girard emphasized the same points. "The real secret of conflict and violence . . . is the mimetic desire and the ferocious rivalries it engenders." This means that the Third World does not simply reject the West but also attempts, with much ambivalence, to imitate it. "The hatred of the West and all it represents is not due to its spirit being truly foreign to these people," writes Girard. On the contrary, the West's ethos is completely familiar to them. "Far from turning away from the West, they cannot keep from imitating it, from adopting its values without admitting to themselves what they are doing."[104]

This seems more than half right. Muslims—and not only the fundamentalists—feel threatened by Western economic and cultural power. Insofar as the extreme Islamists sense their world imitating the West, they respond with enmity. It is not so much the "other" as its absence that spurs anger. Resemblance embitters them. They fear losing themselves by mimicking the West. A Miss World beauty pageant in Nigeria, for instance, spurred widespread riots by Muslims that left hundreds dead.[105] This could be considered a violent rejection of imitation. "It is now on a planetary scale that the game of mimetic rivalry will play itself out," writes a follower of Girard. "The image that appears to emerge—in place of the 'clash of civilizations' slogan invoked by those who do not understand the state of the world—is that of a civil war within a single global civilization."[106]

The sensible as well as the less sensible of the Muslim world fear copying the West. It is not the distance between "them" and "us" that disturbs them, but its reduction or absence. Miscellaneous evidence supports the notion. A Moroccan engineer who works for an American company in Morocco may speak for many. "I want my daughter to live the traditions of Islam," he stated, "and not copy Western women. Copying the Western culture is our biggest sin."[107] What appears to be an ineluctable imitation provokes Muslim extremists.

Malise Ruthven, in *A Fury for God* (2002), underlines the embattled identity of the lead hijacker of 9/11. Mohamed Atta studied architecture and Western city planning, but imitation haunted him. The Islamic metropolises he loved seem organized on principles diametrically opposed to those of Western cities. The old urbanscape boasted narrow alleys with merchants who displayed goods in open booths and often dispensed tea to customers. The new Westernized districts were characterized by broad avenues with sleek stores staffed by cool professionals.

After Atta studied architecture, he went to Germany, where he wrote a master's thesis on urban planning. This move itself is revealing. Atta was not an outsider to Western education or mores, but a successful player. His German thesis adviser had the highest praise for him and considered him a skillful and attentive city planner. "I know him very well and vouch for Mohamed in every situation," he stated in a letter of recommendation.[108] He also noted that Atta believed that "modernization" threatened the "Islamic heritage" and that high-rise towers destroyed the warren of alleys and courtyards that had constituted the old cities.[109]

Atta's thesis for his Hamburg studies, which has not been published, is subtitled "Neighborhood Development in an Islamic-Oriental City." It examines an old quarter in Aleppo, one of Syria's oldest and best-preserved cities. According to Atta, Western planners were destroying the neighborhood. The cover of the thesis sports opposing photos and maps. An image of a taxi-clogged street is set against one of smiling boys in an alleyway; an aerial view of straight avenues, traffic circles, and high-rises is juxtaposed with one of the honeycombed streets of the old town.[110]

In *Newsweek,* a former acquaintance also spoke of Atta's belief that the new high-rise, Westernized apartment buildings undermined the old neighborhoods, with their intimacy and dignity. "It may have been particularly galling to Atta," reported this associate, "that his own family had moved into an eleventh-floor apartment in just such a hulking monstrosity in 1990, as he was graduating with an engineering degree from Cairo University. To Atta, the boxy building was a shabby symbol of Egypt's haphazard attempts to modernize and its shameless embrace of the West."[111] It is all here, imitation and the rage at imitation, which spells loss of identity.

It can also spell loss of manhood, which brings us back to Freud, his "minor differences" and fratricidal fury. This is not a blind leap. Osama bin Laden often evokes the Western threat to Muslim manhood. A despised imitation of the West signifies the surrender not simply of identity but also of masculinity. The Arab regimes and their media, Bin Laden said, want to "strip us of our virility—we believe we are men, Muslim men." The "American and Jewish whores" steal our land and oil. The Arab leaders do nothing. "The virility of the rulers in this region has been stolen," Bin Laden declared, "and they think people are women."[112] In his supposed last will and testament, Bin Laden stated, "If every Muslim asks himself why has our nation reached this state of humiliation and defeat, then his obvious answer is because . . . the Jews and Christians have tempted us with the comforts of life and its cheap pleasures and invaded us with their materialistic values before invading us with their armies while we stood like women doing nothing."[113]

Training in hermeneutics is not required here. We—the Muslim peoples—are unable to resist imitating the West. Inasmuch as we lack courage, our men are women; they are castrated. Several clauses in Atta's will radiate with disdain of women. "I don't want a pregnant woman or a person who is not clean to come and say goodbye to me. . . . I don't want women to come to my house to apologize for my death. . . . I don't want any women to go to my grave at all during my funeral or any occasion thereafter."[114]

Women threaten groups like Al-Qaeda and the Taliban. When the Taliban came to power, they subjugated women to a thousand prohibitions and regulations. In Kabul in 1996 the Taliban forbade women to work outside the home, attend school, or leave their house unless accompanied by a husband, father, brother, or son. In effect, women could not be seen. "Houses and buildings in public view," noted a Physicians for Human Rights report, "must have their windows painted over if females are present in these places."[115] If women did (with permission) leave their houses, the situation hardly improved. A United Nations report cited Taliban regulations: apart from what they must wear, the edicts ordered that women "must not walk in the middle of the streets" or "talk to" or "look at strange men. . . . If it is necessary to talk, they must talk in a low voice and without laughter."[116]

Though extreme, the Taliban stand in a long tradition of misogyny that is hardly confined to Islam. *The World's Oldest Prejudice*, reads the subtitle of a recent history of misogyny.[117] An anthropologist summarizes: "The Christian Bible, the Muslim Qur'an, the Hebrew Torah, and the Buddhist and Hindu scriptures condemn woman, not only for her spiritual defects, but also for her body, which they deride in the crudest terms." All these religions "blame" woman for bringing about "lust, licentiousness, and depravity."[118] In his book on misogyny, Jack Holland notes that he was raised in Belfast, Northern Ireland, whose "sectarian animosities . . . have made it a byword for violence and bloodshed." But the warring Catholics and Protestants agreed upon one thing—their contempt for women.

Misogyny brings us back to the "narcissism of minor differences," which Freud linked to the "dread of woman." A woman is as familiar—and as strange—as a wife or girlfriend. "For men, women are the original 'Other,'" writes Holland. But, he continues, women present a more difficult case than foreign races or religions. "She is 'the Other' that cannot be excluded." She is "the other" whom men live with. Or she is the other which is not an other. He continues:

Tribesmen in the highlands of New Guinea and aborigines in the Amazon basin may bar her from their sleeping quarters. Athenian gentlemen may lock her in the remotest part of the home, Catholic theologians seclude her behind convent doors, and Moslem fanatics hide her behind the head-to-toe veil, but intimacy with her is as unavoidable as it is essential.[119]

Is misogyny the crux of fratricide? Does the fear of women drive fraternal violence? Does the dread of effeminacy in particular and the loss of identity in general provoke bloodletting? Perhaps.

Where are the women themselves in all of this? Of course, much has been written about this absence, an absence that might be better characterized as partial. Indeed, an archetypal Western fratricide led women to enter the stage of history. After Romulus killed his brother Remus and founded Rome, the men of the new settlement discovered they needed females. The Romans abducted young women of Sabine, a neighboring settlement. Years later—the women were now mothers—the Sabines attacked Rome in revenge. The battle seesawed. After a momentary victory, the leading Sabine exulted in the manner of male warriors through the ages. We have beaten our "feeble" foes. "They know now that catching girls is a different matter from fighting against men!"

But the tide turned in favor of the Romans with the fratricidal Romulus rallying his troops. Amid the slaughter of the neighboring warriors, in the account of the Roman historian Livy, the Sabine women "with loosened hair and rent garments" pushed their way between the battling armies. "They parted the angry combatants; they besought their fathers on one side, their husbands on the other, to spare the curse of shedding kindred blood."[120] The curse still troubles the world. The women of Sabine may have something to teach us.

ACKNOWLEDGMENTS

Over thirty years my circle of close readers has hardly grown. Perhaps—to quote an old revolutionary—better fewer, but better. Paul Breines and Elliott Eisenberg are still reading what I write and still encouraging me. I salute them. A number of people in the UCLA Department of History have read assorted chapters and corrected or buoyed me, notably Ra'anan Boustan, Gabi Piterberg, Teo Ruiz, and Ron Mellor, who has helped me locate and translate more than one passage from Latin. I want to thank Kurt Jacobsen and Sung-eun Choi for their observations, and Bob Hullot-Kentor for his incisive remarks on the last chapter. I owe much to my daughter, Sarah, and to my son, Sam, who went through many pages with his sharp pen. Sara Lippincott, editor extraordinaire, burnished the writing and saved me from innumerable gaffes. My thanks to Hilary Redmon, my editor at the Free Press, for taking on my proposal after many publishers (names on request) turned it down. My thanks, also, to Steve Wasserman, venerable friend and indefatigable agent, who believed in this book and, despite setbacks, never flagged in his support. When she could, the intrepid Cristina Nehring, my love and companion of many years, worked her magic on my prose—and worked her magic in general. She and her lovely daughter Eurydice ("Dice") lengthened the process of writing this book—and sweetened it.

NOTES

PREFACE

1. Elie Wiesel, *Messengers of God: Biblical Portraits and Legends,* trans. from French by Marion Wiesel (New York: Random House, 1976), 37.

2. Daniel L. Byman and Kenneth M. Pollack, *Things Fall Apart: Containing the Spillover from an Iraqi Civil War* (Washington, DC: Brookings Institution Press, 2007), 17.

3. "Movie on WWII Jewish Massacre Shocks Poles," Associated Press, April 4, 2001.

4. Jan T. Gross, *Neighbors* (New York: Penguin, 2002), xix, 114, 54. The book elicited, mainly in Poland, heated controversy, and the number of those immolated is disputed. See *The Neighbors Respond: The Controversy over the Jadwabne Massacre in Poland,* ed. Antony Polonsky and Joanna B. Michlic (Princeton, NJ: Princeton University Press, 2004). This volume includes Gross's reply to the critics, "Critical Remarks Indeed," 344–70. See also Frank Fox, "A Skel-

eton in Poland's Closet: The Jedwabne Massacre," *East European Jewish Affairs* 31, no. 1 (2001): 77–94.

5. Gérard Prunier, *Africa's World War: Congo, the Rwandan Genocide, and the Making of a Continental Catastrophe* (New York: Oxford University Press, 2009), 1.

6. "Rates of Slayings and Gun Violence Are Up," *Los Angeles Times,* September 11, 2006, A13.

7. See "New York Killers, and Those Killed, by Numbers," *New York Times*, April 28, 2006.

8. "Personal Crimes of Violence, 2006: Number and percent distribution of incidents, by type of crime and victim-offender relationship," U.S. Department of Justice, Bureau of Justice Statistics, *Criminal Victimization in the United States, 2006 Statistical Tables,* August 2008.

9. "The majority of victims of gang homicides and drive-by shootings are gang members," writes a researcher. Malcolm W. Klein, *Street Gang Patterns and Policies* (New York: Oxford University Press, 2006), 83.

10. Sigmund Freud, "The Taboo of Virginity," *Collected Papers*, vol. 4, trans. by Joan Riviere (London: Hogarth Press, 1957), 224.

11. René Girard, *Violence and the Sacred,* trans. Patrick Gregory (Baltimore, MD: Johns Hopkins University Press, 1977), 146.

12. "Saudi Magazine Publishes 'Important Parts' of Usama Bin Ladin's 'Will,'" in *Compilation of Usama Bin Ladin Statements 1994–January 2004* (Washington, DC: FBIS, 2004), 223.

13. Randall Collins, *Violence: A Micro-Sociological Theory* (Princeton, NJ: Princeton University Press, 2008), 19, 82.

14. See Kurt Jacobsen, *Freud's Foes: Psychoanalysis, Science and Resistance* (Lanham, MD: Rowman & Littlefield, 2009).

15. Bradley A. Thayer, *Darwin and International Relations: On the Evolutionary Origins of War and Ethnic Conflict* (Lexington: University Press of Kentucky, 2004), 10.

16. Azar Gat, *War in Human Civilization* (New York: Oxford University Press, 2006), 662–63. To be fair, Gat includes cultural and historical factors.

17. Randolph Roth, *American Homicide* (Cambridge, MA: Harvard University Press, 2009), 474.

18. William T. Vollmann, *Rising Up and Rising Down,* 7 volumes (San Francisco: McSweeney's Press, 2003).

19. T. W. Adorno, "Resignation," in *Critical Models: Interventions and Catchwords,* ed. and trans. Henry W. Pickford (New York: Columbia University Press, 1998), 293.

CHAPTER ONE: "KINSMEN, NEIGHBORS, AND COMPATRIOTS"

1. My account draws upon the thorough narrative of Boehmer and of Longhurst: Edward Boehmer, *Spanish reformers of two centuries from 1520. Their lives and writings, according to the late Benjamin B. Wiffen's plan and with the use of his materials, described by Edward Boehmer* [1st ed. 1874] (reprinted New York: B. Franklin, [1962]). John E. Longhurst, *Luther's Ghost in Spain, 1517–1546* (Lawrence, KS: Coronado Press, 1969). Both follow closely the contemporary account, which was translated from Latin into Spanish and printed in the eighteenth century: *Historia de la muerte de Juán Díaz: por determinazión tomada en Roma, le hizo matár su hermano Alfonso Díaz, en la madrugada del sábado 27 iiim. del año 1546* (Madrid: Reformista Antigüos Españoles, 1865). Longhurst translates swatches of it, which I am using. See also Marcelino Menéndez y Pelayo, *Historia de los heterodoxos españoles,* 2nd ed., vol. 4 (Madrid: V. Suárez, 1928), 257–72; Jules Bonnet, *Récits du seizième siècle* (Paris: Grassart, 1875), 177–239.

2. Longhurst, *Luther's Ghost,* 80.

3. Eells calls this Raitsbon gathering "a funeral of lost hopes." Hastings Eells, *Martin Bucer* (New Haven, CT: Yale University Press, 1931), 373. Eells also summarizes the Díaz murder, 379–80.

4. Cited in J. H. (Jean Henri) Merle d'Aubigné, *History of the reformation in Europe in the time of Calvin,* vol. 8 (London: Longman, Green and Co., 1878), 123.

5. Longhurst, *Luther's Ghost,* 77.

6. See Edward Peters, *Inquisition* (Berkeley: University of California Press, 1989), 88–90; Henry Kamen, *The Spanish Inquisition: A*

Historical Revision (New Haven, CT: Yale University Press, 1997), 83–102.

7. Juan Ginés de Sepúlveda, as cited in Thomas M'Crie, *The Reformation in Spain* [1824] (Rapidan, VA: Hartland Publications, 1998), 120. See Eells, *Bucer,* 380.

8. Bucer, Preface, cited in Longhurst, 74.

9. Boehmer believes that Senarcleo only "reported" the events, while the book was actually written by another friend of Díaz's, Franzisco de Enzinas, *Spanish reformers,* 147.

10. John Foxe, *The acts and monuments of John Foxe: with a life of the martyrologist, and vindication of the work* by George Townsend, vol. 4 (London: Seeley and Burnside, 1846), 888.

11. After Alfonso was released, he proceeded to Italy and later to Spain. Five years later he returned to Germany and apparently committed suicide. See Boehmer, 198–99. C. A. Wilkens, in *Spanish Protestants in the Sixteenth Century,* ed. Rachell Challice (London: William Heinemann, 1897), also reports that he killed himself, 28.

12. For instance, an 1879 book designed for young Christian readers, James Macaulay, *All True—Records of Adventure by Sea and Land— Remarkable Escapes and Deliverances—Missionary Enterprises— Wonders of Nature and Providence—Incidents of Christian History and Biography* (London: Oxford University, 1879), includes a chapter "The Assassination of Juan Díaz," 122–33. Frank J. Sulloway in his *Born to Rebel: Birth Order, Family Dynamics and Creative Lives* (New York: Random House, 1996) gives a paragraph to the Díaz brothers (273) and throughout his book refers to fratricide and sibling rivalry. Yet Sulloway subordinates fratricide to a Darwinian approach that focuses on birth order. For all his research and arresting vignettes, scientistic bluster overwhelms the book. For a convincing critique, which also takes up the Díaz brothers, see Gary R. Johnson, "Science, Sulloway, and Birth Order: An Ordeal and an Assessment," *Politics and the Life Sciences* 19, no. 2 (September 2000): 211–45. This piece includes a lengthy account of how Sulloway sought to block critical reviews of his book.

13. Marguerite de Valois, Queen of Navarre, *Memoirs of Marguerite de*

Valois, Letter IV, Project Gutenberg Ebook, www.gutenberg.org/etext/3841.

14. Cited in Donald Kelley, *François Hotman: A Revolutionary's Ordeal* (Princeton, NJ: Princeton University Press, 1973), 208. For a description of the festivities, see Roy Strong, *Splendour at Court: Renaissance Spectacle and Illusion* (London: Weidenfeld and Nicolson, 1973), 149–51.

15. See the summary of evidence in Arlette Jouanna, *La Saint-Barthélemy. Les mystères d'un crime d'état* (Paris: Gallimard, 2007), 101–15.

16. Fundamental accounts are N. M. Sutherland, *The Massacre of St. Bartholomew and the European Conflict 1559–1572* (London: Macmillan, 1973), and Barbara B. Diefendorf, *Beneath the Cross: Catholics and Huguenots in Sixteenth-Century Paris* (New York: Oxford University Press, 1991). For a revisionist interpretation, see Jean-Louis Bourgeon, *L'Assassinat de Coligny* (Geneva: Droz, 1992). Bourgeon believes that neither the king nor the assassination itself had much role in the ensuing massacre. See also his "Pour une histoire, enfin, de la Saint-Barthélemy," *Revue historique* 571 (1989): 83–142, which argues with great vigor that everyone except Sutherland and himself have been misled. Bourgeon stresses the international and political realities that shaped the massacre.

17. François Hotman (Ernest Varamund of Freseland), *A true and plaine report of the furious outrages of Fraunce & the horrible and shameful slaughter of Chastillion the admiral, and diuers other noble and excellent men, and of the wicked and straunge murder of godlie persons, committed in many cities of Fraunce, without any respect of sorte, kinde, age, or degree* (Striveling, Scotland: 1573), 48–49.

18. *Oeuvres de J. Michelet: Histoire de France au seizième siècle,* vol. 11 (Paris: A. Lemmere, 1887), 423.

19. Diefendorf, *Beneath the Cross,* 96.

20. "The Massacre of St. Bartholomew," in Lord Acton, *The History of Freedom and Other Essays,* ed. John Neville Figgis and Reginald Vere Laurence (London: Macmillan, 1907). For a discussion of Acton's essay and the nineteenth-century debate on the massacre,

see Edwin Jones, *John Lingard and the Pursuit of Historical Truth* (Brighton, UK: Sussex Academic Press, 2001), 39–50.

21. Robert M. Kingdon, *Myths about the St. Bartholomew's Day Massacres 1572–1576* (Cambridge, MA: Harvard University Press, 1988), 30.

22. Mack P. Holt, *French Wars of Religion, 1562–1629* (New York: Cambridge University Press, 2005), 86–87.

23. François Hotman, cited in Donald R. Kelley, "Martyrs, Myths and Massacre: The Background of St. Bartholomew," *American Historical Review* 77, no. 5 (1972): 1338.

24. The classic account by Natalie Z. Davis, "The Rites of Violence," sought mainly to debunk economic interpretations that considered sixteenth-century religious violence to have been provoked by grain shortages or class hatreds. Instead, Davis argued such violence has its own organization, logic, and meaning (in her collection *Society and Culture in Early Modern France* [Palo Alto, CA: Stanford University Press, 1975], 152–87). To be sure, but this does not take us very far.

25. The letter is cited in the appendix to Sir James Mackintosh, *History of England*, vol. 3 (London: Longman, Rees, Orme, Brown, Green & Longman, 1832), 356. The letters of Salviati are discussed in Owen Chadwick, *Catholicism and History: The Opening of the Vatican Archives* (Cambridge: Cambridge University Press, 1978), 59–60. Inasmuch as Salviati was a cousin of the queen, his presence in Paris redoubled accusations that the massacre was orchestrated by the evil Italian Medicis—by strangers. See Gabriel Brizard, *Du massacre de la Saint-Barthelemi, et de l'influence des étrangers en France durant la Ligue* (Paris: Chez Garnéry, 1790?). According to Citizen Brizard, writing during the French Revolution, if it were not for "strangers" leading the government, there would have been no massacre. The notion that strange Italians—the family of Catherine de Medici—bear responsibility for the religious violence arose in the sixteenth century. See, for instance, Nicholas Le Roux, "La Saint-Barthélemy des italiens n'aura pas lieu: un discours envoyé à Catherine de Médicis en 1573," in Bernard Barbiche et al.,

Pouvoirs, contestations et comportements dans l'Europe modern (Paris: PUPS, 2005), 165–79. See also Henry Heller, *Anti-Italianism in Sixteenth-Century France* (Toronto: University of Toronto Press, 2003). Heller notes that popular opinion linked the Italians with the Jews, 85–90.

26. "Letter from Father Joachim Opser, S.J., Sub Prior of the College of Clermont, to the Abbot of Saint Gall, dated 26th August, 1572," cited in Philippe Erlanger, *St Bartholomew's Night*, trans. Patrick O'Brian (London: Weidenfeld and Nicolson, 1962), 251–52. Translation slightly altered. For the Latin and French, see "Deux lettres de couvent à couvent," *Bulletin de la Société de l'histoire du protestantisme français* 8 (1859): 284–94.

27. "Saint Bartholomew's Day," *New Advent Catholic Encyclopedia* (1917), www.newadvent.org/cathen/13333b.htm. See this entry for the standard defense of the pope, to wit, he did not know the extent of the massacres and believed they averted a plot against the royal family.

28. The French as well struck coins to commemorate the event. See Paul Orgels, "Documents relatifs à la Saint-Barthélemy et aux médailles frappées pour la glorification de cet événement," *Bulletin Mensuel de Numismatique et D'Archéologie* 3, nos. 1–2 (July–Aug. 1883): 12–19.

29. See J. Jacquiot, "Médailles et jetons commémorant la Saint-Barthélemy," *Revue d'histoire littéraire de la France* 73, no. 5 (Sept.– Oct. 1973): 791–92.

30. See the comments of Nigel J. Spivey, *Enduring Creation: Art, Pain, and Fortitude* (Berkeley: University of California Press, 2001), 98.

31. Philipp Fehl, "Vasari's 'Extirpation of the Huguenots': The Challenge of Pity and Fear," *Gazette des Beaux-Arts* 84 (1974): 264. For a criticism of Fehl's interpretation of these paintings, see Alexandra Herz, "Vasari's 'Massacre' Series in the Sala Regia," *Zeitschrift für Kunstgeschichte* 49, no. 1 (1986): 41–54.

32. "Saint Bartholomew's Day" and "The Vatican" in *New Advent Catholic Encyclopedia* (1917), www.newadvent.org/cathen/13333b .htm.

33. Acton, "Massacre of St. Bartholomew," 135.

34. Kingdon, *Myths about the St. Bartholomew's Day Massacres*, 46.

35. *Oeuvres de J. Michelet. Histoire de France au seizième siècle*, vol. 11 (Paris: A. Lemmere, 1887), 442.

36. Donald Kelley, *The Beginning of Ideology: Consciousness and Society in the French Reformation* (New York: Cambridge University Press, 1981), 80.

37. Hotman, *A true and plaine report*, lxvii–lxviii.

38. Giovanni Michiel, "Report to the Venetian Senate," in Barbara B. Diefendorf, *The Saint Bartholomew's Day Massacre: A Brief History with Documents* (Boston: Bedford/St. Martin's, 2009), 89.

39. Christopher Marlowe, *Massacre at Paris* (Whitefish, MT: Kessinger, 2004), 16.

40. Marguerite Christol, "La dépouille de Gaspard de Coligny," *Bulletin de la Société de l'Histoire du Protestantisme français* 111 (1965): 136–40. Cf. Bourgeon, *L'Assassinat de Coligny*.

41. Cited in and see Janine Estèbe, *Tocsin pour un massacre. La saison des Saint-Barthélemy* (Paris: Centurion, 1968), 197.

42. Giovanni Michiel, Venetian ambassador, cited in Erlanger, *St. Bartholomew's Night*, 168. This is the same report as in Diefendorf, *Saint Bartholomew's Day Massacre*, with a slightly different translation.

43. See generally Anthony Pagden, *The Fall of Natural Man: The American Indian and the Origins of Comparative Ethnology* (Cambridge: Cambridge University Press, 1982), and J. G. A. Pocock, *Barbarism and Religion*, vol. 4: *Barbarians, Savages and Empires* (Cambridge: Cambridge University Press, 2008). Pocock is concerned with a later period, the eighteenth century, and the literature on barbarism and savagery as refracted through the work of Gibbon.

44. The longest boulevard in Los Angeles is named after him.

45. Cited in and see Lewis Hanke, *All Mankind Is One: A Study of the Disputation between Bartolomé de Las Casas and Juan Ginés de Sepúlveda* (DeKalb: Northern Illinois University Press, 1974), 68.

46. Bartolomé de las Casas, *In Defense of the Indians* [1552], trans. and ed. Stafford Poole (DeKalb: Northern Illinois University Press, 1992), 28–29, 53.

47. Bartolomé de las Casas, *The Devastation of the Indies*, trans. Herma Briffault (Baltimore, MD: Johns Hopkins University Press, 1992), 126–27, 117.

48. Alonso de Zorita, *Life and Labor in Ancient Mexico: The Brief and Summary Relation of the Lords of New Spain*, trans. Benjamin Keen (Norman: University of Oklahoma Press, 1994), 171–73. See Ralph H. Virgil, *Alonso de Zorita: Royal Judge and Christian Humanist 1512–1585* (Norman: University of Oklahoma Press, 1987), 281.

49. The book is available in a recent French edition: Richard Vestegan, *Théâtre des cruautés des hérétiques de notre temps* [1587], ed. Frank Lestringant (Paris: Éditions Chandeigne, 1995). See "Un Récit catholique des trois premières guerres de religion. *Les Acta Tumultuum Gallicanorum*," ed. H. Hauser, *Revue historique* 108 (1911): 314–16.

50. Nicolas Barnaud (Nicolas Froumenteau), *Le secret des finances de France, descouuert, & departi en trois liures par N. Frovmenteav, & maintenant publié, pour ouurir les moyens legitimes & necessaires de payer les dettes du roy, descharger ses suiets des subsides imposez depuis trente vn ans, & recouurer tous les deniers prins à Sa Maiesté* (Paris?, 1581), unpaged section: "Av Roy de France et de Pologne, Henri," access via http://galenet.galegroup.com/servlet. Froumenteau sought to assess the economic damage caused by the religious wars. For discussion of this work, see James B. Wood, "The Impact of the Wars of Religion: A View of France in 1581," *Sixteenth Century Journal* 15, no. 2 (Summer 1984): 131–68.

51. Denis Crouzet, *Les Guerriers de Dieu: La Violence au temps des troubles de religion*, vol. 2 (Seyssel, France: Champ Vallon, 1990), 152, and his "Sur le concept de barbarie au XVIe Siècle," in *La Conscience européenne au XVe et au XVIe siècle*, actes du colloque international organisé à l'Ecole normale supérieure de jeunes filles [30 septembre–3 octobre 1980] (Paris: L'Ecole, 1982), 103–26. See Patricia Gravatt, who draws heavily on Crouzet, *Le Nouveau monde et le vieux monde* (Paris: L'Harmattan, 2005), and Angela Enders, *Die Legende von der 'Neuen Welt.' Montaigne und die 'lit-*

térature géographique' im Frankreich des 16. Jahrhunderts (Tübingen: Max Niemeyer, 1993).

52. Prince of Conde, cited in Jean de Serres, *The three partes of commentaries containing the whole and perfect discourse of the ciuill warres of Fraunce*, trans. from Latin by Thomas Timme (London: Frances Coldocke, 1574), Fourth Book, 119, access via Early English Books On-Line.

53. See Mark Greengrass, "Hidden Transcripts: Secret Histories and Personal Testimonies of Religious Violence in the French Wars of Religion," in *The Massacre in History,* ed. Mark Levene and Penny Roberts (New York: Berghahn Books, 1999), 69–70.

54. Jean de Serres, *Three partes of commentaries,* Tenth Book, 21–22.

55. For a discussion of the word *massacre* and Marlowe, see Graham Hammill, "Time for Marlowe," *ELH,* vol. 75, no. 2 (2008): 291–314; Julia Briggs, "Marlowe's Massacre at Paris: A Reconsideration," *Review of English Studies* 34, no. 135 (1983), especially 268–69; and David Riggs, *The World of Christopher Marlowe* (New York: Henry Holt, 2004), 31–34.

56. See Frank Lestringant, *Cannibals: The Discovery and Representation of the Cannibal from Columbus to Jules Verne,* trans. Rosemary Morris (Berkeley: University of California Press, 1997). The issue among the anthropologists is whether cannibalism existed in the New World or was imagined to exist by Western observers and missionaries. That is not the issue here. The postcolonial anthropologists believe—surprise!—that cannibalism did not exist but was "invented" by Western missionaries and exploiters. For a good overview, see Iris Gareis, "Cannibals, Bons Sauvages and Tasty White Men: Models of Alterity in the Encounter of South American Tupi and Europeans," *Medieval History Journal* 5 (2002): 247–66. See also Peter Hulme, *Colonial Encounters: Europe and the Native Caribbean, 1497–1797* (New York: Methuen, 1986).

57. Jean de Léry, *History of a Voyage to the Land of Brazil,* trans. Janet Whatley (Berkeley: University of California Press, 1990), 6. This translation is based on the 1580 or second edition.

58. Jean de Léry, *L'histoire mémorable de la ville de Sancerre*, 291. The whole text is reprinted in Géralde Nakam, *Au lendemain de la Saint-Barthélemy: Guerre civile et famine* (Paris: Éditions anthropos, 1975).

59. For a summary of some of the changes in later editions, see Lestringant, *Cannibals*, 73–74.

60. Léry, *History of a Voyage*, 131–33.

61. See François Rigolot, "Saint Barthélemy l'Indien," *Bulletin de la Société des Amis de Montaigne* 37–38 (Jan.–June 2005): 51–66. David Quint in *Montaigne and the Quality of Mercy* (Princeton, NJ: Princeton University Press, 1998) seeks to tease out all references to the civil wars. See also José Alexandrino de Souza Filho, "Civilisation et barbarie en France au temps de Montaigne": Thèse pour obtenir le grade de docteur de l'université Bordeaux III (Lille: ANRT, Atelier national de reproduction des thèses, 2005), 298–307.

62. Michel de Montaigne, "On the Bad Means to a Good End," in *The Complete Essays*, trans. and ed. M. A. Screech (London: Penguin Books, 1991), 776.

63. Montaigne, "On Cruelty," *Complete Essays*, 484.

64. Montaigne did not explicitly cite Léry, but most scholars conclude he read and indeed copied from him. See, for instance, Bernard Weinberg, "Montaigne's Readings for *Des Cannibales*," in *Renaissance and Other Studies in Honor of William Leon Wiley*, ed. George Bernard Daniel, Jr. (Chapel Hill: University of North Carolina Press, [1968]), 261–79; Géralde Nakam, *Les "Essais" de Montaigne, miroir et procès de leur temps: témoignage historique et création littéraire*, new edition with new preface (Geneva: Éditions Slatkine, 2001), 334–43; Marcel Françon, "On a Source of Montaigne's 'Essays,'" *Modern Language Review* 48, no. 4 (Oct. 1953), 443–45; Gérard Defaux, "Un cannibale en haut de chausses: Montaigne, la différence et la logique de l'identité," *MLN* 97, no. 4, French issue (May 1982), 919–57.

65. Montaigne, "On the Cannibals," *Complete Essays*, 235–36. See de Souza Filho, "Civilisation et barbarie," for a very careful reconstruction of the historical material used (and misused) in "On the Cannibals," 90–206.

66. Jerome Friedman, *Michael Servetus: A Case Study in Total Heresy* (Geneva: Librarie Droz, 1978), 133.

67. Cited in Roland H. Bainton, *Hunted Heretic: The Life and Death of Michael Servetus, 1511–1553* (Boston: Beacon Press, 1960), 70.

68. See generally Marcel Bataillon, "Michel Servet poursuivi par l'Inquisition espagnole," *Bulletin hispanique* 27 (1925): 5–17. See as well Marian Hillar, *The Case of Michael Servetus (1511–1533)* (Lewiston, NY: Edwin Mellen Press, 1977), 206–8.

69. Verdict cited in Bainton, *Hunted Heretic*, 207–9.

70. See Luisa Simonutti, "Après Michel Servet," in *Michel Servet (1511–1553): Hérésie et pluralisme du xvie au xxie siècle*, ed. Valetine Zuber (Paris: Honoré Champion, 2007), 185–204. See also Lawrence and Nancy Goldstone, *Out of the Flames: The Remarkable Story of a Fearless Scholar, a Fatal Heresy and One of the Rarest Books in the World* (New York: Broadway Books, 2002), 221ff.

71. See Earl M. Wilbur, *A History of Unitarianism* (Cambridge, MA: Harvard University Press, 1947), for several excellent chapters on Servetus.

72. Montaigne, "Something Lacking in Our Civil Administrations," *Complete Essays*, 250 (I:35).

73. Sebastian Castellio, *Concerning Heretics: Whether They Are to Be Persecuted and How They Are to Be Treated*, ed. and trans. Roland H. Bainton (New York: Octagon Books, 1979), 119. See Hans R. Guggisberg, *Sebastian Castellio 1515–1563*, ed. and trans. Bruce Gordon (Aldershot, UK: Ashgate, 2003), 81–96.

74. Castellio, *Concerning Heretics*, 218.

75. Sebastian Castellio, *Advice to a Desolate France* (1562), ed. Marius F. Valkoff (Shepherdstown, WV: Patmos Press, 1975), 1.

76. Bainton, *Hunted Heretic*, 211–14, and Bainton's Introduction to *Concerning Heretics*, especially 108–9.

77. Benjamin J. Kaplan, *Divided by Faith: Religious Conflict and the Practice of Toleration in Early Modern Europe* (Cambridge, MA: Harvard University Press, 2007), 35.

78. Castellio, *Concerning Heretics*, 266.

79. See the fair-minded discussion in Edwin Rabbie, "Hugo Grotius and Judaism," in *Hugo Grotius Theologian: Essays in Honor of G. H. M. Posthumus Meyjes*, ed. Henk J. M. Nellen and Edwin Rabbie (Leiden: E. J. Brill, 1994), 99–120.

80. See generally Jacob Meijer, "Hugo Grotius' *Remonstrantie*," *Jewish Social Studies* 17, no. 2 (April 1955): 91–104. See Kaplan, *Divided by Faith*, 327–28. The Tacitus reference derives from his *Histories*, Book IV, chapter 70.

81. Thomas More, *Utopia*, trans. and ed. Robert M. Adams (New York: Norton, 1992), 72.

82. "The Dialogue Concerning Heresies," in Thomas More, *Utopia and Other Essential Writings*, ed. James J. Greene and John P. Dolan (New York: NAL, 1984), 208–16.

83. See the summary in J. A. Guy, "Sir Thomas More and the Heretics," *History Today* 30, no. 2 (1980): 11–15.

84. More, "Dialogue Concerning Heresies," 214–16. For a good discussion of the Christian as worse than the Turk, which takes up More, see Norman Housley, *Religious Warfare in Europe, 1400–1536* (Oxford: Oxford University Press, 2002), 149–59.

85. See Clarence Dana Rouillard, *The Turk in French History, Thought and Literature (1520–1660)* (Paris: Boivin, 1940), 395–418.

86. Luther and the papal nuncio cited in and see Kenneth M. Setton, "Lutheranism and the Turkish Peril," *Balkan Studies* 3, no. 1 (1962): 133–68. Luther later moderated his opinion inasmuch as he equated the Catholic and the Turk. "But just as the pope is the Antichrist, so the Turk is the very devil incarnate," Luther, "On War Against the Turk, 1529," in *Luther's Works*, volume 46, ed. Robert C. Shultz (Philadelphia: Fortress Press, 1967), 181.

87. Las Casas, *Devastation of the Indies*, 58. For a discussion of the image of the "Turk" in Las Casa and Sepúlveda, see Tomaz Mastnak, "Fictions in Political Thought: Las Casas, Sepúlveda, the Indians, and the Turks," *Filozofski Vestnik* 15 (1994): 127–49. At the same time, Las Casas offered a defense of the Inquisition, which suppressed Christian heretics, not outsiders. "The Inquisition does very well," he believed, in using against heretics "every kind of

punishment." Las Casas cited in and see the discussion in Angel Losada, "The Controversy between Sepúlveda and Las Casas in the Junta of Valladolid," in *Bartolomé de Las Casas in History*, ed. Juan Friede and Benjamin Keen (DeKalb: Northern Illinois University Press, 1971), 309–49.

88. Fehl, "Vasari's 'Extirpation of the Huguenots,'" 264, and A. W. Whitehead, *Gaspard de Coligny: Admiral of France* (London: Methuen, 1904), 272–73.

89. For a reproduction of the woodcut, the caption, and the relationship to Léry, see Scott D. Juall, "Draculean Dimensions of Early Modern French Politics and Religion: Vlad III Ţepeş 'the Impaler' and Jean de Léry's Political Project in *Histoire d'un voyage faict en la terre du Brésil* (1599/1600)," *Exemplaria* 21, no. 2 (2009): 202–24.

90. The new chapter is included as an appendix in the edition of Léry, *Histoire d'un voyage faict en la terre du Brésil*, ed. F. Lestringant (Paris: Livre de Poche, 1994), "Appendice I," 571–95. Some of the material is repeated from his chapter 15, and I take the translation of the verses from the English edition by Janet Whatley, since it also appeared in the earlier chapter (*Léry, History of a Voyage*, 133). For a thoughtful discussion of the new chapter 16, see Scott D. Juall, "'Beaucoup plus barbares que les Sauvages mesmes': Cannibalism, Savagery, and Religious Alterity in Jean de Léry's *Histoire d'un voyage faict en la terre du Brésil* (1599–1600)," *L'Esprit Créateur* 48, no. 1 (2008): 58–71.

91. Perez Zagorin, *How the Idea of Religious Tolerance Came to the West* (Princeton, NJ: Princeton University Press, 2003), 1.

92. Voltaire, *Philosophical Dictionary, J–Z*, ed. and trans. Peter Gay (New York: Basic Books, 1962), 485.

93. *A Monk's Confession: The Memoirs of Guibert of Nogent*, ed. Paul J. Archambault (University Park, PA: Penn State University Press, 1996), 111. I am using part of the translation of Norman Golb, Appendix III ("Guibert of Nogent's Account of the Persecution of the Jews of Rouen in 1096"), 557, in his *The Jews in Medieval Normandy: A Social and Intellectual History* (Cambridge: Cambridge

University Press, 1998). See his discussion (117–35) of the reliability of Guibert's account.

94. See generally Robert Chazan, *European Jewry and the First Crusade* (Berkeley: University of California Press, 1987).

95. "The Chronicle of Solomon bar Simson," in *The Jews and the Crusaders: The Hebrew Chronicles of the First and Second Crusades,* ed. Shlomo Eidelberg (Madison: University of Wisconsin Press, 1977), 21–72. For a revisionist and more literary analysis of these chronicles, see Jeremy Cohen, *Sanctifying the Name of God: Jewish Martyrs and Jewish Memories of the First Crusade* (Philadelphia: University of Pennsylvania Press, 2004).

96. "*Sefer Zekhirah* or *The Book of Remembrance* of Rabbi Ephraim of Bonn,*" in *The Jews and the Crusaders,* 122.

97. Cited in Cohen, *Sanctifying the Name of God,* 3, and in H. Graetz, *History of the Jews,* vol. 3 (Philadelphia: Jewish Publication Society of America, 1902), 350. See Dominique Iogna-Prat, *Ordonner et exclure: Cluny et la société chrétienne face à l'hérésie, au judaïsme et à l'islam 1000–1150* (Paris: Aubier, 1998), 276–79, and Jean-Pierre Torrell, "Les juifs dan l'oeuvre de Pierre le Vénérable," *Cahiers de civilisation médiévale* 30 (1987): 331–46.

98. See Shmuel Shekaru, *Jewish Martyrs in the Pagan and Christian Worlds* (New York: Cambridge University Press, 2006), 215–21. For a brief survey of the violence of the crusaders in Germany, see Christopher Tyerman, *God's War: A New History of the Crusades* (Cambridge, MA: Harvard University Press, 2006).

99. Mark Gregory Pegg, *A Most Holy War: The Albigensian Crusade and the Battle for Christendom* (Oxford: Oxford University Press, 2008), 191.

100. See Mark Gregory Pegg, *The Corruption of Angels: The Great Inquisition of 1245–1246* (Princeton, NJ: Princeton University Press, 2001), 15–19, for a discussion of the terminology.

101. Carl Joseph Hefele, *Histoire des conciles d'après les documents originaux,* vol. 5, 2nd part (Paris: Letouzey et Ané, 1913), 1261–70.

102. Pope Innocent cited in the chronicle Peter of Les Vaux-de-Cernay, *The History of the Albigensian Crusade,* trans. W. A. and M. D. Sibly (Suffolk, UK: Boydell Press, 1998), 37.

103. "Innocent to King Philip II of France, 17 November 1207" and "Innocent to the faithful in the provinces of Narbonne, Arles, Embrun, Aix and Vienne, 10 March 1208," in Louise and Jonathan Riley-Smith, *The Crusades: Idea and Reality, 1095–1274* (London: Edward Arnold, 1981), 78–85.

104. Canon 3, Fourth Lateran Council (1215), Medieval Sourcebook, www.fordham.edu/ha/sall/source/lat4-c3.html.

105. Peter of Les Vaux-de-Cernay, *History of the Albigensian Crusade*, 60.

106. To be sure, the Cathars enjoyed an afterlife in the scholarly world, and increasingly in tourism and mythology. For a recent overview, see Emily McCaffrey, "Imagining the Cathars in Late-Twentieth-Century Languedoc," *Contemporary European History* 11, no. 3 (2002): 409–27

107. William of Tudela, *The Song of the Cathar Wars*, trans. Janet Shirley (Hants, UK: Scolar Press, 1996), 20–21.

108. Peter of Les Vaux-de-Cernay, *History of the Albigensian Crusade*, 50–51.

109. Arnaud Amalric to Innocent III, August 1209, cited in Pegg, *Corruption of Angels*, 6. Pegg offers a slightly different translation in his *Most Holy War*, 77.

110. Caesarius of Heisterbach, *Dialogue on Miracles*, trans. H. Von E. Scott and C. W. Swinton Brand, vol. 1 (New York: Harcourt, Brace, 1929), Book V, chap. 21, 345–46, translation slightly altered. The biblical allusion is to 2 Timothy 19, "The Lord knoweth them that are his." For a careful discussion of the quotation—in its original Latin—and the likelihood of its veracity, see Jacques Berlioz, *'Tuez-les tous, Dieu reconnaîtra les siens.' Le massacre de Béziers (22 juillet 1209) et la croisade contre les Albigeois vus par Césaire de Heisterbach* (Portet-sur-Garonne, France: Loubatières, 1994), especially 76–83.

111. Michael Ott, "Caesarius of Heisterbach," in *The Catholic Encyclopedia* (New York: Robert Appleton Company, 1908), www.newadvent.org/cathen/03137a.htm.

112. See Michel Roquebert, *L'Épopée cathare, 1198–2120: L'invasion* (Toulouse: Edouard Privat, 1970), 258–61.

113. See James A. Brundage, "Holy War and the Medieval Lawyers," in *The Holy War,* ed. Thomas P. Murphy (Columbus: Ohio State University, 1976), 123, and Frederick H. Russell, *The Just War in the Middle Ages* (Cambridge: Cambridge University Press, 1975), 209.

114. For a discussion, see "Appendix B: The Massacre at Béziers, 22 July 1209," in Peter of Les Vaux-de-Cernay, *History of the Albigensian Crusade,* 289–93. For a revisionist account, which closely examines the numbers killed, see Laurence W. Marvin, "The Massacre at Béziers July 22, 1209," in *Heresy and the Persecuting Society in the Middle Ages: Essays on the Work of R. I. Moore,* ed. Michael Frassetto (Leiden: Brill, 2006), 195–225.

115. "Preface to the French Bible," in Castellio, *Concerning Heretics,* 257–58.

116. Stefan Zweig, *The Right to Heresy: Castellio against Calvin* (New York: Viking Press, 1936), 227–28.

117. Zweig to Romain Rolland, June 2, 1935, in Zweig, *Briefe 1932–1942,* ed. Knut Beck and Jeffrey B. Berlin (Frankfurt: Fischer Verlag, 2005), 124.

118. Étienne Giran, *Sébastien Castellion et la réforme calviniste* (Geneva: Slatkin Reprints, 1970, 1st ed. 1914).

119. Zweig to Arnold Zweig, May 1938, *Briefe,* 223.

120. "In dieser dunklen Stunde" (1941), in Stefan Zweig, *Schlaflose Welt. Aufsätze und Vorträge aus den Jahren 1909–1941* (Frankfurt/Main: S. Fischer Verlag, 1983), 276–78.

121. Joseph Roth, "The Auto-da-fé of the Mind" (1933), in his collection *What I Saw,* trans. Michael Hofmann (New York: Norton, 2003), 210.

122. See Knut Beck, "Nachbermerkung des Herausgebers," in Stefan Zweig, *Castellio gegen Calvin* (Frankfurt: Fischer Taschenbuch, 1996), 243–44.

123. Zweig, letter to Felix Braun, March 21, 1938, in *Briefe,* 218.

124. Cited in and see D. A. Prater, *European of Yesterday: A Biography of Stefan Zweig* (Oxford: Oxford University Press, 1972), 288–89.

125. See Alberto Dinos, "Death in Paradise: A Postcript," in *Stefan Zweig: Exil und Suche nach dem Weltfrieden,* ed. Mark H. Gelber and Klaus Zelewitz (Riverside, CA: Ariadne Press, 1995), 309–26.

126. Étienne Giran, who wrote that book on Castellio in 1914 in order to save him from "obscurity" (Giran, *Sébastien Castellion*, xii), himself deserves to be rescued. While Giran wrote several other books and led what appears to be an exemplary life both before and during the Resistance, virtually nothing exists about his life and contribution. Unfair! A few sources mention his arrest and death at Buchenwald at the age of seventy-three (see, for instance, Iorwerth Jones, "Sébastien Castellion: Apostle of Religious Liberty," *Expository Times*, 95 [1983]: 75), and one book devotes a few paragraphs to his life. That is it. See "Étienne Giran 1871–1944" in *Anthologie des écrivains morts à la guerre 1939–1945* (Paris: Association des écrivains combattants, 1960), 380–84.

CHAPTER TWO: UNCIVIL WARS

1. Paul Collier, V. L. Elliott, et al., *Breaking the Conflict Trap: Civil War and Development Policy* (Washington, DC: World Bank/ Oxford University Press, 2003), 1.

2. *UNESCO Universal Declaration on Cultural Diversity, Adopted by the 31st Session of the General Conference of UNESCO,* Paris, 2 November 2000 (Paris: UNESCO, 2002), http://unesdoc.unesco. org/images/0012/001271/127160m.pdf.

3. The index, eHRAF, "is produced by the Human Relations Area Files, Inc. (HRAF) at Yale University. The mission of HRAF, a nonprofit consortium of universities and colleges, is to encourage and facilitate worldwide and other comparative studies of human behavior, society, and culture." http://ehrafworldcultures.yale.edu/ ehrafe/index.do?browseSelect=1&topSelect=0&context=main.

4. *Encyclopedia of World Cultures,* vol. 4, ed. Linda A. Bennett (Boston: G. K. Hall, 1992), 109, 273–75, 98–100.

5. *Letters from the Kaiser to the Czar,* ed. Isaac Don Levine (New York: Frederick A. Stokes, 1920), letter LXXIII (March 18, 1913), 259.

6. "Princess Weds in Dazzling Pomp," *New York Times,* May 25, 1913.

7. *Letters from the Kaiser,* LXXIV (January 1, 1914), 261.

8. The Willy-Nicky Telegrams are available on many sites, e.g., wwi .lib.byu.edu/index.php/The_Willy-Nicky_Telegrams.

9. Erich Maria Remarque, *All Quiet on the Western Front*, trans. A. W. Wheen (New York: Random House/Fawcett, 1982), 223.

10. L. S. Stravianos, *Balkan Federation: A History of the Movement toward Balkan Unity in Modern Times* (Hamden, CT: Archon Books, 1964), 172.

11. Commander Hubert Cardale, R.N., cited in D. J. Cassavetti, *Hellas and the Balkan Wars* (London: T. Fisher Unwin, 1914), 342–44. See also Theodoros Zaimes, *The Crimes of Bulgaria in Macedonia: An Authentic Document Based on Facts and Records* (Washington, DC: NP, 1914), a translation of a quasi-official Greek government publication.

12. Christ Anastasoff, *The Tragic Peninsula: A History of the Macedonian Movement for Independence since 1878* (St. Louis: Blackwell Wielandy, 1938), 233, 211.

13. *Report of the International Commission to Inquire into the Causes and Conduct of the Balkan Wars*, Carnegie Endowment for International Peace, Publication No. 4 (Washington, DC: 1914), 265–66, 16.

14. Joachim Remak, "1914—The Third Balkan War: Origins Reconsidered," *Journal of Modern History* 43, no. 3 (Sept. 1971): 354–66. "The Balkan Wars were the first phase of the First World War. They were the same war," writes Richard C. Hall in his *The Balkan Wars 1912–1913: Prelude to the First World War* (London: Routledge, 2000), 132.

15. The concept of a "European civil war" of the twentieth century has had a checkered history. See Tom Lawson, "The Myth of the European Civil War," in *Myths of Europe*, ed. Richard Littlejohns and Sara Soncini (Amsterdam: Rodopi, 2007), 275–89. Leftist historians such as Paul Preston, Isaac Deutscher, and, with slightly different emphasis, Eric Hobsbawm have used the term. For instance, here is Hobsbawm: "We may regard the period from 1914 to 1945 as a single 'Thirty Years' War'" ("War and Peace in the 20th Century," in *War and Peace in the 20th Century and Beyond*, ed. Geir

Lundestad and Olav Njølstad [London: World Scientific, 2002], 25). However, the term is mainly associated with conservative and far-right writers and thinkers. The conservative German historian Ernst Nolte used the idea in part to justify an equivalence between Nazism and Communism. See his *Der europäische Bürgerkrieg 1917–1945: Nationalsozialismus und Bolschevismus* (Frankfurt: Ullstein, 1987). Along with many others such as Preston, however, he begins the civil war in 1917, with the Bolshevik Revolution and its opposition. F. J. P. Veale, a writer (and supporter of the British fascist Oswald Mosley), gets it right, however, in his *Advance to Barbarism.* "Popularly, and even officially, the war of 1914–1918 has come to be known as the First World War. This is a plain misnomer. It began as a European civil war. . . . On the one side were the peoples of Central Europe and on the other side the chief Atlantic Powers" (Appleton, WI: C. C. Nelson, 1953), 56. Luciano Canfora uses the term in his recent *Democracy in Europe: A History of Ideology,* trans. Simon Jones (Malden, MA: Blackwell, 2006), but only in quotes, and mainly as a critique of Nolte's argument. See "The 'European Civil War,'" chap. 12, 152–73, in *Democracy in Europe.* On this book see Adam Krzeminski, "Canfora's Scandalous History of Democracy," signandsight.com, 22/03/2006, www.signandsight.com/features/669.html.

16. For the prolongation of civil wars, see Ann Hironaka, *Neverending Wars: The International Community, Weak States and the Perpetuation of Civil War* (Cambridge, MA: Harvard University Press, 2005).

17. Karl Derouen and Uk Heo, eds., *Civil Wars of the World: Major Conflicts since World War II* (Santa Barbara, CA: ABC-CLIO, 2007).

18. James D. Fearon and David D. Laitin, "Ethnicity, Insurgency, and Civil War," *American Political Science Review* 97, no. 1 (Feb. 2003): 75. There is a burgeoning scholarly literature on the "new" or not-so-new civil wars. For an overview of the issues, see Christopher Cramer, *Civil War Is Not a Stupid Thing: Accounting for Violence in Developing Countries* (London: Hurst, 2006), 49–86.

19. Of course the number of deaths in all these conflicts is difficult to calculate, and famously contentious. For Russia, see Michael

Haynes and Rumy Husa, *A Century of State Murder? Death and Policy in Twentieth-Century Russia* (London: Pluto Press, 2003).

20. Evan Mawdsley, *The Russian Civil War* (Boston: Allen & Unwin, 1987), 281.

21. See Michael Malet, *Nestor Makhno in the Russian Civil War* (London: Macmillan, 1982).

22. Arno J. Mayer, *The Furies: Violence and Terror in the French and Russian Revolutions* (Princeton, NJ: Princeton University Press, 2000), 323. Mayer overstates the absence of theories of civil wars. In 1904, for instance, a French political thinker tackled the issue. He complained that the problem had been ignored but believed that the American Civil War had prompted attention to the subject. See Antoine Rougier, *Guerre civiles et les droit des gens* (Paris: L. Larose, 1903). Rougier in turn refers to Carlos Wiesse, a Peruvian scholar, as leading the way. See Wiesse's *Le Droit international appliqué aux guerres civiles* (Lausanne: B. Benda, 1898), trans. from Spanish by Donat Sautter.

23. Carl von Clausewitz, *On War,* ed. and trans. Michael Howard and Peter Paret (New York: Knopf, 1993), 100, 700, 85.

24. Scholars have expended much time on the meaning of faction or *stasis* in Greek thought. *Stasis* encompasses more than just civil wars. See Jonathan J. Price, *Thucydides and Internal War* (Cambridge: Cambridge University Press, 2001), 1–78, and Nicole Loraux, *The Divided City: On Memory and Forgetting in Ancient Athens* (New York: Zone Books, 2002), 64–68, as well as her "Corcyre 427, Paris 1871: La 'guerre civile grecque' entre deux temps," *Les temps modernes* 49 (Dec. 1993): 82–119 and (March 1994): 188–90.

25. *Republic,* V, 470–71 in *Collected Dialogues of Plato,* ed. Edith Hamilton and Huntington Cairns (New York: Bollingen Foundation/ Pantheon, 1963), 709–10.

26. Price, *Thucydides,* 60–61. I'm following Price's translation and discussion here.

27. Thucydides, *History of the Peloponnesian War,* trans. Rex Warner (London: Penguin Books, 1972), 241–45; Book III, 81–85. For a close reading of this passage and the issues of civil war and *stasis,* see Price, *Thucydides.*

28. Giovanni Michiel, "Report to the Venetian Senate," 90 (see chap. 1, n. 38).

29. "Separate Opinion of Judge Shahabuddeen," International Tribunal for the Prosecution of Persons Responsible for Serious Violations of International Humanitarian Law Committed in the Territory of the Former Yugoslavia since 1991, Case: IT-94-1-A, July 15, 1999, "The Prosecutor v. Duško Tadić," 150. http://icr.icty .org/LegalRef/CMSDocStore/Public/English/Judgment/Not Indexable/IT-94-1-A/JUD62R0000067347.TIF.

30. *The Memoirs of François René, Vicomte de Chateaubriand, Sometime Ambassador to England,* trans. by Alexander Teixeira de Mattos, vol. 5 (London: Freemantle, 1902), 153–54. René Gérin, a twentieth-century French pacifist, concurred. "Individuals who fight against their compatriots have real things to win or lose. . . . In a civil war, one knows why one fights." *Pacificisme intégral et guerre civile* (1937), cited in Paul Jal, *La guerre civile à Rome* (Paris: Presses Universitaires de France, 1963), 423. See Jal for a good discussion of Roman ideas of civil war.

31. Leonardo Sciascia, *Sicilian Uncles,* trans. N. S. Thompson (Manchester: Carcanet Press, 1986), 188–89.

32. Ibid., 174.

33. Italo Calvino, "Conscience," in *Numbers in the Dark,* trans. Tim Parks (New York: Vintage Books, 1996), 18–19.

34. "The First Memorial Day," *New York Times,* May 30, 1887.

35. John R. Neff, *Honoring the Civil War Dead: Commemoration and the Problem of Reconciliation* (Lawrence: University Press of Kansas, 2005), 222–41.

36. "McDonnell's Confederate History Month Proclamation Irks Civil Rights Leaders," *Washington Post,* April 7, 2010.

37. See Anastasia Karakasidou, "Protocol and Pageantry: Celebrating the Nation in Northern Greece," in *After the War Was Over: Reconstructing the Family, Nation and State in Greece, 1943–1960,* ed. Mark Mazower (Princeton, NJ: Princeton University Press, 2000), 221–46, and Kostantinos Charamis, "'Nothing and no one has been forgotten': commemorating those who did not give in during

the Greek civil war (1946–1949)," *Cahiers de la Méditerranée* 70 (2005), http://cdlm.revues.org/index915.htm.

38. Prime Minister Tzannis Tzannetakis, cited in David Close, who also summarizes the findings of anthropologists on the consequences of the war in his "The Road to Reconciliation? The Greek Civil War and the Politics of Memory in the 1980s," in *The Greek Civil War*, ed. Philip Carabott and Thanasis D. Sfikas (Aldershot, UK: Ashgate Publishing, 2004), 260–62.

39. Anne Dolan, *Commemorating the Irish Civil War* (Cambridge: Cambridge University Press, 2003), 56, and David Fitzpatrick, "Commemoration in the Irish Free State: A Chronicle of Embarrassment," in *History and Memory in Modern Ireland*, ed. Ian McBride (Cambridge: Cambridge University Press, 2001), 198–203.

40. "Civil War Anniversary Opens Old Wounds: Franco's Ghosts Still Haunt Nation after 70 Years," *Times* (London), April 1, 2009.

41. Dionisio Ridruejo, cited in Paloma Aguilar, *Memory and Amnesia: The Role of the Spanish Civil War in the Transition to Democracy*, trans. Mark Oakley (New York: Berghahn Books, 2002), 90–91.

42. See Aguilar, "Agents of Memory: Spanish Civil War Veterans and Disabled Soldiers," in Jay Winter and Emmanuel Sivan, eds., *War and Remembrance in the Twentieth Century* (New York: Cambridge University Press, 1999), 84–87, and Aguilar's *Memory and Amnesia*, 206–8, 138–39.

43. Paul Preston, *The Spanish Civil War: Reaction, Revolution and Revenge* (New York: Norton, 2006), 8–9.

44. "Spain's Dilemma: To Toast Franco or Banish his Ghost?" *New York Times*, October 8, 2006.

45. "Franco's face and name erased from public view in Spain," *Guardian* (UK), October 6, 2009.

46. Michael Kimmelman, "In Spain, a Monumental Silence," *New York Times*, January 13, 2008.

47. "The New Civil War," *Economist*, February 20, 2010, 48. This article concerns the inquiry of Judge Baltasar Garzón into crimes against humanity of the Franco period—and the opposition it has incurred.

48. Drew Gilpin Faust, *This Republic of Suffering: Death and the American Civil War* (New York: Knopf, 2008), xi, and her "'Numbers on Top of Numbers': Counting the Civil War Dead," *Journal of Military History* 70, no. 4 (2006): 995–1009.

49. "What Secession Has Done," *Missouri Statesman,* October 4, 1961, cited in Amy Murrell Taylor, *The Divided Family in Civil War America* (Chapel Hill: University of North Carolina Press, 2005), 3.

50. Jacob Merritt Howard, 38th Congress 1st Session, *Cong. Globe* 344 (1864), Wednesday, January 27, 1864, 344. Nor was this just sentiment. Brothers often faced brothers. See also Taylor, *Divided Family,* 72–81, and George B. Forgie, *Patricide in the House Divided: A Psychological Interpretation of Lincoln and His Age* (New York: W. W. Norton, 1979), 201–41.

51. William G. Stevenson, *Thirteen months in the Rebel Army: being a narrative of personal adventures in the infantry, ordnance, cavalry, courier, and hospital services . . . By an impressed New Yorker* (New York: A. S. Barnes & Burr, 1862), 148–49.

52. *Walt Whitman's Memoranda during the War & Death of Abraham Lincoln,* ed. Roy P. Balser (Bloomington: Indiana University Press, 1962), 53.

53. Amalendu Misra, *Politics of Civil Wars: Conflict, Intervention and Resolution* (New York: Routledge, 2008), 59. Stathis N. Kalyvas, in "'New' and 'Old' Civil Wars: A Valid Distinction?" *World Politics* 54 (Oct. 2001): 99–118, argues with great vigor that nothing distinguishes the "new" from the "old" civil wars.

54. Nikos Kazantzakis, *The Fratricides,* trans. Athena G. Dallas (New York: Simon and Schuster, 1984), 8.

55. Nicholas Gage, *Eleni* (New York: Ballantine Books, 1984), 2, 605.

56. Ramón Sender Barayón, *A Death in Zamora* (Albuquerque: University of New Mexico Press, 1989), 148–64.

57. Edward N. Luttwak in *Times Literary Supplement,* June 16, 1995. I was led to this piece by its reference in Stathis N. Kalyvas's *The Logic of Violence in Civil War* (New York: Cambridge University Press, 2006), which is, among other things, an extraordinary survey of scholarship and writings on civil wars.

58. William Finnegan, *A Complicated War: The Harrowing of Mozambique* (Berkeley: University of California Press, 1992).

59. Stephen C. Lubkemann, "Migratory Coping in Wartime Mozambique: An Anthropology of Violence and Displacement in 'Fragmented' Wars," *Journal of Peace Research* 42, no. 4 (2005): 493–508.

60. René Lemarchand, *The Dynamics of Violence in Central Africa* (Philadelphia: University of Pennsylvania Press, 2009), xi. The minister is cited in Mahood Mamdani, *When Victims Become Killers: Colonialism, Nativism, and the Genocide in Rwanda* (Princeton, NJ: Princeton University Press, 2001), 6.

61. Ian Fisher, "Congo's War Overshadows Tribal Fight," *New York Times*, Feb. 13, 2000.

62. Hussein M. Adam, *From Tyranny to Anarchy: The Somalian Experience* (Trenton, NJ: Red Sea Press, 2008), 42, 82.

63. "New Somali Government Faces Old Problem: Clans," *New York Times*, Jan. 22, 2007.

64. "The Global Menace of Local Strife," *Economist*, May 24, 2003.

65. Archbishop of Juba cited in Bill Berkeley, *The Graves Are Not Yet Full: Race, Tribe and Power in the Heart of Africa* (New York: Basic Books, 2001), 219–23.

66. E. E. Evans-Pritchard, *The Nuer: A Description of the Modes of Livelihood and Political Institutions of a Nilotic People* (Oxford: Oxford University Press, 1940), 125, 130–31.

67. For the documents and a discussion of their credibility, see Neil Caplan, "Faisal Ibn Husain and the Zionists: A Re-examination with Documents," *International History Review* 5, no. 4 (Nov. 1983): 561–614.

68. Avner Falk, *Fratricide in the Holy Land: A Psychoanalytic View of the Arab-Israeli Conflict* (Madison: University of Wisconsin Press, 2004), 5.

69. Ibid., 128.

70. Yigal Amir, cited in Ehud Sprinzak, *Brother Against Brother: Violence and Extremism in Israeli Politics from "Altalena" to the Rabin Assassination* (New York: Free Press, 1999), 282.

71. Matt Rees, *Cain's Field: Faith, Fratricide and Fear in the Middle East* (New York: Free Press, 2004), 300–302.

72. Donald Harman Akenson, *Small Differences: Irish Catholics and Irish Protestants, 1815–1922: An International Perspective* (Kingston, ON: McGill-Queen's University Press, 1988), 108–9.

73. Peter Hart, *The I.R.A. and Its Enemies: Violence and Community in Cork, 1916–1923* (Oxford: Clarendon Press, 1998), 264–65.

74. Seán Ó Faoláin, *Vive Moi!* (Boston: Little Brown, 1964), 195, 189.

75. Nenad Miscevic, "Close Strangers: Nationalism, Proximity and Cosmopolitanism," *Studies in East European Thought* 51, no. 2 (June 1999), 109–25.

76. Michael Ignatieff, *The Warrior Honor: Ethnic War and the Modern Conscience* (New York: Henry Holt, 1997), 36.

77. Vamik Volkan, *Blood Lines: From Ethnic Pride to Ethnic Terrorism* (Boulder, CO: Westview Press, 1997), 109.

78. Chris Hedges, *War Is a Force That Gives Us Meaning* (Oxford: PublicAffairs, 2002), 26, 32.

79. George F. Kennan, "Introduction: The Balkan Crises: 1913 and 1993," in *The Other Balkan Wars: A 1913 Carnegie Endowment Inquiry in Retrospect* (Washington, DC: Carnegie Endowment for International Peace, 1993), 9.

80. Milovan Djilas, *Land without Justice* (New York: Harcourt, Brace, 1958), 8. See Christopher Boehm, *Blood Revenge: The Anthropology of Feuding in Montenegro and Other Tribal Societies* (Lawrence: University Press of Kansas, 1984).

81. Hannah Arendt, *On Revolution* (London: Penguin Books, 1990), 20.

82. I am following here Loraux, *Divided City*, 200–221. See her chapter "Politics of Brothers," 197–214. The prevailing English translation of Herodotus reads that the brothers quarreled "in spite of the fact that they were brothers." (Herodotus, *The Histories*, trans. Aubrey de Sélincourt [London: Penguin Books, 2003], 378, VI.52.) Loraux argues that this might be misleading and could just as well be rendered, "because they were brothers."

83. Hesiod, "Work and Days," 371, in *Theogony, Work and Days, Shield*, trans. Apostolos N. Athanassakis (Baltimore, MD: Johns Hopkins University Press, 1983), 76.

84. *Thebaid*, in *Greek Epic Fragments*, ed. Martin L. West (Cambridge, MA: Harvard University Press, 2003), 45. Word in brackets added; ellipses in original.

85. *Oedipus at Colonus, Complete Plays of Sophocles*, trans. Richard Claverhouse Jebb, ed. Moses Hadas (New York: Bantam Books, 1982), 229.

86. Aeschylus, *Seven Against Thebes*, in *Prometheus Bound and Other Plays*, trans. Philip Vellacott (London: Penguin Books, 1961), 108, 110.

87. See Publius Papinius Statius, *The Thebaid: Seven against Thebes*, trans. Charles Stanley Ross (Baltimore, MD: Johns Hopkins University Press, 2004).

88. See T. P. Wiseman, *Remus: A Roman Myth* (Cambridge: Cambridge University Press, 1995), for a full discussion of the myth and its vagaries. See also Anthony G. Pontone, "Fratricide as the Founding Myth of Rome: The Roman Historiographical Perspective," Ph.D. dissertation, 1986, NYU, and T. J. Cornell, "Aeneas and the Twins: The Development of the Roman Foundation Legend," *Proceedings of the Cambridge Philological Society* 21 (1975): 1–32; Cynthia J. Bannon, *The Brothers of Romulus: Fraternal Pietas in Roman Law, Literature and Society* (Princeton, NJ: Princeton University Press, 1997), especially 158–73; and J. N. Bremmer, "Romulus, Remus and the Foundation of Rome," in J. N. Bremmer and N. M. Horsfall, eds., *Roman Myth and Mythology* (London: Institute of Classical Studies, 1987), 25–48.

89. See in general Otto Rank, *The Myth of the Birth of the Hero* (New York: Vintage Books, 1959), 65.

90. Plutarch, "Romulus," *Plutarch's Lives*, Dryden translation, ed. Arthur Hugh Clough, vol. 1 (New York: Modern Library, 2001), 30.

91. Livy, *The Early History of Rome*, Introduction by R. M. Ogilvie, trans. Aubrey de Sélincourt (London: Penguin Books, 2002), 36–37.

92. Horace, Epode 7, in *The Odes and Epodes of Horace*, trans. Joseph P. Clancy (Chicago: University of Chicago Press, 1960), 212.

93. See generally Ricardo J. Quinones, *The Changes of Cain: Violence and the Lost Brother in Cain and Abel Literature* (Princeton, NJ: Princeton University Press, 1991). For an old and thorough survey, see Oliver F. Emerson, "Legends of Cain, Especially in Old and Middle English" *PMLA* 21, no. 4 (1906): 831–929. For references and ideas, I owe much to Quinones's book.

94. John Steinbeck, *East of Eden* (New York: Penguin Books, 2002), 264.

95. Wiesel, *Messengers of God*, 40 (see Preface, n. 1).

96. See Fredrick E. Greenspahn, *When Brothers Dwell Together: The Preeminence of Younger Siblings in the Hebrew Bible* (New York: Oxford University Press, 1994), especially 111–12.

97. See the discussion in Adiel Schremer, *Brothers Estranged: Heresy, Christianity, and Jewish Identity in Late Antiquity* (New York: Oxford University Press, 2010), 134–41.

98. See Alfred Bertholet, *Die Stellung der Israeliten und der Juden zu den Fremden* (Freiburg: J. C. B. Mohr, 1896), especially 303–49.

99. I am following here Benjamin Nelson's *The Idea of Usury: From Tribal Brotherhood to Universal Otherhood* (Chicago: University of Chicago Press, 1969), 1st ed. 1949.

100. There is no good translation. "Mount of Piety" means nothing in English. See generally Carol B. Menning, *Charity and State in Late Renaissance Italy: The Monte di Pietà of Florence* (Ithaca, NY: Cornell University Press, 1993).

101. P. Heribert Holzapfel, *Die Anfänge der Montes Pietatis* (Munich: J. J. Lentner'schen Buchhandlung, 1903), 26.

102. See Giacomo Todeschini, "Franciscan Economics and Jews in the Middle Ages," in *Friars and Jews in the Middle Ages and Renaissance*, eds. Steven J. McMichael and Susan E. Myers (Leiden: Brill, 2004), 99–118.

103. Anonymous play, cited in and see Menning, *Charity and State*, 26.

104. See John T. Noonan, *The Scholastic Analysis of Usury* (Cambridge, MA: Harvard University Press, 1957), 305.

105. Nelson, *Idea of Usury*, 19.

106. Armin Ehrenzweig, "Kain und Lamech," *Zeitschrift für die alttes-tamentliche Wissenschaft* 35 (1915): 1ff. For a rejoinder, see Norbert Strosetzki, "Kain und Romulus als Stadtgründer," *Forschungen und Fortschritte* 29, no. 6 (1955): 184–88.

107. Jacques Ellul, *The Meaning of the City*, trans. Dennis Pardee (Grand Rapids, MI: William B. Eerdman's, 1970), 5.

108. Leon R. Kass, "Farmers, Founders, and Fratricide: The Story of Cain and Abel," *First Things* 62 (April 1996): 19–26. See George M. Shulman, "The Myth of Cain: Fratricide, City Building, and Politics," *Political Theory* 14, no. 2 (May 1986): 215–38, and Gerhard Wallis, "Die Stadt in den Überlieferungen der Genesis," *Zeitschrift für die alttestamentliche Wissenschaft* 78, no. 2 (1966): 133–48.

109. N. O. Brown, "Rome—A Psychoanalytical Study," *Arethusa* 7, no. 1 (1974): 97.

110. Lewis Mumford, *The City in History: Its Origins, Its Transformations, and Its Prospects* (New York: Harvest/HBJ, 1961), 37.

111. Livy, *Early History of Rome*, Book 1, §7, 37.

112. *Matthew Henry Complete Commentary on the Whole Bible*: www .studylight.org/com/mhc-com/.

113. Augustine, *The City of God against the Pagans*, ed. and trans. R. W. Dyson (Cambridge: Cambridge University Press, 1998), Book xv, chap. 8, 646.

114. Ibid., Book xvi, chap. vi, 634–41.

115. Lucan, *Civil War*, trans. and ed. Susan H. Braund (Oxford: Oxford University Press, 1992), Book One, lines 2–4, 30–34, 3–4.

116. "Political thinkers in America have spoken of liberty and equality . . . but they have rarely spoken of fraternity," William C. McWilliams, *The Idea of Fraternity in America* (Berkeley: University of California Press, 1973), 95.

117. Donald Greer, *The Incidence of the Terror During the French Revolution: A Statistical Interpretation* (Cambridge, MA: Harvard University Press, 1935), 38, and the chapter "The Geographic Incidence," 38–70. See the summary in Colin Jones, "Synopsis of the Geog-

raphy of Terror," *The Longman Companion to the French Revolution* (London: Longman, 1988), 119.

118. Jean-Clément Martin, "Est-il possible de compter les morts de la Vendée?" *Revue d'histoire moderne et contemporaine* 38, no. 1 (1991): 119. The figure of 250,000 does not include deaths of the Revolutionary army.

119. David Bell, *The First Total War: Napoleon's Europe and the Birth of Warfare as We Know It* (Boston: Houghton Mifflin, 2007), 196, 153.

120. Edward J. Woell, *Small-Town Martyrs and Murderers: Religious Revolution and Counterrevolution in Western France, 1774–1914* (Milwaukee: Marquette Press, 2006), 153. Woell provides a complete reconstruction of the events from the contrasting positions of both rebels and patriots.

121. Alexandre Dumas, *My Memoirs,* trans. E. M. Waller, vol. III (London: Methuen, 1908), 282.

122. Jean Tabeur, *Paris contre la province! Les guerres de l'Ouest, 1792–1796* (Paris: Economica, 2008).

123. Indictment cited in Bronislaw Baczko, *Ending the Terror: The French Revolution after Robespierre,* trans. M. Petheram (Cambridge: Cambridge University Press, 1994), 144.

124. Cited in Élie Fournier, *Turreau et les colonnes infernales* (Paris: Albin Michel, 1985), 43–47.

125. Both quotations from Reynald Secher, *A French Genocide: The Vendée,* trans. George Holoch (Notre Dame, IN: University of Notre Dame Press, 2003), 118–19. Secher's writings on the Vendée, which dub the violence genocidal—and draw parallels to the genocide of the Jews by the Nazis—have spurred much controversy. See Bell, *First Total War,* 157–61, and Jean-Clément Martin, "A propos du 'génocide vendéen,'" in his *La Vendée et la révolution* (Paris: Perrin, 2007), 61–85. For numerous reasons, to label the violence in the Vendée a genocide cannot be justified.

126. Cited in Jean-Clément Martin, *La Vendée et la France* (Paris: Éditions du Seuil, 1987), 192.

127. Martin, *La Vendée et la France,* 218–24; Secher, *French Genocide,* 111–14.

128. François-Joseph Westermann, in J. Crétineau-Joy, *Histoire de la Vendée militaire*, 2nd ed., vol. 2 (Paris: Maison de la Bonne Presse, 1896), 6. Westermann himself was caught up in the Terror and executed. Turreau, however, was spared and led a charmed career. His name is carved on the Arc de Triomphe in Paris. See Bell, *First Total War*, 183.

129. Duc de Lauzun (also known as Biron) in *Compte rendu au Comité de Salut public et au Conseil exécutif provisiore—De la guerre en Vendée*, cited in Comte R. De Gontaut Biron, *Un Célèbre méconnu: Le duc de Lauzun* (Paris: Librairie Plon, 1937), 309.

130. Louis-Marie Turreau, *Memoirs for the History of the War of La Vendée*, trans. from French (London: M. Peltier, 1796), 33, 163.

131. Jean-Baptiste Carrier, *Suite du rapport* (Paris: Imprimerie nationale, Brumaire, l'an III [1794]), 28.

132. Baczko, *Ending the Terror*, 195.

133. Merlin (from Thionville), cited in ibid., 144.

134. Cited in Secher, *French Genocide*, 118.

135. This according to Marcel David in his *Fraternité et révolution française 1789–1799* (Paris: Aubier, 1987), 145, 173–74. Apparently only a few prints survive. David's book is essential for the issue of fraternity in the Revolution.

136. See Mona Ozouf, "Liberté, égalité, fraternité," in *Les Lieux de Mémoire*, ed. Pierre Nora, vol. 3 (Paris: Gallimard, 1992), 592.

137. Cited in and see Alphonse Aulard, "La Devise 'Liberté, égalité, fraternité,'" in his *Études et leçons sur la Révolution française*, vol. 6 (Paris: Félix Alcan, 1910), 20–21. Aulard pays attention to the vagaries of the "or death" phrase.

138. M. Mercier, *New Picture of Paris*, trans. from the French, vol. 1 (London: H. D. Symonds, 1800), 412.

139. François de Chateaubriand, *Mémoires d'outre-tombe*, trans. A. S. Kline, Book XIII, chap. 3: "The year 1800," http://tkline.pgcc.net/PITBR/Chateaubriand/Chathome.htm.

140. Aulard, "La Devise," 19.

141. Cited in Claude Arnaud, *Chamfort: A Biography*, trans. Deke Dusinberre (Chicago: University of Chicago Press, 1992), 250.

142. See the recent edition of his *Mustapha et Zéangir* and the introduction by Simon Davies (Exeter, UK: University of Exeter Press, 1992).

143. Chamfort, *Reflections on Life, Love and Society,* ed. and trans. Douglas Parmée (London: Short Books, 2003), 69.

144. See Pierre-Louis Ginguené, "La Vie and l'oeuvre de Chamfort," in Chamfort, *Produits de la civilisation perfectionnée* (Paris: Société du Mercure, 1905), 373–74. See Maurice Pellison, *Chamfort: Étude sur sa vie, son caractère et ses écrits* (Paris: Lecène, Oudin, 1895), 275. David, in his *Fraternité et révolution française,* is very anxious to minimize the importance of the phrase "Fraternity or Death" and Chamfort's comments about it. I think he protests too much.

145. Mona Ozouf, "Liberty, Equality, Fraternity," in *Realms of Memory,* vol. 3, ed. Pierre Nora, trans. Arthur Goldhammer (New York: Columbia University Press, 1998), 81.

146. "Fraternité," *Encyclopédie, ou Dictionnaire raisonné des sciences, des arts et des métiers, par une société de gens de lettres.* Mis en ordre & publié par M. Diderot, vol. 7 (Geneva, 1772), 290; "Liberté," vol. 9, 462–76.

147. For a discussion of the Masonic origins, see Robert Amadou, "'Liberté, égalité, fraternité': La Devise republicaine et La Franc-Maconnerie," *Renaissance traditionelle* (1973): 1–24. Amadou finds little evidence of "fraternity" in the Masonic tradition before the Revolution.

148. See in general Alphonse Aulard, "Le Serment du jeu de paume," in his *Études et leçons sur la Révolution française,* vol. 1 (Paris: Félix Alcan, 1909), 55–70.

149. See Philippe Bordes, *Le Serment du jeu de paume de Jacques-Louis David* (Paris: Éditions de la Réunion de la musées nationaux, 1983).

150. Cited in John R. Roberts, "Liberté, Égalité, Fraternité: Sources and Development of a Slogan," *Tijdschrift voor de studie van de verlichting,* 3–4 (1976): 332.

151. See Jacques André, "L'assemblée des frères. Au commencements de la Révolution française," *Psychanalyse à l'université* 13, no. 52

(Oct. 1988): 537–74, and his *La révolution fratricide: Essai de psychoanalyse du lien social* (Paris: Presses Universitaires de France, 1993), 181–85. See also Lynn Hunt, *The Family Romance of the French Revolution* (Berkeley: University of California Press, 1992) for a psychoanalytic-inflected interpretation of regicide and fratricide in the French Revolution.

152. Jean-Sylvain Bailly, *Mémoires*, in *Avant-Moniteur ou Tableau sommaire des huit premiers mois de Révolution française* (Paris: Levrault, Schoell, 1805), xxviii.

153. Cited in Mona Ozouf, "La Révolution française et l'idée de fraternité," in her *L'homme régénéré* (Paris: Gallimard, 1989), 163.

CHAPTER THREE: GENOCIDE IN HISTORY: KILL THY NEIGHBOR

1. Montaigne, "On Conscience," *Complete Essays*, 411–12 (see chap. 1, n. 62). Montaigne says nothing more about the "mishap" or slaying. His biographers do not mention it. The Pléiade edition of his essays reports that nothing is known about the encounter. Montaigne, *Les Essais*, ed. Jean Balsamo, Michel Magnien, and Catherine Magnien-Simonin (Paris: Gallimard, 2007), 1517.

2. John Cleveland, *Rustick Rampant or Rurall Anarchy affronting monarchy: in the insurrection of Wat Tiler* (London: Westminster Hall and the Royall Exchange, 1658), 36. This chronicle is apparently based on an earlier and contemporary account, the anonymous "Julius BII," which states that many Flemish lost their heads because they could not say "Breede and Chese, But Case and Brode." "Julius BII, 1365–1381," in *Chronicles of London*, ed. Charles L. Kingsford (Gloucestershire, UK: Alan Sutton, 1977, 1st ed. 1905), 15. See Alastair Dunn, *The Peasants' Revolt: England's Failed Revolution of 1381* (Stroud, UK: Tempus, 2004), 113–14. During World War II the U. S. Army briefly published a comic for American troops in China. It included linguistic tips to identify enemy Japanese among the allied Chinese. Even when they speak English well, "most Japanese hiss when they pronounce the letter 'S.'" It advised

American officers to demand of the presumed spy to "repeat a sentence like 'Smith left the fortress.'" See "How to Spot a Jap," included in *Pocket Guide to China*, 1942, www.ep.tc/howtospot ajap/howto01.html.

3. See Ed Cairns, *A Welling Up of Deep Unconscious Forces, Psychology and the Northern Ireland Conflict* (Coleraine: University of Ulster, 1994), www.ccruni.gov.uk/research/csc/forces.htm.

4. Avraham Kochavi in the documentary *Genocide* (1975) in the series *The World at War*, directed by Michael Darlow, Thames Television, London.

5. *Der Giftpilz* (1938), partially reproduced and translated in German Propaganda Archive, www.calvin.edu/academic/cas/gpa/thumb.htm.

6. "To Stay Alive, Iraqis Change Their Names," *New York Times*, September 6, 2006.

7. Samantha Power, *"A Problem from Hell": America and the Age of Genocide* (New York: Basic Books, 2002), 58.

8. Lee Ann Fujii, *Killing Neighbors: Webs of Violence in Rwanda* (Ithaca, NY: Cornell University Press, 2009), 31.

9. Human Rights Watch, "Leave None to Tell the Story: Genocide in Rwanda," March 1999, www.hrw.org/legacy/reports/1999/rwanda/rwanda0399.htm.

10. "République Rwanda" findings from 1994, cited in Fujii, *Killing Neighbors*, 110.

11. Rosemary Ruether, *Faith and Fratricide: The Theological Roots of Anti-Semitism* (San Francisco: HarperSanFrancisco, 1984), 30.

12. George Montandon, *Comment reconnaître le Juif?* (Paris: Nouvelle éditions françaises, 1940), 7.

13. For an overview of the contending positions, see Peter Schäfer, *Judeophobia: Attitudes toward the Jews in the Ancient World* (Cambridge, MA: Harvard University Press, 1997), 1–8.

14. Victor Tcherikover, *Hellenistic Civilization and the Jews*, trans. S. Applebaum (Philadelphia: Jewish Publication Society of America, 1959), 358.

15. Wiesel, *Messengers of God*, 37 (see Preface, n. 1).

16. Ambrose, "Hexameron, Paradise, and Cain and Abel," in *The Fathers of the Church,* vol. 42, trans. John J. Savage (Washington, DC: Catholic University of America Press, 1961), 361–62.

17. Augustine, *City of God,* 646 (see chap. 2, n. 113). See, generally, Bernhard Blumenkranz, *Die Judenpredigt Augustins: Ein Beitrag zur Geschichte der jüdisch-christlichen Beziehungen in den ersten Jahrhunderten* (Basel: Helbing & Lichtenhahn, 1946). Elsewhere he stated, "God says to Cain: 'Thou art cursed from the earth. . . . A mourner and an abject shalt thou be on the earth.' It is not, Cursed is the earth, but, Cursed art thou from the earth. . . . So the unbelieving people of the Jews is cursed from the earth, that is, from the Church . . . the Church admits and avows the Jewish people to be cursed, because after killing Christ they continue to till the ground of an earthly circumcision, an earthly Sabbath, an earthly Passover." Augustine, *Reply to Faustus the Manichaean [Contra Faustum Manichaeum],* Book xi, paragraph 11, Nicene and Post-Nicene Fathers, Series I, Vol. 4 (ECF Vol. 13): Augustine Volumes: Anti-Manichaean and Anti-Donatist Writings, www.aroundomaha.com/ecf/volume13/. The key new book on the subject is Paula Fredriksen's *Augustine and the Jews.* As a nonexpert on the subject, I find that she is too generous to Augustine. See also Jeremy Cohen, *Living Letters of the Law: Ideas of the Jew in Medieval Christianity* (Berkeley: University of California Press, 1999), which argues for an Augustinian and moderate tradition of Christian ideas of the Jew. For a careful consideration of Fredriksen and the issues, see Ra'anan S. Boustan, "Augustine as Revolutionary? Reflections on the Continuity and Rupture in Jewish-Christian Relations in Paula Fredriksen's *Augustine and the Jews,*" *Jewish Quarterly* 99 (Winter 2009): 74–87.

18. Augustine cited in Leopold Lucas, *The Conflict between Christianity and Judaism: A Contribution to the History of the Jews in the Fourth Century* (Warminster, UK: Aris & Phillips, 1993), 90, first German ed. 1910. Another Church father states, "Today the glory has passed from the people of Israel and they stand among the nations ashamed, as Cain was, at the unnatural deed." Ephrem, cited in Ruether, *Faith and Fratricide,* 134.

19. G. Dahan, "L'exégèse de l'histoire de Caïn et Abel du XIIe au XIVe siècle en Occident," *Recherches de théologie, ancienne et médiévale*, vol. 49 (1982): 21–89. This is a comprehensive survey.

20. Cited in and see Ruth Mellinkoff, "Cain and the Jews," *Journal of Jewish Art* 6 (1979), 22–23.

21. Philo, "The Worse Attacks the Better," in *The Works of Philo*, ed. C. D. Yong (Peabody, MA: Hendrikson, 1997), 131.

22. See Ruth Mellinkoff, *The Mark of Cain* (Berkeley: University of California Press, 1981), a book to which I am indebted. For a recent consideration, see R. W. L. Moberly, "The Mark of Cain—Revealed at Last?" *Harvard Theology Review* 100 (2007): 11–28.

23. Film *The Eternal Jew / Der Ewige Jude* (1940). English subtitles 1988 by International Historic Film, Chicago.

24. See Laurence Sigal-Klagsbald, "Au-delà du miroir figures bibliques du juif errant," in *Le juif errant. Un témoin du temps* (Paris: Musée d'art et d'histoire du Judaïsme, 2001), 35–39.

25. I am citing the lines from the slightly later French edition of 1650, from George K. Anderson, *The Legend of the Wandering Jew* (Providence, RI: Brown University Press, 1965), 56. In a crowded field, this is an exemplary study.

26. *The First Book of Adam and Eve, Also Called The Conflict of Adam and Eve with Satan*, trans. and ed. Rev. S. C. Malan (London: Williams and Northgate, 1882), 101–3.

27. Cited in and see Mellinkoff, *Mark of Cain*, 57.

28. Augustine, *Reply to Faustus*.

29. "Letter Innocent III, January 17, 1208" in Solomon Grayzel, *The Church and the Jews in the XIIIth century* (Philadelphia: Dropsie College for Hebrew and Cognate Learning, 1933), 127. See Robert Chazan, "Pope Innocent III and the Jews," in *Pope Innocent III and His World*, ed. John C. Moore (Aldershot, UK: Ashgate, 1999), 187–204.

30. Cited in Robert Chazan, *Medieval Stereotypes and Modern Antisemitism* (Berkeley: University of California Press, 1997), 49.

31. See Joachim Radkau, *Das Zeitalter der Nervosität: Deutschland zwischen Bismarck und Hitler* (Munich: Carl Hanser, 1998), 324–

39, and his essay, "Nationalismus und Nervosität," in *Kulturge-schichte Heute*, ed. Wolfgang Hardtwig and Hans-Ulrich Wehler (Göttingen: Vandenhoeck & Ruprecht, 1996), especially 299–303.

32. Édouard Drumont, *La France juive; essai d'histoire contemporaine* (Paris: C. Marpon & E. Flammarion, 1886), vol. I, 105. See Pierre Birnbaum, "Le Retour du Juif errant," in *Le juif errant. Un témoin du temps*, 130–31.

33. Frank G. Hyde, "Notes on the Hebrew Insane," *American Journal of Insanity* 58, no. 3 (1902): 469. See Sander L. Gilman, "Hysteria, Race and Gender," in Sander L. Gilman, Helen King, Roy Porter, G. S. Rousseau, and Elaine Showalter, *Hysteria Beyond Freud* (Berkeley: University of California Press, 1993), 406ff.

34. Cecil F. Beadles, "The Insane Jew," *Journal of Mental Science* 46 (1900): 731–36.

35. Maurice Fishberg, *The Jews: A Study of Race and Environment* (New York: Walter Scot Publishing, 1911), 324–25.

36. Anatole Leroy Beaulieu, *Israel Among the Nations: A Study of the Jews and Antisemitism*, trans. F. Hellmann (New York: G. P. Putnam's Sons, 1904), 176, 168–9, 1st French ed. 1895.

37. See Georg Hofer, "Juden und Nervosität," in *Jüdische Identitäten: Einblicke in die Bewusstseinslandschaft des österreichischen Judentums*, ed. Klaus Hödl (Innsbruck: StudienVerlag, 2000), 95–119.

38. Elcan Isaac Wolf and David Friedländer, both cited in Michael A. Meyer, "Normality and Assimilation," *Acculturation and Modern German Jewry*, ed. Rainer Liedtke and David Rechter (Tübingen: Mohr Siebeck, 2003), 19. See also Meyer's essay on Friedländer in his *The Origins of the Modern Jew* (Detroit: Wayne State University Press, 1967), 57–84.

39. Quotations from Petra Zudrell, *Der Kulturkritiker und Schrift-steller Max Nordau: Zwischen Zionismus, Deutschtum und Judentum* (Würzburg: Königshausen & Neumann, 2003), 186–91.

40. Several Zionists, including Herzl, moved "not from Judaism to Zionism but the other way around," notes Gabriel Piterberg. "They were completely alienated from Judaism and knew very little about it. Their rejection by an increasingly anti-Semitic society made

them convert to Zionism, which was an adequate substitution to the Romantic nationalism." Gabriel Piterberg, *The Returns of Zionism: Myths, Politics and Scholarship in Israel* (London: Verso, 2008), 82–83.

41. Cited in and see my *Picture Imperfect: Utopian Thought for an Anti-Utopian Age* (New York: Columbia University Press, 2005), 89–92.

42. Theodor Herzl, *Altneuland: Old-New Land,* trans. Paula Arnold (Haifa: Haifa Publishing, 1960), 62.

43. The term did not originate with him. Nordau took it from Bénédict Morel, a French psychiatrist, who was alarmed at what he considered accelerating cretinism and insanity. For a nice overview, see Richard D. Walter, "What Became of the Degenerate? A Brief History of a Concept," *Journal of the History of Medicine,* vol. 11 (Oct. 1956): 422–29, and Daniel Pick, *Faces of Degeneration: A European Disorder, c. 1848–1918* (New York: Cambridge University Press, 1989).

44. Max Nordau, *Degeneration* [1892], trans. from 2d ed., Introduction by George L. Mosse (New York: Howard Fertig, 1968), 17.

45. See Peter Baldwin, "Liberalism, Nationalism, and Degeneration: The Case of Max Nordau," *Central European History* 13, no. 2 (June 1980), 99–120. Baldwin argues that Nordau never fit together the pieces of his thinking—his rationalistic liberalism and his Volkish Zionism.

46. See Paul Breines, *Tough Jews: Political Fantasies and the Moral Dilemma of American Jewry* (New York: Basic Books, 1990).

47. Max Mandelstamm at the Fourth Zionist Conference, cited in (p. 106) and see Mitchell B. Hart, *Social Science and the Politics of Modern Jewish Identity* (Palo Alto, CA: Stanford University Press, 2000), for a discussion on debates about Jewish degeneration and anthropological types. See also Martin Englander, *Die auffallend häufigen Kranksheitsersheinungen der jüdischen Rassen* (Vienna: J. Pollak, 1902). This lecture-pamphlet was delivered at the Zionist convention, and replies to Mandelstamm.

48. Cited and see Todd S. Presner, *Muscular Judaism: The Jewish Body and the Politics of Regeneration* (New York: Routledge, 2007),

122–23. See also Daniel Wildmann, "Jewish Gymnasts and their Corporeal Utopias in Imperial Germany," in *Emancipation through Muscles: Jews and Sports in Europe*, ed. Michael Brenner and Gideon Reuveni (Lincoln: University of Nebraska Press, 2006), 27–43.

49. Max Nordau, "Jewry of Muscle," originally *Jüdische Turnzeitung* (1900), in *The Jew in the Modern World*, ed. Paul R. Mendes-Flohr and Jehuda Reinharz (New York: Oxford University Press, 1980), 434–35. Nordau himself was aware that he was repeating the charges of anti-Semites that Jews lacked physical strength and vigor, but he maintained this was a product of ghetto life and lack of "physical education." He spelled this out in another article, "Was bedeutet das Turnen für uns Juden?" for the Jewish gymnast journal *Jüdische Turnzeitung*, 1902, reprinted in his *Zionistische Schriften*, 2nd ed. (Berlin: Jüdischer Verlag, 1923), 427–33. On the subject of Jewish gymnasts and Nordau, see Daniel Wildmann, *Die Veränderbare Körper: Jüdische Turner, Männlichkeit und das Wiedergewinnen von Geschichte in Deutschland um 1900* (Tübingen: Mohr Siebeck, 2009).

50. Cited in and see Presner, *Muscular Judaism*, 106–23. See also his "'Clear Heads, Solid Stomachs, and Hard Muscles': Max Nordau and the Aesthetics of Jewish Regeneration," *Modernism/modernity* 10, no. 2 (2003): 269–96, and Moshe Zimmermann, "Muscle Jews versus Nervous Jews," in *Emancipation through Muscles*, 13–26.

51. Joseph Jacobs, "On the Racial Characteristics of Modern Jews," *Journal of the Anthropological Institute of Great Britain and Ireland* 15 (1886), 25–26.

52. Francis Galton, "Eugenics and the Jew," *Jewish Chronicle*, July 29, 1910, reprinted in *Mankind Quarterly* 48, no. 2 (Winter 2007). These words of Galton appear in various of his writings. For a recent consideration, see David M. Levy and Sandra J. Peart, "Statistical Prejudice: From Eugenics to Immigrants," *European Journal of Political Economy* 20, no. 1 (2004): 5–22. See also Mitchell B. Hart, *The Healthy Jew: The Symbiosis of Judaism and Modern Medicine* (Cambridge: Cambridge University Press, 2007), 110–13.

53. Jacobs, "Racial Characteristics of Modern Jews," 39, 53. On Jacobs and the English debate on Jewish racial features, which includes

material on Jewish "doubles," see Deborah Cohen, "Who Was Who? Race and Jews in Turn-of-the-Century Britain," *Journal of British Studies* 41, no. 4 (2002): 460–83.

54. See Klaus Hödl, *Die Pathologisierung des jüdischen Körpers* (Vienna: Picus Verlag, 1997), John M. Efron, *Defenders of the Race: Jewish Doctors and Race Science in Fin-de-Siècle Europe* (New Haven, CT: Yale University Press, 1994), and in general the many books of Sander Gilman. "The Jewish, or Hawk nose," wrote one self-proclaimed expert from an earlier period, "is very convex, and preserves its convexity like a bow, throughout its whole length from eyes to the tip. . . . It indicates considerable shrewdness in worldly matters." It is a good "money-getting nose, a good commercial nose, and perhaps the latter term would be an apt secondary designation for it," since its owner may attain a weighty "purse" but not an "exalted" intellectuality. (The author scoffs at Jewish scholars as "curious wranglers, ingenious cabalists, fine splitters of hair, shrewd perverters of texts, sharp detectors of discrepancies, clever concocters of analogies.") George Jabet, "Of the Jewish Nose," in his *Notes on Noses* (London: Richard Bentley, 1852), 89–98.

55. Maurice Fishberg, *Materials for the Physical Anthropology of the Eastern European Jews*, in *Memoirs of the American Anthropological Association* 1 (1905–1907), 16, 39–45, 50–51.

56. See the collection *Jewish Tradition and the Challenge of Darwinism*, ed. Geoffrey Cantor and Marc Swetlitz (Chicago: University of Chicago Press, 2006).

57. See Piterberg, *Returns of Zionism*, 81–88. For some other Jewish partisans of eugenics, see Kamila Uzarczyk, "'Moses als Eugeniker'? The Reception of Eugenic Ideas in Jewish Medical Circles in Interwar Poland," ed. Marius Turda and Paul J. Weindling, *"Blood and Homeland": Eugenics and Racial Nationalism in Central and Southeast Europe, 1900–1940* (Budapest: Central European University Press, 2007), 283–97.

58. All my information on Bychowski derives from the work of Raphael Falk; see his "Three Zionist Men of Science: Between Nature and Nurture" in *Jews and Sciences in German Contexts*, ed.

Ulrich Charpa and Ute Deichmann (Tübingen: Mohr Siebeck, 2007), 131–37.

59. Cited in and see Jan Goldstein, "The Wandering Jew and the Problem of Psychiatric Anti-Semitism in Fin-de-Siècle France," *Journal of Contemporary History* 20, no. 4 (Oct. 1985): 521–52. See Gilman, "The Image of the Hysteric," in Gilman et al., *Hysteria Beyond Freud*, 402–36.

60. Henry Meige, *Le juif-errant a la Salpêtrière. Étude sur certains néuropathes voyageurs* (Paris: L. Battaille, 1893), 6, 21, 61. See Roland Auguet, *Le juif errant: Genèse d'une légende* (Paris: Payot, 1977), which begins with Meige. Auguet considers these visions of the wandering Jew anti-Semitic, 7–11.

61. See for instance C. P. Jones, "Tattooing and Branding in Graeco-Roman Antiquity," *Journal of Roman Studies* 77 (1987): 139–55. For more general reflections, see Valentin Groebner, *Who Are You? Identification, Deception and Surveillance in Early Modern Europe* (New York: Zone Books, 2007). Groebner reminds us that some brandings and markings indicated positive features.

62. Justice William Harper cited in Marina Wikramanayake, *A World in Shadow: The Free Black in Antebellum South Carolina* (Columbia: University of South Carolina Press, 1973), 51.

63. See David S. Bogen, "The Maryland Context of Dred Scott: The Decline of Legal Status of Maryland Free Blacks 1776–1810," *American Journal of Legal History* 34, no. 4 (1990): 381–411.

64. Ira Berlin, *Slaves without Masters: The Free Negro in the Antebellum South* (New York: Vintage Books, 1976), 317. In apartheid South Africa the same type of restrictions for the same reasons existed. By order of the Pass Law Act of 1952, all "natives," which meant a person "generally accepted as a member of any aboriginal race or tribe of Africa," had to carry a much-despised "reference book" with full particulars of his or her status. See Statutes of the Union of South Africa, Natives (Abolition of Passes and Co-ordination of Documents) Act, Act No. 67 of 1952, www.disa.ukzn.ac.za:8080/DC/leg19520711.028.020.067/leg19520711.028.020.067.pdf.

65. See Laurent Joly, *Vichy dans la "solution finale": Histoire du commissariat général aux questions juives* (Paris: Bernard Grasset, 2006), 542–62.

66. A reproduction of one can be found at http://commons.wikimedia .org/wiki/File:Certificat_de_non_appartenance_%C3%A0_la_ race_juive.jpg.

67. See Bruno Halioua, *Blouse blanches, étoiles jaunes* (Paris: Liana Levi, 2000), 112–16.

68. Carmen Callil, *Bad Faith: A Forgotten History of Family, Fatherland and Vichy France* (New York: Knopf, 2006), 232.

69. Richard H. Weisberg in his *Vichy Law and the Holocaust in France* (New York: New York University Press, 1996) cites the case of Weiller and others in which circumcision was employed to settle disputes over Jewish identity on the basis of French (Vichy) law, 72–73. Weisberg states that Weiller, although circumcised, "escaped" deportation because, among other things, of his baptism certificate. But the Mémorial de la Shoah lists a Marcel Weiller as deported to Drancy and Auschwitz, and his name has been inscribed on "Le mur des noms" as a victim of Nazism. Could there be two Marcel Weillers? Information about Weiller's fate comes from the data bank of Centre de documentation juive contemporaine (CDJC): www.memorialdelashoah.org.

70. Solomon Perel, *Europa, Europa,* trans. Margot B. Dembo (New York: John Wiley, 1997), 21–22.

71. Jakov Lind, *Counting My Steps: An Autobiography* (Toronto: Macmillan, 1969), 182.

72. To the extent that Muslims are circumcised, amid fratricidal violence their circumcision might also lead to death. "Where on earth except in India would a man's life depend on whether or not his foreskin has been removed?" asks the Sikh in Khushwant Singh's novel *Train to Pakistan* (London: Chatto & Windus, 1956), 188. In the novel, a classic account of the violence sparked by the partition of India and Pakistan, the Hindus threaten the life of the Sikh, whom they believe is a Muslim because he is circumcised.

73. "The Queen of Sheba in the *Midrash Mishle* (Proverbs)," Appendix to Jacob Lassner, *Demonizing the Queen of Sheba: Boundaries of Gender and Culture in Postbiblical Judaism and Medieval Islam* (Chicago: University of Chicago Press, 1993), 162.

74. Cited in and see especially chap. 2, 26–69, of Shaye J. D. Cohen, *The Beginnings of Jewishness: Boundaries, Varieties, Uncertainties* (Berkeley: University of California Press, 1999).

75. Chase F. Robinson, "Neck-Sealing in Early Islam," *JESHO* 3, no. 48 (2005): 401–41.

76. Alexander Scheiber, "The Origins of 'Obadyah, the Norman Proselyte,'" *Journal of Jewish Studies* 5 (1954): 32–37. This piece includes a translation of the four pages of the manuscript. For a recent discussion of Obadiah and another translation, see Norman Golb, "The Autograph Memoirs of Obadiah the Proselyte of Oppido Lucano," *Convegno internazionale di Studi,* 2004, http://oi.uchicago.edu/pdf/autograph_memoirs_obadiah.pdf.

77. Cited in and see the excellent piece by Danièle Sansy, "Marquer la différence: l'imposition de la rouelle au XIIIe and XIVe siècles," *Médiévales* 20, no. 41 (2001): 15–36.

78. See generally Raymonde Foreville, *Latran I, II, II et Latran IV* (Paris: Éditions de L'Orante, 1965), 227–317.

79. Canon 68 cited from *Medieval Sourcebook: Twelfth Ecumenical Council: Lateran IV 1215,* www.fordham.edu/halsall/basis/lateran4.html.

80. Ibid.

81. Petition to Cortes of Toro, cited in Benzion Netanyahu, *The Origins of the Inquisition in Fifteenth Century Spain* (New York: Random House, 1995), 119.

82. Cited in and see the comprehensive article by Guido Kisch, "The Yellow Badge in History," *Historia Judaica* 19 (Oct. 1957): 89–146.

83. See Benjamin Ravid, "From Yellow to Red: On the Distinguishing Head-Covering of the Jews of Venice," in his *Studies on the Jews of Venice, 1382–1797* (Aldershot, UK: Ashgate, 2003), 179–210.

84. Nichols de Fer, *Voyages and travels over all Europe: Containing all that is most curious in that part of the world,* trans. from French

(London: Rhodes & Harris, 1693), vol. 1, 23. The city was Avignon, which at the time belonged to the papacy.

85. William Lithgow, *Travels and voyages through Europe, Asia, and Africa: For nineteen years* (Edinburgh: J. Meuros, 1770), 42–43. This is the 11th edition. Presumably the first edition was during Lithgow's life. He is believed to have died in 1645.

86. *Travels of Clarissa Trant,* cited in and see "The Jewish Badge and Garb" in Rev. Dr. A. Cohen, *An Anglo-Jewish Scrapbook* (London: M. L. Cailigold, 1943), 249–59.

87. For the background and text of this and other related directives, see León Poliakov, *L'étoile jaune,* Pref. de Justin Godart (Paris: Éditions du Centre, 1949).

88. Dawid Sierakowiak, *The Diary of Dawid Sierakowiak: Five Notebooks from the Lodz Ghetto,* ed. Alan Adelson (New York: Oxford University Press, 1996), 63. He died in the ghetto four years later, not yet nineteen.

89. Lucien Rebater in "Je suis partout," cited in Serge Klarsfeld, *L'étoile des juifs* (Paris: Crif/L'Archipel, 2002), 35.

90. Cited in and see Maurice Rajsfus, *Opération étoile jaune,* suivi de *Jeudi noir* (Paris: Cherche midi, 2002), 97.

91. Michael R. Marrus and Robert O. Paxton, *Vichy France and the Jews* (New York: Basic Books, 1981), 92.

92. *Le Procès de Xavier Vallat présenté par ses amis,* preface by Marie-Madeleine Martin (Paris: Éditions du Conquistador, 1948), 74–77. To be sure, when Vallat cites these Church doctrines, he also points out that he disagrees with them. See Laurent Joly, *Xavier Vallat 1891–1972: Du nationalisme chrétien à l'antisémitisme d'Etat* (Paris: Bernard Grasset, 2001), 259.

93. See Callil, *Bad Faith,* 228–29.

94. Jean Contoux in "L'Appel," cited in Rajsfus, *Opération étoile jaune,* 98.

95. See generally Serge Klarsfeld, *L'étoile des juifs.*

96. *Le Petit Parisien,* June 8, 1942, http://perso.orange.fr/d-d.natanson/etoile_juive.htm.

97. *Cri du Peuple,* cited in Jeremy Josephs, *Swastika over Paris* (New York: Arcade, 1989), 41.

98. Rebatet, "Je suis partout," June 6, 1942, cited in Klarsfeld, *L'etoile des juifs,* 70.

99. Susan Zuccotti, *The Holocaust, the French, and the Jews* (Lincoln: University of Nebraska Press, 1999), 91.

100. Maurice Rajsfus, *Jeudi noir: 16 juillet 1942, l'honneur perdu de la france profonde* (Paris: L'Harmattan, 1988), 20–26. The book deals with the "raid" of Jews in July 1942 that swept up the parents of Rajsfus, who never returned. The first pages of the book recall his memories of first wearing the yellow star.

101. *The Journal of Hélène Berr,* trans. and ed. David Bellos (New York: Weinstein Books, 2008), 54–56.

102. Paul Steinberg, *Speak You Also: A Survivor's Reckoning,* trans. Linda Coverdale (New York: Holt, 2001), 5. Steinberg was picked up, however, because someone informed about him.

103. Primo Levi, *Survival in Auschwitz,* trans. Stuart Woolf (New York: Touchstone, 1996), 98–99.

104. Poliakov, *L'étoile jaune,* 53.

105. Information on the fate of Gleidmann comes from the data bank of Centre de documentation juive contemporaine (CDJC), www.memorialdelashoah.org.

106. Poliakov prints a list of some twenty individuals interned at Drancy for parodying the Jewish badge, *L'étoile jaune,* 87–88. See Rajsfus, *Opération étoile jaune,* for a more complete listing, 77–96.

107. Jeanette in Serge Lapidus, *Étoiles jaunes dans la France des années noires. Onze récits parallèles de jeunes rescapés* (Paris: L'Harmattan, 2000), 189.

108. *Journal of Hélène Berr,* 81.

109. Bernard Lazare, *Antisemitism: Its History and Causes,* 1894, www.fordham.edu/halsall/jewish/lazare-anti.html.

110. Joshua Trachtenberg, *The Devil and the Jews: The Medieval Conception of the Jew and its Relation to Modern AntiSemitism* (Philadelphia: Jewish Publication Society of America, 1961), 3, 1st ed. 1943.

111. Harumi Befu, "Demonizing the 'Other,'" in Robert W. Wistrich, ed., *Demonizing the Other: Anti-Semitism, Racism and Xenophobia* (Amsterdam: Harwood Academic Publisher & Vidal Sassoon In-

ternational Center for the Study of Antisemitism, Hebrew University of Jerusalem, 1999), 26–28.

112. See generally Moshe Zimmermann, *Wilhelm Marr, the Patriarch of Antisemitism* (New York: Oxford University Press, 1986). The league sought "das deutsche Vaterland vor der vollständigen Verjudung zu bewahren." Cited from "Zum Wortgebrauch 'Antisemitismus,'" www.martinblumentritt.de/agr332.htm.

113. Zimmermann, *Marr,* 71–72.

114. See Fred Sommer, *"Halb-Asien": German Nationalism and the Eastern European Works of Karl Emil Franzos* (Stuttgart: Akademischer Verlag Hans-Dieter Heinz, 1984), and Carl Steiner, *Karl Emil Franzos, 1848–1904* (New York: Peter Lang, 1990).

115. Stefan Zweig, *The World of Yesterday* (Lincoln: University of Nebraska Press, 1964), 231.

116. Elisabeth Albanis, *German-Jewish Cultural Identity from 1900 to the Aftermath of the First World War: A Comparative Study of Moritz Goldstein, Julius Bab and Ernst Lissauer* (Tübingen: Max Niemeyer Verlag, 2002), 220.

117. Ernst Lissauer, "Deutschtum und Judentum," *Der Kunstwart* 25 no. 3 (1912): 7. Lissauer used the term *Volksgenossen.*

118. Philip Roth, "Eli, the Fanatic," in *Goodbye, Columbus and Five Short Stories* (New York: Modern Library, 1995), 247–98.

119. František Langer, Foreword to Jiří Langer, *Nine Gates to the Chassidic Mysteries,* trans. Stephen Jolly (New York: Behrman House, 1976), vii, xv–xvi.

120. Steven E. Ascheim, *Brothers and Strangers: The East European Jew in German and German Jewish Consciousness 1800–1923* (Madison: University of Wisconsin Press, 1982). See also Jack Wertheimer, *Unwelcome Strangers: East European Jews in Imperial Germany* (New York: Oxford University Press, 1987).

121. See David A. Brenner, *Marketing Identities: The Invention of Jewish Ethnicity in "Ost und West"* (Detroit, MI: Wayne State University Press, 1998).

122. Gershom Scholem, *From Berlin to Jerusalem: Memories of My Youth,* trans. Harry Zohn (New York: Schocken Books, 1980), 44.

123. See Jakob Wassermann, "Der Jude als Orientale," and Hans Kohn, "Der Geist des Orients," in *Von Judentum: Ein Sammelbuch*, ed. Verein jüdischer Hochschüler Bar Kochba in Prague (Leipzig: Kurt Wolff Verlag, 1913).

124. See the fine essay by Paul Mendes-Flohr, "Fin de Siècle Orientalism, the *Ostjuden*, and the Aesthetics of Jewish Self-Affirmation," 109–21, in his *Divided Passions: Jewish Intellectuals and the Experience of Modernity* (Detroit, MI: Wayne State University Press, 1991).

125. "Changing Face in Poland: Skinhead Puts on Skullcap," *New York Times*, February 28, 2010.

126. See Ascheim, *Brothers and Strangers*, 112–13.

127. See Mendes-Flohr, "Fin de Siècle Orientalism," 77. Little seems known about Arndt, although he married the writer Helene Böhlau, who wrote the preface to his most important (or only?) book, *Das hohe Ziel der Erkenntnis* (Google Books). There is an entry about him in a German encyclopedia of Islam, www.eslam.de/begriffe/a/arndt.htm. See also Ascher D. Biemann's informed review of the diary of Eugen Hoeflich, another Orientalist, in *Modern Judaism* 21 (2001): 175–84.

128. Muhammad Asad, *The Road to Mecca* (New York: Simon and Schuster, 1954), 64. The uncle was Dorian Feigenbaum, usually considered the first psychoanalyst to settle in Palestine.

129. See Günther Windhagen, *Leopold Weiss alias Muhammad Asad: Von Galizien nach Arabien 1900–1927* (Vienna: Böhlau Verlag, 2003); Martin Kramer, "The Road from Mecca: Muhammad Asad (born Leopold Weiss)," in Martin Kramer, ed., *The Jewish Discovery of Islam: Studies in Honor of Bernard Lewis* (Tel Aviv: Moshe Dayan Center for Middle Eastern and African Studies, 1999), 225–47; and Dan Diner, who sees Asad as a reformer who challenged Islamic orthodoxy, *Lost in the Sacred: Why the Muslim World Stood Still*, trans. Steven Rendall (Princeton, NJ: Princeton University Press, 2009), 175–76. See also Florence Heymann, *Un juif pour l'Islam* (Paris: Éditions Stock, 2005). She also stresses Asad's distance at the end of his life from the new Islamic fundamentalism—and notes that he liked to tell Yiddish jokes, a point picked up in

a portrait that first appeared in the *Frankfurter Allgemeine Zeitung* in 2005: Joseph Hanimann, "From Lemberg to Pakistan: The Yiddish Jokes of Mohammad Asad," www.qantara.de/webcom/show_article.php/_c-310/_nr-207/i.html. For a two-volume collection of material by and on Asad, see M. Ikram Chaghatai, ed., *Muhammad Asad: Europe's Gift to Islam* (Lahore, Pakistan: Truth Society/Sang-e-Meel Publications, 2006).

130. Tom Reiss, *The Orientalist: Solving the Mystery of a Strange and Dangerous Life* (New York: Random House, 2006), xxii.

131. Essad Bey, *"Allah ist Gross": Niedergang und Aufstieg der Islamischen Welt von Abdul Hamid Bis Ibn Saud*, with a biographical essay by von Gerhard Höpp (Munich: Matthes & Seitz, 2002), 373. Nussimbaum collaborated with a militant Zionist, Wolfgang von Weisl, on this book. As Höpp notes in his afterword, how the Jewish convert to Islam and the militant Zionist came to work together remains obscure, 400.

132. In "Foreword" to Jiří Langer, *Nine Gates to the Chassidic Mysteries*, xvii.

133. "For most German and Austrian racists, what appeared ominous and even sinister about Jews was no longer their difference but rather their *sameness*. Jewish 'otherness' became even more frightening to antisemites the more it became diluted, adaptable, mobile and able to efface boundaries." Robert S. Wistrich, *Laboratory for World Destruction: Germans and Jews in Central Europe* (Lincoln: University of Nebraska Press, 2007), 21.

134. Anonymous, *Allgemeine Zeitung des Judenthums* 19, no. 33 (Aug. 13, 1855), 418.

135. Wilhelm Marr, cited in Michael A. Meyer, *Judaism within Modernity: Essays on Jewish History and Religion* (Detroit, MI: Wayne State University Press, 2001), 158.

136. Carl Schmitt, *Glossarium: Aufzeichnungen der Jahre 1947–1951*, ed. Eberhard Freiherr von Medem (Berlin: Dunker & Humblot, 1991), 18. See Raphael Gross, *Carl Schmitt und die Juden* (Frankfurt: Suhrkamp, 2000), 366–81.

137. "Goldhagen ultimately offers readers a representation of 'Germans' and 'Jews' as two absolutely distinct, essentially opposed, and ul-

timately abstract principles that have been locked in an eternal struggle whose outcome can only be total victory or total defeat," writes the historian Jane Caplan, in "Reflections on the Reception of Goldhagen in the United States," in Geoff Eley, ed., *The "Goldhagen" Effect: History, Memory, Nazism—Facing the German Past* (Ann Arbor: University of Michigan Press, 2000), 158.

138. Daniel Goldhagen, *Hitler's Willing Executioners* (New York: Vintage, 1997), 77–78.

139. Amos Elon, *The Pity of It All: A History of Jews in Germany, 1743–1933* (New York: Metropolitan Books, 2002), 12.

140. Fritz Stern, *Five Germanys I Have Known* (New York: Farrar, Straus and Giroux, 2006), 98–101.

141. Theodor Lessing, *Einmal und Nie Wieder* (Gütersloh: Bertelsmann Sachbuchverlag, 1969), 112, 1st ed. 1935.

142. Martin Freud, cited in Peter Gay, *A Godless Jew: Freud, Atheism and the Making of Psychoanalysis* (New Haven, CT: Yale University Press, 1987), 125.

143. Scholem, *From Berlin to Jerusalem*, 28.

144. See Alexander Waugh, *The House of Wittgenstein: A Family at War* (New York: Doubleday, 2008), 208.

145. Karl Wittgenstein, cited in Brian McGuinness, *Wittgenstein: A Life; Young Ludwig 1889–1921* (Berkeley: University of California Press, 1988), 2.

146. See Ray Monk, *Ludwig Wittgenstein: The Duty of Genius* (New York: Penguin Books, 1990), 5.

147. Moses Mendelssohn, *Jerusalem*, trans. Allan Arkush, Introduction by Alexander Altmann (Hanover, NH: Brandeis University Press, 1983), 133.

148. Abraham to Felix, June 8 and July 8, 1829, cited in Jeffrey S. Sposato, "The price of assimilation: The oratorios of Felix Mendelssohn and the nineteenth-century anti-semitic tradition" (Ph.D. diss., Brandeis University, 2000), vol. 1, 22, 69–70.

149. Felix Gilbert, "Einleitung" to his *Bankiers, Künstler und Gelehrte: Unveröffentliche Briefe der Familie Mendelssohn* (Tübingen: J. C. B. Mohr, 1975), xvi. See in general Herbert Kupferberg, *The Mendels-*

sohns: Three Generations of Genius (New York: Charles Scribner's Sons, 1972).

150. Sebastian Panwitz, "Otto (von) Mendelssohn Bartholdy," *Mendelssohn Studien* 16 (2009): 439–66. How Otto (von) Mendelssohn Bartholdy was "nobilized" remains controversial, at least to Otto (von) Mendelssohn Bartholdy scholars. For a careful study of German Jewish elite integration—partial and imperfect, according to its author, himself the son of a prosperous German Jewish family—see W. E. Mosse, *The German-Jewish Economic Elite 1820–1935: A Socio-cultural Profile* (Oxford: Clarendon Press, 1989).

151. Hans-Joachim Schoeps, "Der Jude im neuen Deutschland" (1933), reprinted in his collection *"Bereit für Deutschland!" Der Patriotismus deutscher Juden and der Nationalsozialismus: Frühe Schriften 1930 bis 1939* (Berlin: Haude & Spenersche, 1970), 105–6, 114. See Richard Faber, *Deutschbewusstes Judentum und jüdischbewusstes Deutschtum: Der Historische und Politische Theologe Hans-Joachim Schoeps* (Würzburg: Königshausen & Newmann, 2008), 23–37.

152. For this fact and details of Schoeps's group, see Carl J. Rheins, "Deutscher Vortrupp, Gefolgschaft deutscher Juden 1933–1935," *Leo Baeck Institute Year Book* 26 (1981): 207–30.

153. See Christhard Hoffmann, "Constructing Jewish Modernity: Mendelssohn Jubilee Celebrations within German Jewry, 1829–1929," especially 48–50, in Rainer Liedtke and Thomas Lackmann, eds., *Acculturation and Modern German Jewry* (Tübingen: Paul Mohr Verlag, 2003), and Thomas Lackmann, *Das Glück der Mendelssohns: Geschichte einer deutschen Familie* (Berlin: Aufbau-Verlag, 2005), 426–29.

154. Leo Baeck, *Mendelssohn Gedenkfeier: Der jüdischen Gemeinde zu Berlin am 8. September 1929* (Berlin: M. Rosenthal, 1929), 14, 17, 19.

155. See Shulamit Volkov, *Jüdisches Leben und Antisemitism im 19. und 20. Jahrhunder* (Munich: Beck, 1990), 130–45, and her *Germans, Jews and Antisemites: Trials in Emancipation* (New York: Cambridge University Press, 2006), 175.

156. For a summary of figures, see Marvin Perry and Frederick M. Schweitzer, *Antisemitism: Myth and Hate from Antiquity to the Present* (New York: Palgrave, 2002), 137–43.

157. Saul Friedländer compares Fischer to Random House or Scribner's in his *Nazi Germany and the Jews,* vol. 1 (New York: Harper-Collins, 1997), 79. See Friedländer for other statistics of the Jewish role in German society.

158. Volkov, *Jüdisches Leben,* 146–65.

159. Yuri Slezkine, *The Jewish Century* (Princeton, NJ: Princeton University Press, 2004), 50. For Vienna, see Steven Beller, *Vienna and the Jews 1867–1938: A Cultural History* (New York: Cambridge University Press, 1989), 33–70. For Budapest, which often has been neglected in comparison to Vienna, see Kati Vörös, "How Jewish Is Jewish Budapest?" *Jewish Social Studies* 8, no. 1 (2002): 88–125.

160. *Juden im deutschen Kulturbereich: Ein Sammelwerk,* ed. Siegmund Kaznelson, introduction by Richard Willstätter, 3rd ed. (Berlin: Jüdischer Verlag, 1962), 454. Goldschmidt was honored with a plaque by a local mountaineering club in 1922. The Nazis destroyed the plaque and a local club replaced it in 1971 with one that read "Botanist of the Rhön." See entry for "Moritz Goldschmidt" in the German Wikipedia.

161. *Juden im deutschen Kulturbereich,* 1043–60.

162. For instance, Friedrich Gundolf, Richard Borchardt, and Hugo von Hofmannsthal—all poets and writers, and all wholly or partly Jewish—have been advanced as representing the pure Aryan spirit. See Peter Gay, *Freud, Jews and Other Germans* (Oxford: Oxford University Press, 1979), 178–81.

CHAPTER FOUR: FEARFUL SYMMETRIES

1. Mary Kingsley, *Travels in West Africa: Congo Français, Corisco and Cameroons* (New York: Macmillan, 1898), 324–28.

2. For instance Mary Slessor; see Brian O'Brien, *She Had a Magic: The Story of Mary Slessor* (New York: E. P. Dutton, 1959).

3. Cited in and see Misty L. Bastian, "'The Demon Superstition': Abominable Twins and Mission Culture in Onitsha History," *Ethnology* 40, no. 1 (Winter 2001): 13–27.

4. John Lasch, *Twins and the Double* (London: Thames and Hudson, 1993), 11. The scholarship on the subject is vast. One useful study

is C. F. Keppler, *The Literature of the Second Self* (Tucson: University of Arizona Press, 1972).

5. Alessandra Piontelli, *Twins in the World: The Legends They Inspire and the Lives They Lead* (New York: Palgrave Macmillan, 2008), 99–101, 117–26.

6. "William Wilson," in *Complete Stories and Poems of Edgar Allan Poe* (New York: Doubleday, 1966), 156–70.

7. Fyodor Dostoevesky, *Notes from Underground, The Double and Other Stories,* ed. Deborah A. Martinsen (New York: Barnes & Noble, 2003), 52, 115.

8. Oscar Wilde, *The Picture of Dorian Gray* (Mineola, NY: Dover, 1993).

9. Thomas De Quincey, *On Murder,* ed. Robert Morrison (Oxford: Oxford University Press, 2006), 13.

10. De Quincey, "Milton *versus* Southey and Landor" in *Note Book of an English Opium-Eater,* ebook, Project Gutenberg, www.gutenberg .org/etext/6881.

11. A. E. Crawley, "Doubles," in *Encyclopedia of Religion and Ethics,* ed. James Hastings, vol. iv (Edinburgh: T & T Clark, 1911), 858.

12. Bronislaw Malinowski, *The Father in Primitive Psychology* (New York: W. W. Norton, 1927), 90. As Malinowski understood it, this shock at resemblance was true only in regard to maternal kinsmen.

13. For a survey of popular beliefs on doubles, see Crawley, "Doubles," 858–60.

14. Hugh Haughton, Introduction to Sigmund Freud, *The Uncanny,* trans. David McLintock (New York: Penguin Books, 2003), xliii.

15. *The Metamorphoses of Ovid,* trans. Allen Mandelbaum (San Diego: Harcourt, 1993), 91 (Bk III, 345–66).

16. Freud, *The Uncanny,* 142.

17. Wilde, *Dorian Gray,* 77.

18. See Otto Rank, *The Double: A Psychoanalytic Study,* trans. Harry Tucker, Jr. (New York: New American Library, 1979), 75–78.

19. Freud, *The Uncanny,* 148.

20. For a scholarly romp on twins and copies, see Hillel Schwartz, *The Culture of the Copy: Striking Likenesses, Unreasonable Facsimiles* (New York: Zone Books, 1998).

21. William S. Sax, "The Hall of Mirrors: Orientalism, Anthropology and the Other," *American Anthropology* 100, no. 2 (1998): 292. Of course some anthropologists buck the trend. I want to salute in particular Anton Blok and his piece "The Narcissism of Minor Differences," *European Journal of Social Theory* 1, no. 1 (1998): 33–56. See also, for some reflections by an anthropologist on resemblances between cultures, Simon Harrison, *Fracturing Resemblances: Identity and Mimetic Conflict in Melanesia and the West* (New York: Berghahn Books, 2006).

22. Edward Said, *Orientalism* (New York: Vintage Books, 1979), 43–46.

23. Robert Irwin, *For Lust of Knowing: The Orientalists and their Enemies* (New York: Allen Lane, 2006), 290–91. See also Ibn Warraq, *Defending the West: A Critique of Edward Said's "Orientalism"* (Amherst, NY: Prometheus Books, 2007), and Daniel Martin Varisco, *Reading* Orientalism: *Said and the Unsaid* (Seattle: University of Washington Press, 2007), especially 251–66. "Said can be criticized . . . for embracing the very dichotomy he wishes to attack," 49.

24. Bernard Lewis, cited by Samuel Huntington, "The Clash of Civilizations?" *Foreign Affairs* 72, no. 3 (Summer 1993): 32.

25. Samuel P. Huntington, *The Clash of Civilizations and the Remaking of the World Order* (New York: Simon & Schuster, 1996), 217.

26. See Jytte Klausen, *The Cartoons That Shook the World* (New Haven, CT: Yale University Press, 2009). Klausen estimates the dead at about 250, injured at about 800 (p. 107). Although Klausen's manuscript included the cartoons, a craven Yale University Press declined to reprint them because doing so "ran a serious risk of instigating violence." "Publisher's Statement," vi.

27. *Messages to the World: The Statements of Osama bin Laden,* ed. Bruce Lawrence, trans. James Howarth (London: Verso, 2005), 124–25.

28. Sadhvi Rithambara, cited in Sudhir Kakar, *The Colors of Violence: Cultural Identities, Religion, and Conflict* (Chicago: University of Chicago Press, 1996), 165.

29. Jonathan Swift, *Gulliver's Travels and Other Writings,* ed. Miriam K. Starkman (New York: Bantam Dell, 2005), 271, 74–75.

30. See Martin Kallich, *The Other End of the Egg: Religious Satire in "Gulliver's Travels"* (Bridgeport, CT: Conference of British Studies, 1970), 26–36.

31. See David S. Werman, "Freud's 'Narcissism of Minor Differences': A Review and Reassessment," *Journal of the American Academy of Psychoanalysis* 16 (1988): 451–59. Werman notes that psychoanalysts have "paid insufficient attention to the narcissism of minor differences," 458.

32. Sigmund Freud, *Moses and Monotheism*, trans. Katherine Jones (New York: Vintage Books, 1967), 66–67.

33. "Unity Is Stressed," *New York Times*, March 15, 1938.

34. I'm using a second translation here, "Moses and Monotheism," in Freud, *Origins of Religion, Pelican Freud Library*, vol. 13 (Middlesex, UK: Penguin, 1985), 334–35. The phrase runs, "gegen kleine Unterschiede stärker als gegen fundamentale Differenzen." Freud, *Der Mann Moses und die Monotheistische Religion* (Frankfurt: Fischer, 1989), 96–97.

35. "Civilization and Its Discontents," in Freud, *Civilization, Society and Religion, Pelican Freud Library*, vol. 12 (Middlesex, UK: Penguin, 1985), 304–5.

36. "Group Psychology and the Analysis of the Ego," in Freud, *Civilization, Society and Religion*, 130–31.

37. Ernest Jones, *The Life and Work of Sigmund Freud*, vol. 2 (New York: Basic Books, 1957), 59.

38. Arthur Schopenhauer, *Parerga und Paralipomena: kleine philosophische Schriften*, vol. 2 (Berlin: A. W. Hahn, 1851), 524–25.

39. A. E. Crawley, *The Mystic Rose: A Study of Primitive Marriage and of Primitive Thought in Its Bearing on Marriage*, ed. Theodore Besterman (London: Methuen, 1927), 259.

40. Sigmund Freud, *Totem and Taboo*, in *Pelican Freud Library*, vol. 13, 71.

41. Two points: I do not find in Crawley exactly that "small differences" provoke antagonisms, and I have altered the Freud translation to make clearer the (possible) links to Crawley. The prevailing English translation has it that "it is precisely the little dissimi-

larities in persons" that provoke hostility. Freud, "The Taboo of Virginity," 224 (see Preface, n. 10). In German the parallels are clearer: "das gerade die kleinen Unterschiede." See "Das Tabu der Virginität," in Sigmund Freud, *Gesammelte Werke*, vol. 12 (London: Imago Publishing, 1947), 169.

42. Freud, "The Taboo of Virginity," 224.

43. Karen Horney, "The Dread of Woman: Observations on a Specific Difference in the Dread Felt by Men and Women Respectively for the Opposite Sex" (1932); originally in *International Journal of Psycho-analysis*, reprinted in *Female Sexuality: The Early Psychoanalytic Controversies*, ed. Russell Grigg et al. (New York: Other Press, 1999), 242–43.

44. For a general discussion and summary, see Gerald K. Gresseth, "The Homeric Sirens," *Transactions and Proceedings of the American Philological Association*, 101 (1970): 203–18.

45. Homer, *The Odyssey*, trans. Robert Fagles, ed. Bernard Knox (New York: Penguin, 1997), 276–77, Book XII, lines 172–214. See the discussion in Max Horkheimer and Theodor W. Adorno, *Dialectic of Enlightenment*, trans. John Cumming (New York: Herder and Herder, 1972), 34–35.

46. Rebecca Comay, "Adorno's Siren Song," *New German Critique* 81 (Autumn 2000): 27.

47. Freud, "The Taboo of Virginity," 224.

48. Jane Marie Todd, "The Veiled Woman in Freud's 'Das Unheimliche,'" *Signs* 11, no. 3 (1986): 527.

49. In the annals of writers who commit suicide, Weininger is neither the most nor the least important. For an upbeat survey of literary suicides, which includes a discussion of Weininger, see Gary Lachman, *The Dedalus Book of Literary Suicides: Dead Letters* (Sawtry, UK: Dedalus, 2008).

50. Jacques Le Rider, *Le cas Otto Weininger: Racines de l'antiféminisme et de l'antisémitisme* (Paris: Presses universitaires de France, 1982), 35.

51. For a summary of responses to Weininger, see Chandak Sengoopta, *Otto Weininger: Sex, Science and Self in Imperial Vienna* (Chicago: University of Chicago Press, 2000), 137–56.

52. Mark Anderson, reviewing Alberto Cavaglion, *Otto Weininger in Italia* in *MLN* 99, no. 1 (Jan. 1984), 172–75. For some comments on Weininger in Italy and his relationship to Lombroso, see Nancy A. Harrowitz, *Antisemitism, Misogyny and the Logic of Cultural Difference: Cesare Lombroso and Matilde Serao* (Lincoln: University of Nebraska Press, 1994), especially 77–80.

53. Wittgenstein to G. E. Moore, August 28, 1931, *Wittgenstein in Cambridge: Letters and Documents 1911–1951*, ed. Brian McGuinness (Malden, MA: Blackwell Publishing, 2008), 193.

54. Freud later said his relations to Weininger were "very complicated. It is not possible to describe them in a short letter. A long thesis would be necessary." Freud to David Abrahamsen, March 14, 1938, cited in David Abrahamsen, *The Mind and Death of a Genius* (New York: Columbia University Press, 1946), 202.

55. For a recent assessment and overview, see David S. Luft, *Eros and Inwardness in Vienna: Weininger, Musil, Doderer* (Chicago: University of Chicago Press, 2003), 45–90. See also *Jews and Gender: Responses to Otto Weininger*, eds. Nancy A. Harrowitz and Barbara Hyams (Philadelphia: Temple University Press, 1995), and Susan C. Anderson, "Otto Weininger's Masculine Utopia," *German Studies Review* 19, no. 3 (Oct. 1996): 433–53.

56. "Publisher's Note," Otto Weininger, *Sex and Character* (London: William Heinemann, 1906), vii.

57. To be sure, he can be insightful—sometimes about himself, for instance, in this aphorism: "Der Hass gegen die Frau ist immer nur noch nicht überwundener Hass gegen die eigene Sexualität." ("Hatred of woman is always unmastered hatred of one's own sexuality.") The aphorisms are included in the appendix to Weininger, *Geschlecht und Charakter*, with essays by Annegret Stopczyk, Gisela Dischner, and Roberto Calasso (Munich: Matthes & Seitz, 1980), 626.

58. Rosa Weininger to Abrahamsen, August 27, 1938, cited in Abrahamsen, *Mind and Death of a Genius*, 204.

59. As recorded by his friend Moriz Rappaport in his preface, "Vorwort zur zweiten Auflage," *Über die Letzten Dinge* (Vienna: Wilhelm Braumüller, 1918), xvi.

60. Otto Weininger, *Sex and Character*, trans. Ladislaus Löb, ed. Daniel Steuer (Bloomington: Indiana University Press, 2005), 14–15.

61. Ibid., 45.

62. Ibid., 69–70.

63. Ibid., 79–80.

64. Ibid., 163, 230.

65. Ibid., 274–76.

66. Ibid., 272–300.

67. For instance, Harold P. Blum, "Little Hans: A Centennial Review and Reconsideration," *Journal of the American Psychoanalytic Association* 55 (2007): 749–65, mentions the footnote only in passing at the end of a long review of the literature. Conversely, historians increasingly attend the footnote. See for instance Jay Geller, "The Godfather of Psychoanalysis: Circumcision, Antisemitism, Homosexuality and Freud's 'Fighting Jew,'" *Journal of the American Academy of Religion* 67 (1999): 355–85. Geller is mainly interested in the anti-Semitic dimension.

68. Weininger appears perhaps because a discussion at the Vienna Psychoanalytic Society had recently mentioned him. See Geller, "The Godfather of Psychoanalysis," 365.

69. Sigmund Freud, "A Phobia in a Five-Year-Old Boy," Sigmund Freud, *Collected Papers*, vol. 3, eds. Alix and James Strachey (New York: Basic Books, 1959), 179.

70. Sigmund Freud, *Leonardo da Vinci and a Memory of his Childhood*, trans. Alan Tyson (New York: Norton, 1964), 45–46.

71. Freud, *Moses and Monotheism*, 116.

72. Otto Fenichel, "Elements of a Psychoanalytic Theory of Anti-Semitism," in *Anti-Semitism: A Social Disease*, ed. Ernst Simmel (New York: International Universities Press, 1946), 27–28.

73. See Leonard B. Glick, *Marked in Your Flesh—Circumcision from Ancient Judea to Modern America* (New York: Oxford University Press, 2005).

74. For a recent discussion of the texts, see Shaye J. D. Cohen, *Why Aren't Jewish Women Circumcised? Gender and Covenant in Judaism* (Berkeley: University of California Press, 2005), 9–21.

75. See in general David L. Gollaher, *Circumcision: A History of the World's Most Controversial Surgery* (New York: Basic Books, 2000).

76. Paolo Mantegazza, *The Sexual Relations of Mankind* [1885], trans. Samuel Putnam (New York: Eugenics, 1939), 99.

77. I am drawing on Ra'anan Abusch [Boustan], "Circumcision and Castration under Roman Law in the Early Empire," in *The Covenant of Circumcision: New Perspectives on an Ancient Jewish Rite,* ed. Elizabeth W. Mark (Waltham, MA: Brandeis University Press, 2003), 75–86, and his "Negotiating Difference: Genital Mutilation in Roman Slave Law and the History of the Bar Kokhba Revolt," in *The Bar Kokhba War Reconsidered,* ed. Peter Schäfer (Tübingen: Mohr Siebeck, 2003), 72–79. In the latter piece Abusch discusses the proper dating and translation of the Roman law. In the former he is using his own translation of Horace Satire I. 9. See *The Complete Odes and Satires of Horace,* trans. Sidney Alexander (Princeton, NJ: Princeton University Press, 1999), 237.

78. Benedict de Spinoza, *Theological-Political Treatise,* ed. Jonathan Israel, trans. Michael Silverthorne and J. Israel (Cambridge: Cambridge University Press, 2007), 55.

79. I switched to a nineteenth-century English translation here: Spinoza, *A Theologico-Political Treatise* [Part I], trans. R. H. M. Elwes, July 1997, sentence 105, www.gutenberg.org/etext/989.

80. See Jay Geller, "Spinoza's Election of the Jews: The Problem of Jewish Persistence," *Jewish Social Studies* 12, no. 1 (2005): 39–63.

81. *The Operated Jew: Two Tales of Anti-Semitism,* trans. and ed. Jack Zipes (New York: Routledge, 1991), 47–74.

82. Daniel Paul Schreber, *Memoirs of My Nervous Illness,* ed. and trans. Ida Macalpine and Richard A. Hunter, Introduction by Samuel M. Weber (Cambridge, MA: Harvard University Press, 1988), 73–76. See Eric L. Santer, *My Own Private Germany: Daniel Paul Schreber's Secret History of Modernity* (Princeton, NJ: Princeton University Press, 1996), 103–45.

83. Sander L. Gilman, *Freud, Race, and Gender* (Princeton, NJ: Princeton University Press, 1993), 142. Gilman's work is an essential source for these topics. In this book he also argues that Freud was

unable to grasp the nexus of woman, Jew, and circumcision. See also Jay Geller, *On Freud's Jewish Body: Mitigating Circumcisions* (New York: Fordham University Press, 2007), and Daniel Boyarin, *Unheroic Conduct: The Rise of Heterosexuality and the Invention of the Jewish Man* (Berkeley: University of California Press, 1997), and Diane Jonte-Pace, *Speaking the Unspeakable: Religion, Misogyny and the Uncanny Mother in Freud's Cultural Texts* (Berkeley: University of California Press, 2001). Jonte-Pace provides a very thoughtful and careful exposition of the issues. She posits that Freud alluded to but failed to develop "an association of both Judaism and anti-Semitism with the uncanny and its accompaniments, that is, the ideology of dangerous and deadly female or maternal difference," 107.

84. Freud, *Totem and Taboo*, 204–5.

85. Stephen Frosh, "Freud, Psychoanalysis and Anti-Semitism," *Psychoanalytic Review* 91 (2004): 327.

86. See Eric Kline Silverman, *From Abraham to America: A History of Jewish Circumcision* (Lanham, MD: Rowman & Littlefield, 2006), 41–42.

87. Peter Riga, cited in Mellinkoff, *Mark of Cain*, 94–95 (see chap. 3, n. 22). Some scholars and psychoanalysts have argued as well that circumcision was the mark of Cain. See for instance H. Zeydner, "Kainszeichen, Keniter und Beschneidung," *Zeitschrift für die alttestamentliche Wissenschaft* 18 (1898): 120–26, and Theodor Reik, "Das Kainszeichen," *Imago* 5 (1917–1919): 31–42.

88. "Germany Voting," *New York Times*, July 31, 1932.

89. Albert Einstein, "Why War?" in Freud, *Civilization, Society and Religion, Pelican Freud Library*, vol. 12, 345–48.

90. Ibid., 355, 357.

91. Letter to Max Eitingon, Sept. 8, 1932, in Jones, *Life and Work of Sigmund Freud*, vol. 3, 175.

92. Fenichel, "Elements of a Psychoanalytic Theory," 12.

93. Sandor Rado, cited in Otto Friedrich, *Before the Deluge: A Portrait of Berlin in the 1920s* (New York: Harper Perennial, 1995), 325.

94. Franco Fornari, *The Psychoanalysis of War* (Garden City, NY: Anchor/Doubleday, 1974), 186.

95. *Contagion*, subtitled *Journal of Violence, Mimesis, and Culture.*

96. For instance, *The New York Review of Books* rarely mentions his books. The only time he was reviewed in its pages was in 1992. *The New Republic* reviewed him only once, in 1978.

97. Chris Fleming, *René Girard: Violence and Mimesis* (Cambridge: Polity, 2004), 2–4.

98. René Girard, *Violence and the Sacred,* 50, 146, 49 (see Preface, n. 11).

99. Ibid., 61–63.

100. René Girard, *Oedipus Unbound: Selected Writings on Rivalry and Desire,* ed. Mark R. Anspach (Palo Alto, CA: Stanford University Press, 2004), 63, 146.

101. Girard, *Violence and the Sacred,* 51.

102. Eugen Weber, *Peasants into Frenchmen: The Modernization of Rural France, 1870–1914* (Palo Alto, CA: Stanford University Press, 1976).

103. René Girard, "What Is Occurring Today Is a Mimetic Rivalry on a Planetary Scale," *Le Monde,* November 6, 2001. English trans. Jim Williams for the Colloquium on Violence and Religion, www .uibk.ac.at/theol/cover/girard/le_monde_interview.html.

104. René Girard, *Celui par qui le scandale arrive* (Paris: Desclée de Brouwer, 2001), 23–24.

105. "Hundreds Flee Nigerian City Swept by Riots," *New York Times,* November 25, 2002.

106. Jean-Pierre Dupuy, "Anatomy of 9/11: Evil, Rationalism and the Sacred," *SubStance* 37, no. 115 (2007): 42.

107. Interviewed by and cited in Fathali M. Moghaddam, *How Globalization Spurs Terrorism: The Lopsided Benefits of "One World" and Why That Fuels Violence* (Westport, CT: Praeger Security International, 2008), 23.

108. Cited in Cordula Meyer, "Der Professor und der Terrorist," *Spiegel OnLine,* September 29, 2009, www.spiegel/spiegelspecial/ 0,1578,435654,00.html.

109. Professor Dittmar Machule, Hamburg, Thursday, 18 October 2001. Liz Jackson interviews Professor Dittmar Machule, Atta's thesis supervisor at the Technical University of Hamburg-Harburg, www.abc.net.au/4corners/atta/interviews/machule.htm.

110. All information on the thesis derives from Daniel Brook, "The Architect of 9/11," www.slate.com/id/2227245.

111. Malise Ruthven, *A Fury for God: The Islamist Attack on America* (London: Granta Books, 2002), 260–61.

112. *Messages to the World,* 89–90.

113. "Saudi Magazine Publishes 'Important Parts' of Usama Bin Ladin's 'Will,'" in *Compilation of Usama Bin Ladin Statements 1994–January 2004* (Washington, DC: FBIS, 2004), 223.

114. English version of Atta's will as released by the FBI, available at www.abc.net.au/4corners/Atta/resources/documents/will1.htm. "The issue of women . . . lies at the heart of Islamic Occidentalism," write Ian Buruma and Avishai Margalit in *Occidentalism: The West in the Eyes of Its Enemies* (New York: Penguin Books, 2004), 128. For Buruma and Margalit, Occidentalism signifies anti-Western sentiment.

115. Physicians for Human Rights, *The Taliban's War on Women: A Health and Human Rights Crisis in Afghanistan* (Washington, DC: Physicians for Human Rights, 1998), 11.

116. United Nations, General Assembly, "Human Rights Questions: Human Rights Situations and Reports of Special Rapporteurs and Representatives: Situation of Human Rights in Afghanistan," UN Document A/49/65 (08 November 1994), 19.

117. Jack Holland, *Misogyny: The World's Oldest Prejudice* (Philadelphia: Running Press, 2007).

118. David D. Gilmore, *Misogyny: The Male Malady* (Philadelphia: University of Pennsylvania Press, 2001), 4. Of course, each religion has its defenders from the charge of misogyny. For instance, the liberal Tunisian sociologist Abdelwahab Bouhdiba writes that "Islamic civilization is essentially feminist. One ought to be able to deduce from this that a Muslim cannot be a misogynist." Yet he admits that this is *"de jure"* and the facts of the situation are otherwise. *Sexuality in Islam,* trans. Alan Sheridan (London: Routledge & Kegan Paul, 1985), 116.

119. Holland, *Misogyny,* 3, 272.

120. Livy, *Early History of Rome,* 42–46 (see chap. 2, n. 91).

INDEX

ABOUT THE AUTHOR

Russell Jacoby is the author of seven previous books, including *The Last Intellectuals* and *The End of Utopia*. He has published articles and reviews in *Harper's Magazine*, the *Los Angeles Times*, *The Nation*, and elsewhere, and is an occasional columnist at the *Chronicle of Higher Education*. He teaches history at UCLA and lives in Los Angeles.